REPORT

OF THE

COMMISSIONER OF AGRICULTURE

ON

THE DISEASES OF CATTLE

IN

THE UNITED STATES.

WASHINGTON:
GOVERNMENT PRINTING OFFICE.
1871.

IN THE SENATE OF THE UNITED STATES, *June* 3, 1870.

Resolved by the Senate, (the House of Representatives concurring,) That there be printed six thousand extra copies of the reports on the "Diseases of Cattle in the United States," presenting the results of investigations ordered by Congress and conducted under the direction of the Commissioner of Agriculture, with illustrations representing various stages of disease, including six photo-micrographs, and not exceeding eight colored plates; of which one thousand five hundred copies shall be for the use of the members of the Senate, three thousand for the use of the members of the House of Representatives, and one thousand five hundred for the Commissioner of Agriculture.

Attest:

GEO. C. GORHAM,
Secretary.

IN THE HOUSE OF REPRESENTATIVES, *July* 14, 1870.

Resolved, That the House concur in the foregoing resolution of the Senate in relation to the printing of the reports on the "Diseases of Cattle in the United States."

Attest:

EDWARD McPHERSON, *Clerk,*
By CLINTON LLOYD, *Chief Clerk.*

CONTENTS.

ILLUSTRATIONS.

CHROMO-LITHOGRAPHS.

MICRO-PHOTOGRAPHS.

CHROMO-LITHOGRAPHS.

LITHOGRAPH.

REPORT OF THE COMMISSIONER OF AGRICULTURE.

SIR: I have the honor to present for publication a series of reports on various diseases of cattle, giving the results of investigations undertaken, first as a duty imposed by the organic law originating this Department, and subsequently continued in pursuance of the direct authority of Congress, and with the aid of an appropriation in furtherance of the work.

About the middle of June, 1868, a disease broke out at Cairo, Illinois, at a point where large numbers of Texas cattle had been landed. It was the disease sometimes called "Spanish fever," but generally known as "Texas cattle disease." This epizoötic, long known and dreaded by owners of herds in Missouri and Kansas, and to some extent in Kentucky, Tennessee, and Virginia, became unusually serious in the track of Texas cattle beyond the Mississippi, in 1867 and 1868. While it was practically unknown in more eastern States, general interest in its manifestations was not aroused; but, when a new channel for the Texas cattle trade was opened, and the river steamboats landed their living freight in the heart of the West, the ravages of the strange disease extended rapidly, carrying infection along the pathway of transportation to the seaboard, filling the public mind with alarm for the safety of farm stock, and even exciting apprehensions that the public health might become involved in the future progress of the disease.

From Cairo the disease spread rapidly, breaking out among the native cattle exposed to the migrating stock, at all points of railroad transshipment. My attention was called to the serious nature of this disease when visiting the fair of the State Agricultural Society at Springfield, Illinois, and I immediately secured the services of Professor Gamgee, of London, England, who was at the time in this country, to make full investigation, under the following instructions:

> In view of the alarming and continued ravages of the cattle disease in Illinois, known popularly as the "Spanish fever," and assumed to be communicated by cattle recently from Texas, I hereby authorize you to make investigations into its cause and character, and to ascertain and report, if possible, a practicable remedy or means of prevention.

In accordance with this letter, the professor visited the infected districts in Illinois and vicinity, and extended his observations to the cattle depot at Abilene, in Kansas.

In the spring of 1869, in company with Mr. H. W. Ravenel, of South Carolina, an accomplished botanist, he visited that part of Texas on and near the Gulf coast, and examined into the conditions of food and management of the native cattle of Texas at those points at which transportation begins. The observations made are embodied in the accompanying reports of Messrs. Gamgee and Ravenel.

Four chromo-lithographs, illustrating the effects of splenic fever on the internal organs, are presented in connection with the report upon that disease.

As many forms of contagious disease are supposed to be due to zymotic or fermentative changes in the blood, in connection with which a microscopic cryptogamous vegetation is constantly present in a growing condition, and as European and American microscopists have asserted that this epizoötic is a disease of this character, it became essential to the success of this investigation that such microscopic examination should be skillfully made. A request was accordingly made by this Department to Brevet Brigadier General J. K. Barnes, Surgeon General United States Army, that Doctors J. S. Billings and E. Curtis, assistant surgeons United States Army, might be authorized to assist Professor Gamgee in his experiments upon the subject of the cryptogamic causes of disease. The Surgeon General authorized these gentlemen to enter upon that duty, and their report is appended.

The rapid extension of pleuro-pneumonia during the summer of 1868, and its increased fatality at points where cattle were collected in numbers, made it the duty of the Department to ascertain its nature, extent, and the possible means of checking or wholly obliterating it. I therefore authorized Professor Gamgee, in the autumn of 1868, to make a full investigation of the disease then spreading through many States of the Union. In December of that year Professor Gamgee presented a preliminary report, which was published in the monthly reports of 1868. His final report was first published with the preliminary reports of cattle diseases issued in the autumn of 1869, of which this is an enlarged edition.

By the favor of Surgeon General Barnes, and under his direction, a further scientific investigation of this disease has been made by Lieutenant Colonel J. J. Woodward, assistant surgeon United States Army, whose report on the pathological anatomy and histology of the respiratory organs in the pleuropneumonia of cattle, just received, is here presented, in connection with six micro-photographs illustrating the condition of the diseased organs.

Three chromo-lithographs accompany the report upon pleuropneumonia.

These reports are followed by a statistical history of the splenic fever, or Texas cattle disease, by J. R. Dodge, statistician of this Department, in which the devastations of this peculiar and native malady are unmistakably traced back into the eighteenth century.

It need not be presumed that these investigations are conclusive or final; on the contrary, some practical problems not yet fully demonstrated urgently demand examination. Among these are the best mode of arresting contagion and the proper regulation of cattle transportation northward. A general law in the interest of the public health, of an enlightened humanity, and of the cattle trade, should regulate the transportation of cattle, not only from the Gulf States, but on the great eastern routes and throughout the country.

HORACE CAPRON,
Commissioner.

Hon. SCHUYLER COLFAX,
President of the Senate.

REPORT OF PROFESSOR GAMGEE ON THE LUNG PLAGUE.

SIR: The lung plague of cattle, developed alone as the result of contagion, recedes and is extinguished wherever the people are fully informed of its origin and nature, and measures based on such knowledge are adopted and enforced. Americans can learn this from Massachusetts. It is, however, the most insidious and the most deceptive of all malignant bovine disorders. It penetrates and travels far and wide, where unsuspecting farmers and dairymen are far from skilled in the veterinary art. It kills, and yet there are survivors which resist all further attacks, and in the course of time they tend to form a small but useful nucleus of insusceptible stock, which enables the people to go on, though in poverty, and hope for better luck. Every one strives, but in secret, lest the publication of facts should prevent the sale and transfer of unhealthy or infected stock. Long Island, New Jersey, Pennsylvania, Maryland, the District of Columbia, and Virginia, furnish wide fields in which to determine the truth of these statements.

In perusing the history of contagious pleuropneumonia, it will be found that the experiences of the New World are but repetitions of those recorded by Europeans.

In advising as to the most certain means whereby so destructive a malady may be eradicated from this country, I have been actuated by the belief that the diffusion of knowledge, in a form that will carry conviction home to every intelligent American, is the most certain means whereby to deal a death blow to the lung plague. There are many prudent and earnest leaders of the agricultural body in every State, who can work, and will work, if armed with reliable information; and it is my belief in this that has induced me to spare no labor in rendering this as complete and satisfactory a record as possible of all the knowledge on the subject that is at present at our disposal. Farmers must not be alarmed at the scientific garb which must necessarily invest such a work. If they follow me through, without a dictionary, they will not be left in doubt as to my meaning, and I hope not a few will rise, after a perusal of what follows, even though they may inhabit the far distant prairies and the mountains of California, and exclaim that it is the duty of every American, and especially of every American farmer, to manifest his interest in the extinction of a malady that may for centuries, if left unheeded now, harass the stock-raisers of the entire continent, and bring poverty and ruin to many thousands of families.

The report has been presented, for convenience of reference, under the following heads:

I. Names by which the lung plague is or has been known in different parts of the world.

II. History of the lung plague from the remotest to the present time.

III. Signs or symptoms by which the disease is recognized during life.

IV. Signs or appearances by which it is recognized after death.

V. How the disease is induced, with special reference to predisposing causes and the nature of contagion.

VI. The pathology or nature of lung plague.

VII. Medical or curative treatment of the lung plague.

VIII. Prevention of the lung plague.

NOMENCLATURE.

The popular term "murrain" was applied, in times past, to all fatal cattle diseases that prevailed in an epizoötic form. The first satisfactory description of the lung plague, written by Bourgelat, in 1769, teaches us that the malady has been known for some years in Franche-Comté, under the name "*murie.*" The expression "pulmonary murrain" has been somewhat extensively used in Great Britain of late years, especially when reference has been made to the outbreaks of the last century, which have been considered as due to the simultaneous introduction into the British Isles of the Steppe murrain, commonly known as the rinderpest and cattle plague, and contagious lung disease.

When free trade first admitted continental cattle and the lung plague into the British Isles within this century, the dairymen who first observed the new fatal foot and mouth disease at once became alarmed at the "new disease," which proved incurable. Professor Hertwig, of Berlin, and correspondents of agricultural papers, soon enabled our veterinarians to recognize in the "new disease" the *Lungenseuche*, or, literally, lungs' plague of cattle, which had been studied with great ability by the veterinary surgeons of Germany. Haller had termed it *Viehseuche*, and expressed his astonishment that it had not been recognized as a disease of the lungs.

German writers were so numerous that attempts were not rare to give a scientific name to the disease, and Sauberg quotes seven Latin sentences employed by different authorities in accordance with the views of the nature and origin of the disease. They are:

Peripneumonia pecorum epizoötica typhosa—Veith, Tscheulin, Burger.

Peripneumonia exsudativa contagiosa—Rychner, Van Hertum.

Peripneumonia exsudativa enzoötica et contagiosa—Gielen.

Peripneumonia s. pleuropneumonia pecorum enzoötica—Dieterich, Vix.

Pleuritis rheumatico-exsudativa—Wagenfeld.

Pleuropneumonia interlobularis exsudativa—Gluge.

Pneumonia catarrhalis gastrica asthenica—Naumann.

Haller's title of *Viehseuche* is now almost always restricted to the Russian murrain, and the name in universal use in Germany is the popular one of *Lungenseuche*, and on the title-pages of monographs the ordinary expression employed is *Lungenseuche des Rindviehes.* It has, however, also been termed *Lungenfäule* and *Krebsartige Lungenfäule.*

Of the French authors, Chabert first names the malady *Péripneumonie, ou Affection gangréneuse du poumon.* Huzard describes it under the head *Péripneumonie chronique, ou Phthisie pulmonaire*, and in 1844 Delafond designated it *Péripneumonie contagieuse du gros bétail.*

The Dutch called it *Kwaadaardige Slijmziekte*, *Heerschende* or *Besmettelijke Longziekte*, *Slijmziekte*, *Slijmlongziekte*, and *Rotachtige Longziekte.*

In Italy it has been known by the names *Pulmonea dei bovini*, and *Pleuropneumonia essudativa.*

I am disposed to favor, as a popular name, that of "lung plague," in order to avoid any confusion with sporadic and non-contagious affections of the chest. Many years ago Mr. Sarginson, of Westmoreland, England, spoke of it as an epizoötic influenza among cattle, and Mr. Barlow, afterward a much respected professor in the Edinburgh Veterinary College, was among the first to draw attention to the disease under the head epizoötic pleuropneumonia.

HISTORY OF THE LUNG PLAGUE.

Ancient traditions and imperfect records rather tend to bewilder those who, from the inferences warranted by a complete knowledge of recent events, are anxious to place before the world evidence of the laws of nature having been immutable from time immemorial. Our ideas of creation, and the facts bearing on the origin of all things, are too meager to warrant us in being confident of our interpretations of the past; and yet glimpses of light seem to promise a better understanding of even antediluvian phenomena in almost every branch of natural history.

The assertion that plagues known now to be propagated alone by contagion have thus been transmitted from the remotest antiquity, is usually met by objectors with the declaration that the first case must have developed spontaneously. Professor Haubner, of Dresden,* accepting the proposition, says: "It is correct that the lung plague was once developed spontaneously, for no one can suppose that Noah had it with him in the ark." But we can point to a contagious disease, scab in sheep, which, if the words of the Bible are to be accepted, indicate the preservation of the scab insect. It is not my desire to enter on discussions which have no direct practical bearing, and I shall dismiss the objections of those who spare themselves the labor of inquiry after positive truth, by declaring that, so far as science has yet taught us, the great law, that like produces like, operates in the increase of certain animal poisons or forms of specific virus, just as in the case of other living entities whose reproduction is undoubted. Spontaneous generation—the theory of development by an accidental cohesion and vivifying of inert matter—ably as it has been defended up to the present day, is fast passing into oblivion. We are, and must probably remain, in ignorance of that final cause which once molded and gave life to all that is living. All that is living, however, owes that life to parents, and such has been the case ever since the globe became inhabited; and there are no facts to indicate that one form of living matter grew out of another, and a totally different, form, or that there were successive stages in the creation of animals or parts of animals. Animal poisons are known to us, it is true, only as parts of animals. They are undistinguishable except from the results produced by them on the creatures they infest, and yet they are as foreign to them as the countless parasites that are only known to us as abiding in the living tissues of living beings. Indeed, animal poisons may be regarded as parasitic productions, and their difference from the more apparent types of organized entities may be due more to imperfect means of observation than to actual diversity.

Efforts are, indeed, being made to demonstrate the vegetable origin of many animal poisons, and it is supposed by some that cryptogamic plants, fungi, &c., not only approach

* Die Entstehung und Tilgung der Lungenseuche des Rindes, von Dr. Karl Haubner, Leipzig, 1861.

more the nature of many forms of specific virus, but actually constitute the contagium or active principle which breeds and propagates in the development of small-pox, cholera, the plagues of the lower animals, &c. There is one grave objection to all that has yet been done in this interesting field of inquiry. The vegetable forms into which poisons are said to pullulate have not, in a single instance, been successfully employed in the reproduction of the diseases they have been supposed to generate.

Delafond* quotes Aristotle, who wrote his work on the History of Animals three hundred and fifty-four years before Christ, to prove that cattle were then known to suffer from a disease of the lungs. "The cattle," he says, "which live in herds are subject to a malady, during which the breathing becomes hot and frequent. The ears droop, and they cannot eat. They die rapidly, and on opening them the lungs are found spoiled."

In the collection of extracts and writings of the Greek veterinarians, made by order of the Emperor Constantine, descriptions of the lung diseases of cattle are given which may lead us to infer the prevalence even then of the lung plague.†

It would be simply waste of time to discuss the merits of unsatisfactory hints—for they are not records—which have been traced in the writings of Livy, Vegetius, Silius Italicus, Columella, Virgil, and others; hints which, no doubt, demonstrate that which few will question—that pulmonary disorders have existed throughout all time.

The evidence that we need is that definite record of outbreaks of a malady marked by the leading characteristics of the lung plague. We have to skip the age of pure quackery, when nothing but the unsatisfactory prescriptions of ignorant pretenders in veterinary medicine were handed down as valuable additions to human knowledge. A purpose is served, however, by referring to these dark ages, when, in their blindness, men sought to arrest the unrelenting torrents of fierce contagions by pills, draughts, charms, and incantations. It makes one blush for the errors and superstitions which, in the Old World and in the New, have prevailed up to the present hour. For seven and twenty years, at least, the people of Great Britain have, in the main, favored nothing but quackery in this respect, just as much as continental nations that suffered in ignorance did in the seventeen hundred years succeeding the birth of Christ. So late as 1865 the outbreak of a virulent cattle plague in England developed in its train the compounders of drugs and filth, and the believers in the treatment of isolated cases of a plague; of a plague, indeed, which advances in direct ratio to the delay in extinguishing its virulent poison, and the rapidity of whose spread may be likened to that of the confluent mountain waters that form the inland seas and navigable streams. Let the people learn from the ancient history of veterinary medicine, as they can learn from recent events, that to dam the Mississippi and annihilate its waters is quite as easy a process as attempting to save a country from incalculable loss by the medical treatment of isolated cases of a specific and contagious cattle plague.

That is the lesson which the want of knowledge regarding the lung plague in the first seventeen hundred years of the Christian era impresses upon us to-day. The wisdom of that conclusion may be demonstrated by tracing up the progress of the malady from 1693 to 1869.

---

* Traité sur la Maladie de Poitrine du Gros Bétail, connue sous le nom de Péripneumonie Contagieuse, par O. Delafond, Paris, 1844.

† Geoponicorum, seu de Re Rustica, Lib. XX—edited by Peter Needham, Cambridge, 1704—Quoted by Sauberg.

The first notice, that may be declared less unsatisfactory than all preceding ones, of the ravages produced by an epizoötic bovine pleuropneumonia, we owe to Valentini.* There is a fact of great importance in relation to the history and progress of pleuropneumonia that writers generally have overlooked. Valentini's remarks, incomplete as they are, had been anticipated by numerous reports concerning the spread of the foot and mouth disease, or epizoötic aphthæ, from east to west. As contagious cattle diseases travel in the lines of communication established by war or trade, so do they appear together or in succession according to their nature, the length of their period of incubation, and the circumstances under which the movement of cattle is conducted.

It will serve to clear up many points of doubt if this point is understood. Epizoötic aphthæ, or the foot and mouth disease, (*Maul und Klauenseuche* of the Germans,) has a short latent stage of two or three days. It moreover spreads to all warm-blooded animals, so that herds infected with contagious diseases might on their travels, as they often are, be seized by this malady, and then the Steppe murrain or rinderpest, which has a latent stage of a week, or the lung plague, which remains latent for a month, six weeks, or more, may break out wherever signs of communication between cattle of different parts have been furnished by the rapidly-evolving and curable aphthæ. The poison of one disease does not counteract or prevent the accession of either of the other two, and one animal may have the three maladies in succession. In Germany, France, Holland, and England, the foot and mouth disease has usually preceded outbreaks of lung disease, and even rinderpest. In America this has not been the case, inasmuch as the voyage across the Atlantic has usually been sufficient to purge animals of the contagion of epizoötic aphthæ, even if they had been shipped with the disease on them, which is not likely, from its very obvious and rapid manifestations.

It is necessary to make one more remark here, which may serve to facilitate the accurate reading of the history of cattle plagues. Although the lung plague has undoubtedly prevailed more constantly, and produced a total mortality greater than that due to the Steppe murrain, nevertheless the rapid slaughter of cattle by rinderpest at once sets people to adopt repressive measures, and, both by killing and isolating the disease itself, tends to supersede other cattle plagues. When it enters a country like Great Britain, where all animals which had a slight chance of contamination from public markets were more or less infected with the virus of lung plague, rinderpest naturally reached those spots first, cleared the cattle out, and extinguished pleuropneumonia.

Now we shall see that the histories of the three maladies I have alluded to are in many points practically inseparable, so far as their dissemination in Europe is concerned, and this fact alone would suffice to induce me to refer to the American outbreaks separately.

---

* Writing with but a small selection of books from my library, I am in a position to give only a second-hand reference to Valentini's observations, and their importance induces me to reproduce Heusinger's quotation: "Præcedente hyeme pluvioso, sed in fine gelidissimo, sub primo vere et insolitus aëris fervor ingruebat, qualis et per omnem æstatis cursum observabatur; quæ mutatio subitanea non poterat non inæqualem et præternaturalem humorum et spirituum motum causare, quem et hominum et brutorum strages insecuta est. Boves sani et vaccæ catervatim succumbebant, cujus rei causa statuebatur inter alia ros corrosivus, lintea maculis plus minus luteis conspurcans, et omnino corrodens. Ex carnificum observatione plerumque phthisi pulmonali necabantur, ad quam sine dubio haustus frigidæ copiosior post æstum intensissimum multum contribuere poterat. Hominibus præter dysenteriam et febres malignas sub finem Junii et initium Augusti hic locorum infensa erat febris qædam intermittens, ut plurimum tertiana." Ephem. Nat. Cur. et Sydenham, opp. ed Geneva, 1, p. 276—quoted in Recherches de Pathologie Comparée—Cassel, 1853.

In 1686–'87 the foot and mouth disease was noticed in Silesia, and other parts of Eastern Europe. In 1695 Valentini described the coincident inflammation of the feet of cattle and aphthæ in man.* And thus it established, beyond doubt, that the influences operating in the transmission of contagious pleuropneumonia were at work then. Valentini committed the common error of attributing the lung plague to the weather, but his reference to a wide-spread pulmonary disorder among cattle is sufficiently distinct to warrant our dissenting from Delafond when he says that nothing can authorize the conclusion that the disease described by Valentini was the pleuropneumonia which prevails to-day among horned cattle.

Sauberg, whose prize essay on the lung plague is worthy of the highest praise, draws attention to the fact that the propagation westward of the Russian murrain, at the commencement of the eighteenth century, directed the attention of the most learned naturalists and physicians to the investigation of the plagues of animals, and thus a marked influence was exerted in the development of veterinary science.

Kanold, Steurlin, Ramazzini, Lancisi, Bates, Lanzoni, Sebroek, Fischer, Scheuchzer, Bottoni, Muratori, Camper, Haller, and numerous others, have contributed to enrich the science of comparative pathology by references to outbreaks of epizoötic aphthæ, lung plague, rinderpest, variolous fevers, carbuncular, and other diseases, which committed great havoc up to the time that an illustrious Frenchman, Bourgelat, resolved to establish a college for the education of veterinary surgeons. All references to the contagious pleuropneumonia are of little practical moment until we come to the labors of Bourgelat himself. He did not, it is true—as no one ever did—on first studying this disease, recognize its contagious character. He met with it in Franche-Comté, where it had been known for years under the name of "*murie.*" He described it as distinguished by a short dry cough, much fever, great oppression, especially after an animal has eaten anything, loss of appetite, fetor of breath, dryness of nose, and sometimes discharge of thick whitish matter from the nostrils. His description of the pleuritic adhesions, the deposits of gelatinous layers of different colors around the lungs, the lividity and engorgement of the lungs, and distension of the chest by a reddish, frothy, sanious, or purulent liquid, is entirely satisfactory, and indicates how much in advance of his times Bourgelat was in his description of this malady. As there has been a disposition to revive the treatment of the lung plague by fumigations, I may mention that, among other remedies, Bourgelat recommended acetic acid to be used in this way.

The malady which had thus stationed itself in France, had also established secure hold in other parts of Europe, and we learn of its prevalence in 1743 in Zurich and the adjacent cantons of Switzerland. It continued to invade that country by importations from the grand duchy of Baden, and in 1773 the great physiologist, Haller, published the ablest memoir on this disease that appeared during the eighteenth century.† He spoke of it as a lung disease, beginning as an inflammation, which passes into gangrene, or at other times into abscess and ends in a true marasmus. "It is very wonderful," he adds, "that among the many modern physicians who have written on this plague, which has been observed so generally and for so long, that they have not noticed the seat of the disease to be in the

---

*Sub æquinoctio autumnali augusto decrepito, inflammatio gingivarum, linguæ et oris in hominibus, in brutis verum pedum inflammationes, observavi hinc inde.—Loc. Cit.

†Abhandlung von der Viehseuche. Von Herrn Alb. Haller. Bern, 1773.

lungs." Haller determined its cause and said, "*Above all, we must abandon all hope that the lung disease is not a contagious disease.* * * * * * At all events, it is certain that in our land, as often as the lung plague has appeared among cattle, the origin of the disease has always been traced to the purchase of an animal from a suspected market, or to one brought from an infected district into our land. At other times our country people have fattened cattle with other cattle from infected parts."

It is hard to trace the course of a disease during periods when little attention was paid to comparative pathology. From 1774 to 1776 the lung plague prevailed in Istria and Dalmatia.* Epizoötic aphthæ made steady inroads from Eastern Europe into Austria and other parts of the Continent. From 1778 to 1784 pleuropneumonia, no doubt very common in many countries, is specially referred to by Kauset and Orus as in Silesia and Istria. Its course during this and subsequent periods was involved in much obscurity, owing to the more alarming outbreaks of rinderpest, which absorbed the attention of scientific men, and also tended, by the wholesale and rapid destruction of herds, to supersede the more insidious pleuropneumonia. Huzard and Vicq d'Azyr studied the malady in 1791, and report that in the years 1772, 1776, 1780, 1787, 1789, 1791, and 1792 it raged among the milch cows of Paris and its neighborhood. Chabert described the malady in 1793, and recognized its contagious character, cautioning people against placing healthy cattle in communication with sick ones. Ioggia at that time studied the malady in Italy, and it prevailed in Baden during the years 1787, 1788, 1792, 1794, and 1798. It is to be regretted that little or nothing was known of this disease, which no doubt prevailed in Russia during the last century; and we are left to draw our own inference as to its probable prevalence there, from indications of its introduction through Poland to Prussia, but more frequently into Austria, Würtemberg, Switzerland, Northern Italy and France.

Records of outbreaks during the present century are more satisfactory. Bojanus studied the malady in Lithuania, and Jeuen first saw it in Russia in 1824. Haupt witnessed it repeatedly in Siberia, and Bussee observed it in the neighborhood of St. Petersburg in 1843, 1844, 1845, and 1850.

The malady invaded Prussia from 1802 to 1810, and was described by Sick in Rudolphi's Observations in Natural History and Medicine, published in Berlin, 1804. Dieterich witnessed it from 1815 to 1820, and Nogenfeld published in his work on the disease official reports of its manifestations in the Dantzig district from 1821 to 1831. Gielen saw the lung plague in 1832, at Blandenburg, and later, from 1837 to 1843, in Saxony. Sauberg, whose prize essay I have so often quoted, enters into very minute details concerning the outbreaks of pleuropneumonia in the Rhine provinces of Prussia, from 1830 to 1840. Some idea of the extent of the losses he had to report on may be derived from the fact that in the single district of Düsseldorf ten thousand head of cattle were lost from pleuropneumonia in the eight years from 1832 to 1840. Gerlach has drawn attention to this subject in Prussia with peculiar diligence since 1835, and remarks that he has watched personally so many cases, in conjunction with historical researches, that he unhesitatingly pronounces in favor of the view that pleuropneumonia is never developed spontaneously.

The lung plague prevailed severely in Hanover in the years 1807, 1808, 1809, 1810, 1812, 1817, 1818. In 1819 Hausmann suggested and performed experiments in the

* A. Fanti, sopra l'epizoozia bovina in alcuni luoghi della Dalmazia. Modena, 1776. Heusinger also quotes memoirs of Orus and Lotti.

inoculation of the disease, which never resulted in practical good. Outbreaks continued to be recorded in Hanover at short intervals from 1820 to 1843, and the country has never been altogether free since.

The malady appeared in Saxony in 1827, and has often raged there since, as shown in the writings of Haubner, and the observations made by Leisering and others.

In 1862 I made a careful study of the progress of pleuropneumonia toward the British Isles through Holland, and it is from these two countries that the New World, Africa, and the Australian colonies have been contaminated within the past quarter of a century.

The disease entered Holland, according to Numann, the director of the veterinary school at Utrecht, in 1833, by the importation of cattle affected with the disease from Prussia, and purchased by a distiller, Vandenbosch, in Gelderland. In 1835 it was transmitted from Gelderland to Utrecht, thence into South Holland, and it raged especially near the great markets of Rotterdam and Schiedam. The Island of Zeeland then began to suffer wherever cattle were injudiciously imported from South Holland, and some outbreaks were attributed to infected cattle from South Holland, North Brabant, and West Flanders From importations of infected cattle, the lung disease attacked the stock on a few farms scattered through the provinces of Drenthe, Groningen, and Overyssel. It was as late as 1842 that Friesland was attacked. British ports were thrown open to the cattle trade by Sir Robert Peel, and the demands of our markets caused a rush of stock through and from the northern provinces of Holland, which infected them in this year. The first traces of pleuropneumonia were observed at Nejiga and Wurms. The Dutch government ordered the slaughter of all the infected cattle, and Friesland again remained free of the disease until 1845. Then the British trade again increased; cattle were passing from Overyssel to Harlingen, and in the month of December, 1845, the malady appeared at St. Nicolunsga, the following March at Mirus, and soon after at Enkhuysen. Prevention, by slaughtering diseased cattle, was enforced; the authorities in Overyssel were asked to adopt similar measures, that there should be no renewed introduction of disease from that province. The cattle trade was too active, and no sooner was the malady extinguished in one spot than it appeared at others. In the last half of the year 1847 the disease broke out in sixteen stables in sixteen different districts. A last attempt was made to arrest the malady, and seven hundred and three sick or suspected animals were killed and buried. Larger and larger did the number of infected stables become as the cattle dealers' movements increased. In 1848 fifty-eight different outbreaks occurred. By 1863 five to six thousand out of the fourteen thousand stables in which cattle are kept in Friesland had been visited by the disease, and the annual mortality rose from 5.25 per thousand in 1850 to nearly 40 per thousand.

It was probably somewhere between 1839 and 1841 that some Dutch cattle were imported into the county of Cork, Ireland, by gentlemen related to a British consul at the Hague This was before the days of free trade in stock, and the animals were introduced under some special permit. Customs of this early period have their representatives in County Cork at the present day, and my inquiries lead me to believe that the earliest of these importations were followed by the manifestations of pleuropneumonia. It spread from Cork into Limerick in 1844, and thence to Carlow, Kilkenny, Tipperary, Waterford, Wicklow, Meath, Galway, and Roscommon. The losses in Ireland have been enormous, and indeed much larger than in England and Scotland. The north of Ireland has been more free than the south, but in 1844 cattle were imported into the county of Tyrone from Glasgow, communicating the disease, which continued till 1852. Londonderry suffered about 1849–'50, and here and there in all other counties, not excluding Kerry, the introduction of the malady by traveling or purchased cattle has occurred.

While the lung disease was thus lighting up in different parts of Ireland, it was committing great ravages in England. All the large towns containing dairy cows suffered. Speedily did the disease pass from London to Manchester, and Birmingham to Liverpool, Leeds, Sheffield and Newcastle. It was in the month of November, 1843, that English cattle carried the disease into Scotland at All-Hallow Fair, in Edinburgh. It speedily passed to Glasgow, Perth, and Aberdeen. In 1844 it reached Inverness, on cattle taken there by sea. Thus the large towns and their vicinities were first affected, but no great interval elapsed before farms were contaminated. The counties of Norfolk, Lincolnshire, Derbyshire, Lancashire, Yorkshire, and Northumberland were all affected by 1844 and 1845. It was later that the disease entered the breeding districts of Gloucestershire, Herefordshire, and Devon. Cheshire lost early and much. In Scotland it was 1846 or 1847 before many districts in such counties as Lanarkshire and Ayrshire had the disease. It committed great ravages in Wigtown, Renfrew, Fife, Perth, Kincardine, and Aberdeen shires. It has been rarely, and on a few farms, in such counties as Argyle, Banff, Inverness, and Caithness.

The losses by pleuropneumonia have amounted during the past seven-and-twenty years to as high as two million pounds sterling per annum in the United Kingdom of Great Britain and Ireland. The best cattle have been destroyed, inasmuch as the breeding cows and young stocks in breeding districts beyond the range of infection never attain the value of the fine milch cows and fattened steers which exist in milk-producing and fattening districts. I prepared a table of losses in 88 dairies in the city of Edinburgh, from the 1st of July, 1861, to the 1st of July, 1862, and out of 1,839 cows, 791 were sold diseased to butchers, and 284 were sold as food for pigs. The total value of the 1,075 diseased animals when first bought, at the very moderate average of £13 10*s.* each, is £14,512 10*s.* There was realized by their sale, calculating the value of the 791 sold to butchers at an average of £5 each, and the 284 sold for pig-feeding at 10 shillings each, the sum of £4,097. The net annual loss by diseased cows in Edinburgh alone was, therefore, £10,415 10*s.* Similar losses have occurred in all other large cities, such as Dublin, London, Liverpool, Newcastle, &c.

From England and Holland the disease has been propagated far and wide. In 1847 English cattle communicated pleuropneumonia to Sweden, and in 1848, it appears, from Sweden to Denmark. Mr. R. Fenger, a Danish veterinarian, furnished me, in 1862, with the following information: "As to the appearance of this disease in the Kingdom of Denmark, it is an established fact that it has taken place only three times upon three different farms where cattle had been introduced from abroad. No other cattle were affected than those in the three herds alluded to, and for three years no disease has appeared in Denmark. As to the spontaneous origin of pleuropneumonia, I wish to draw your attention to the fact that it is never seen in the town of Copenhagen, notwithstanding that in this place there are large dairies where the cows are fed on draff from distilleries, and are kept in a state contrary to any which sanitary rules might suggest. In the dukedom of Schleswig the disease has been imported several times, and last from England, and occasionally has spread rather widely. This autumn the cattle of thirty different places in Schleswig have been kept in a kind of quarantine."

In 1858 an agricultural society in Oldenburg purchased some Ayrshires to distribute among its members for breeding purposes. Wherever these animals went they communicated disease. Oldenburg has kept very free from pleuropneumonia from the activity with which the infected animals are destroyed at the outbreak of disease. The same remark applies to Mecklenburg-Schwerin and Schleswig-Holstein. With regard to the latter province, it transpires that in 1859 some Ayrshire cattle imported in the vicinity of Tondern communicated pleuropneumonia.

In the month of August, 1860, an agent of the Norwegian government purchased a number of Ayrshire cattle; they were taken to the Royal Agricultural College at Aas, and in the commencement of November pleuropneumonia broke out among them. Dr. Oluf Thesen has informed me that he limited the disease to the college by destroying the native cattle with which the Ayrshire stock had come in contact, and keeping the Ayrshire animals to themselves. Norway had been exempt from this cattle plague, and owing to Professor Thesen's activity it now enjoys the same immunity.

In the month of September, 1858, Mr. Boodle, farmer, near Melbourne, imported a cow from England; she landed in good condition and gave milk. She died of pleuropneumonia six weeks after her arrival. Two other head of cattle belonging to Mr. Boodle died in December, and another in January. The disease continued to spread, and the losses have been enormous and almost incessant in Victoria and even in New South Wales.

HISTORY OF THE LUNG PLAGUE IN AMERICA.

The first notice of the lung plague in the United States dates back to 1843, when a German cow, imported direct from Europe, and taken from shipboard into a Brooklyn cattle shed, communicated the disease, which, it is said and believed, has prevailed more or less in Kings County, Long Island, ever since.

In 1847 Mr. Thomas Richardson, of New Jersey, imported some English stock. Signs of disease were noticed soon, and the whole of Mr. Richardson's stock, valued at $10,000, were slaughtered by him to prevent an extension of the plague.

In 1850 a fresh supply of the lung-plague poison reached Brooklyn from England in the system of an imported cow.

Mr. W. W. Chenery, of Belmont, Massachusetts, has related the history of the introduction of lung plague from Holland into Massachusetts in 1859. Four cows were purchased for him at Purmerend and Beemster, shipped at Rotterdam early in April on board the bark J. C. Humphreys, which arrived in America on the 23d of May, 1859. Two of the cows were driven to Belmont; the other two had to be transported on wagons, owing to their "extremely bad condition," one of them "not having been on her feet during the twenty days preceding her arrival." On the 31st of May, it being deemed impossible that this cow could recover, she was slaughtered, and on the 2d of June following the second cow died. The third cow sickened on the 20th of June, and died in ten days. The fourth continued in a thriving condition. A Dutch cow, imported in 1852, was the next one observed ill, early in the month of August following, and she succumbed on the 20th. "Several other animals were taken sick in rapid succession, and then it was that the idea was first advanced that the disease was identical with that known in Europe as epizoötic pleuropneumonia." Mr. Chenery then did all in his power to prevent the spread of disease from his farm. The last case at the Highland farm, Belmont, occurred on the 8th of January, 1860.

In June, 1859, Curtis Stoddard, of North Brookfield, bought three young cattle, one bull and two heifers, from Mr. Chenery. One calf showed signs of sickness on the way home. Leonard Stoddard, father of Curtis, thinking he could better treat the sick calf, took it to his own barn, where he had forty-eight head, exclusive of calves, and with which the calf mingled. One animal after another was attacked, till the 12th of April, when thirteen head had died, and most of the remainder were sick. The disease continued to spread from farm to farm as rapidly as circumstances favored the admixture of stock. The period of incubation in well-defined cases varied from nineteen to thirty-six days, and averaged twenty-six and two-thirds days.

The people of Massachusetts, a little slow at first, overcame the delays incident to legislation, established a commission for the purpose of exterminating the disease, and an appropriation of $10,000 was placed under the control of the commissioners on the 4th of April, 1860. The disease was gaining ground rapidly, and a bill to extirpate the disease passed its several stages and was approved on the same day. Commissioners were appointed; herds were examined by surgeons, and, if infected, slaughtered; the animals pronounced healthy at the time of inspection were paid for; all the money appropriated was spent, and such was the feeling then in Massachusetts that private gentlemen made themselves responsible for a second amount of nearly $20,000. An extra session of the legislature was called for the 13th of May. Fresh powers were sought and obtained, additional commissioners were appointed, and the disease was apparently exterminated. It reappeared in 1861, a new board of commissioners was appointed, and further successful efforts were made to prevent the disease. On the 24th of December, 1863, Mr. Charles L. Flint, in a letter to Governor Andrew, asserted that pleuropneumonia still existed in twelve or fifteen towns of the Commonwealth of Massachusetts. Mr. E. T. Thayer, to whom the people of Massachusetts owe much for his skill and industry as the veterinary commissioner, and Mr. Charles P. Preston, wrote their final report to the senate and house of representatives of Massachusetts on the 30th of December, 1867. In that report, in tendering their resignations to the governor, they congratulate the people on the success which had been insured by efficient co-operation "in eradicating one of the worst forms of contagious disease which has been found among cattle."

From numerous inquiries there is not the slightest doubt in my mind that the lung disease has continued, ever since its first introduction, to attack some of the numerous dairies on Long Island. One of the best informed dairymen in Brooklyn informed me that, three months after starting in business, sixteen years ago, he lost eleven out of twelve cows he had purchased in Newark, New Jersey. He bought more and began to inoculate with excellent results. Other people were losing, and he established himself on Jamaica Pond to be clear of every one. When he stopped inoculating the disease reappeared. Mr. Benjamin Babbit, of Lafayette avenue, was the first to inoculate after the introduction of this practice in Europe, and many dairymen adopted it. The board of health opposed the practice, as many of the cows lost portions of the tail, and reports were made of blood and matter finding their way into the milk-pail. The disease has never ceased, and I have visited many dairies, in all of which, at one time or another, and in most of which during the present year, the disease has prevailed. In five dairies I examined, within one hundred yards of each other, I found one or two sick cows in each. The Hartford Insurance Company, which has recently suspended operations, lost heavily on the insurance of cows from the prevalence of this disease, and that company objected also to the practice of inoculation.

From Mr. Bedell's statement there is no doubt of the existence of the contagious pleuropneumonia in New Jersey when he first bought his cattle. Mr. Robert Jennings, veterinary surgeon, had his attention drawn to the disease on its appearance in Camden and Gloucester Counties, New Jersey, in the year 1859. In 1860 it crossed the Delaware River into Philadelphia, spreading very rapidly in all directions, particularly in the southern section of the county known as "The Neck"—many of the dairymen losing one-third to one-half of their herds. The sale of sick cattle continued, as it always does, unless prevented by rigid laws. In 1861 the malady appeared in Delaware, and in Burlington County, New Jersey, and the disease could be distinctly traced to the Philadelphia market.

The records of outbreaks are by no means satisfactory, but a gentleman well known in Maryland, Mr. Martin Goldsborough, informs me that the malady has been very destructive on many farms of that State for the past three years. Individuals have lost their entire herds, in some cases numbering twenty-four, thirty, and as high as forty-seven head. Last year an effort was made to direct the attention of the legislature of Maryland to the subject, with a view to the adoption of successful measures, but without effect. Mr. Goldsborough's statement is to the effect that the disease in Maryland is due to the purchase of cattle in the Philadelphia market.

There is no doubt of the great prevalence of the malady for some years in Pennsylvania. I have seen it on two farms in Delaware County, and it has been on several others recently. Bucks County has suffered much for two years. A correspondent informs me that in March, 1867, a drove of cows was taken into that county, and one of them was observed to be sick. These animals were distributed among the farmers, and soon the plague appeared in all directions. An effort was made then to secure the aid of the State legislature, without effect, and to this day the disease is in Bucks County. The last case I have to report is at Newtown, Bucks County, where the disease was introduced by cows bought in the Philadelphia market.

That the malady has attained such proportions as to demand constant attention, apart from the fact that but one case on the whole continent is a source of incalculable danger, is proved by a circular recently issued by gentlemen in Westchester, Pennsylvania, and which is of sufficient importance to be reproduced here:

Pleuropneumonia.—The great increase in the disease known as pleuropneumonia among cattle within a few years past, its highly contagious character, and the acknowledged inability of the most skillful veterinary surgeons to control or in the least mitigate its severity in certain stages of the disease, call for immediate and earnest attention from the community. It is a well-known fact that the cupidity of many induces them as soon as the disease develops itself on their premises to hurry off their stock (diseased as well as those not diseased) to the nearest drove-yard, to be there sold for whatever they will bring; to be either sold as food or driven off to new sections, and there to infect and poison other animals with which they may come in contact.

With the view of arresting this increasing and wide-spreading evil, the undersigned, a committee of the "Mutual Live Stock Insurance Company of Chester County," an institution established purely for mutual assistance and protection, respectfully invite your co-operation in procuring such action at the hands of our next legislature, by the passage of a law authorizing the appointment of a suitable number of qualified and conscientious inspectors throughout the State, whose duty it shall be to examine thoroughly all animals, especially those offered for sale, wherever they may be, and to subject those offering such diseased animals to both fine and imprisonment, and to take such other measures as may be deemed necessary to effect the entire extirpation of the disease from our midst.

I can corroborate the statements made as to the sale of cattle that are infected. Not only has this occurred often where the disease has been most rife for years past, as on Long Island, but recently, in making inquiries in Delaware County, Pennsylvania, I learned of three cows which had been sold "healthy" (?) out of an infected herd. Such a practice explains the progress of the disease even further south than Maryland.

I have been informed that the malady has traveled as far west as Kentucky and Ohio, but of this I have not been able, in the brief time since I commenced the inquiry, to obtain satisfactory evidence. I have taken some pains to ascertain if the disease had reappeared in Massachusetts, and personal inquiries in various parts of the State show that it is quite free from the disease, thanks to the energy of its people and the enlightened action of its legislature.

The conclusions that are warranted by the facts I have gleaned are as follows:

First. That the lung plague in cattle exists on Long Island, where it has prevailed for many years; that it is not uncommon in New Jersey; has at various times appeared in New York State; continues to be very prevalent in several counties of Pennsylvania, especially in Delaware and Bucks; has injured the farmers of Maryland, the dairymen around Washington, D. C., and has penetrated into Virginia.

Second. That the disease travels wherever sick cattle are introduced, and that the great cattle-rearing States of the West, which may not at present be entirely free from the disease, have been protected by the fact that they sell rather than buy and import horned stock.

Third. There are no proper restrictions on the sale of infected stock, and in another year or two, unless some definite and immediate action should be taken, the disease is likely to find its way into so many parts of the country that its eradication will be almost impossible.

Of all the cattle diseases pleuropneumonia is in the long run the most destructive, because the most insidious and the least likely to rouse a people to united action for its effectual suppression. To ignore its presence is, however, to insure that the cattle mortality of America, like that of England, will be at least doubled within a few years. Rational means, energetic action, and earnest co-operation between the different States and the central government, may, with a moderate expenditure now, save many millions annually in the not distant future.

For three years past the city of Washington, and, indeed, the whole District of Columbia, with adjoining parts of Maryland and Virginia, have been seriously affected with the lung plague. It is gleaned from the contractors who clean the city of the carcasses of dead animals, that it is not uncommon to have several dead cows in a day from the Washington dairies; that to have a dozen a week has not been unusual, during certain seasons, and that the supply is constant. Unfortunately, as in other cities of America and Europe, the prevalence of pleuropneumonia results in a wholesale traffic in such animals. Sick cows are sold to butchers, and if in good condition command thirty to sixty dollars; others that are too lean are taken in the early stage, mixed with other stock, and sent by railroad to Baltimore, to be sold as stock cows to farmers. In fact, the active and unremittent traffic in sick cattle insures that Washington, the neighborhood of Alexandria, in Virginia, and Baltimore, will continue to be great breeding centers of pleuropneumonia. Some idea of the heavy losses in the Washington district may be gleaned from a table annexed, prepared by a Washington dairyman. (See Appendix at close of this report.)

SIGNS OR SYMPTOMS DURING LIFE.

It is necessary to draw special attention to the fact that in States or on farms where the lung plague has never before existed it is the more readily recognized, in the earlier stages, as in case of other epizoötics, the more complete the history. The fact that cattle have been recently purchased, or that drift cattle have crossed the farm or prairie, the knowledge of the existence of such a disease in adjoining States or farms, or of sick cattle being sold by auctions or in the markets, are all most important elements in guiding to a correct conclusion as to the nature of the disease.

Very frequently an animal is bought, placed among others, dies, and the remaining cattle cough, get out of condition, and some soon sicken. The purchased animal may show no signs of illness, however; it may be suffering from a latent form of the disease, or it may be in the convalescent stage, and gaining flesh daily.

A dairyman, especially in a large town, may have had pleuropneumonia among his cattle, which had subsided, and his stock, composed of animals that had withstood the disease, might be regarded as healthy. But some still discharge a degree of poison, and infect the atmosphere, and a newly bought animal dates the period of the incubation of the malady from the moment it entered the stable.

The incubation of the disease may be said to vary from eight or nine days to three or four months. In the inoculated malady the exudation commences sometimes as early as the fifth day, more commonly about the ninth or twelfth, and it may be as late as thirty or forty days. In the disease communicated by cohabitation, a cough, to which very special attention was drawn by the experiments of the French commission on contagion, supervenes about the ninth day and later. It is usually noticed by cow-feeders, who buy cows which have just calved, that they drop with the disease about the time they should manifest œstrum, that is to say, six weeks after their admission.

There are false and true periods of incubation of the lung plague. And this has been overlooked too much in descriptions of the disease. The actual incubation is from the period of contamination, by contact or inoculation, to the moment that a special morbid change commences. Our means of observation have not been exact enough, and it is very desirable that thermometric observations should be made on experimental animals, and these, with the ordinary phenomena derived by auscultation, &c., will assure us of the actual length of the stage of the lung disease which is unattended by any appreciable sign. We shall then know the true period of incubation. The false periods of incubation are those derived by persons from observing an animal to sicken, say four months after purchase, and drawing the conclusion that this period represents the incubation stage. As a rule in such cases, two or three latent instances of the disease have preceded the obvious one. Then, again, the period of incubation is not usually stated correctly by farmers, as they overlook the first signs of the disease, which occur several days before cessation of appetite, secretion of milk, &c.

Invasion of the lung plague is characterized by local phenomena which most frequently show themselves by the cough already referred to. With one of Casella's self-registering thermometers it will be found that in an infected herd some animal or animals in apparent health, which no one suspects to be diseased, will manifest a temperature of 104° or 105° Fahrenheit. I have never seen a case in which, when the temperature was thus elevated,

I could not detect friction sounds, loud respiratory murmurs, especially at the lower part of the trachea and involving one lung. It is not a little remarkable to notice the want of faith of some persons who watch the separation of such cattle, with great doubt as to the correctness of the observation. In rinderpest the elevation of temperature occurs before all other signs, and to a less marked extent this is the same with splenic fever; but in pleuropneumonia there is reason to believe that acute observation would reveal first the local change and then the fever.

In order to show the value of the thermometer in this disease, I subjoin the observations made by me on two herds of cows suffering from it, and which I inoculated on the 26th of February, 1869, at Alexandria:

MR. BIEMÜLLER'S COWS.		MR. REID'S COWS.	
No.	Fahr.	No.	Fahr.
1	101.4	1	101.5
2	102	2	101.8
3	102	3	102.6
4	101	4	101.4
5	101.6	5	101
6	102.3	6	102.2
7	102	7	102
8	101.8	8	101.8
9	104.4	9	102
10	102.6	10	102.8
11	101	11	105.2
12	102	12	101.4
13	101.6	13	101.3
14	105.6	14	103
15	103.6	15	100.6
16	101.3	16	101.8
17	101	17	102.2
18	101.3	18	101.8
19	104.4	19	102.6
20	102.2	20	101
21	101		

Of Reid's cows, Nos. 11 and 14 were sick, and of Biemüller's, Nos. 9, 14, 15, and 19. Some doubt exists as to No. 19; I had not opportunity of seeing her again. Mr. Reid thinks she might have been at heat, but from the indications, however slight, associated with the elevation of temperature, I believe it was one of the numerous latent cases which the thermometer alone reveals to us. Nos. 14 and 15 were in the earliest stages of the malady, and both grew worse, suffered for three weeks, and then recovered.

OBVIOUS PREMONITORY SIGNS.

The obvious premonitory signs are shivering fits, as in ordinary fever, but their transient and mild character lead to their often being passed unnoticed. The animal's coat looks dull, staring, and the skin is often rigid. An occasional cough of a dry and harsh character is noticed, and, when inspecting a herd in a field, if the cattle are made to move briskly, several will be found to cough. For some days the cattle appear to thrive well, and milch cows yield a copious amount of milk. It has been remarked that they appear full—indeed fuller in the early morning than other animals which, like them, had not fed since the previous evening. The excrement is dry, and urine somewhat scanty.

An expert dairymaid, in the habit of milking cows where the disease prevails, is apt to notice, as the malady declares itself, that there is some stiffness, and the milk is not so freely drawn as usual. The quantity of this secretion then diminishes.

The progress of the malady is then characterized by loss of appetite, altered gait, segregation of the sick from the healthy in the field, the sick standing with their elbows turned outward, their feet drawn forward, neck and head extended, and nostrils somewhat convulsively expanded at each inspiration. There is quickness of breathing, especially if the animal is even slightly disturbed, and on the slightest movement there is an audible grunt. The expression of countenance indicates uneasiness or absolute pain, and the eyes are prominent and fixed. The pulse rises to seventy, eighty, and even one hundred beats per minute. In hot cow-sheds the pulse is more frequent than in the open field in healthy cattle, and a corresponding increase is seen in this disease under similar circumstances. The respirations rise to thirty-five and forty per minute, are labored, audible, and each expiration is often associated with a short characteristic grunt. This grunt is especially marked if the sides of the chest or the spine are pressed; and many years ago Lecoq showed that graziers regarded this as a decisive symptom of the malady. A somewhat watery discharge from the nose, increased in the act of coughing, is noticed early in the disease, and driving sick cattle in the earliest stage produces much thirst, and there is a ropy saliva discharged from the mouth. The muzzle is hot and dry.

Cattle suffering from this disease are readily identified, as it advances, by persons who have seen a few cases. They stand motionless, with protruding head, arched back, extended fore limbs, with elbows turned as far out as they can be held, and the hind limbs drawn under them, with knuckling at the near hind or both hind fetlocks. When lying, especially in the latter stages of the disease, they rest on their brisket or lie on the affected side, leaving the ribs on the healthy side of the chest as much freedom of motion as possible.

As the disease advances the pulse gets more frequent and feeble, and the heart's beats, which are at first subdued, become marked and palpitating, as in cases of poverty or anæmia. The membranes of the eyes, mouth, and vagina are usually pallid, though the membrane of the nose is often red. The tongue is foul, covered with fur, and the exhaled breath has a nauseous and even fetid odor.

Listlessness, grunting, grinding of teeth, diminished secretions, weakness, and emaciation, increase with the progress of the malady. When the animals become weak they lie more. They sometimes show symptoms of jaundice, have a tendency to heave, or tympanitis from gases accumulating in the paunch, and their gait is so staggering that they appear to suffer from partial paralysis of the hind quarters. As all these aggravated symptoms develop themselves the pulse becomes weak, and often rises to one hundred and twenty per minute; the breathing is more frequent and labored; the animal gasps for breath. The spasmodic action of the nostrils is very marked, the grunt very audible, and there is a peculiar puckering of the angles of the mouth. The temperature, which is elevated during the acute stage of the disease, is irregularly up and down, according to the complications of the disease, and there is great tendency to coldness of the horns and extremities. Abortion is not an uncommon accident. The constipation, which is a very common symptom of the lung disease, is apt to be followed by diarrhea in the later stages, and this is also associated with a considerable discharge of clear-colored urine.

Auscultation and percussion are valuable aids in the diagnosis of lung plague. Most persons can, with a little care, distinguish the sick from healthy cattle by listening to the sides of the chest. It does not require a skillful expert to recognize that the ribs are motionless and flattened over the consolidated lung, that there is an absence of resonance on striking the ribs over the affected region, and that the ear distinguishes a very distinct respiratory murmur wherever the lung is pervious, and an absence of this sound where the lung is transformed into a solid mass.

At an early stage of pleuropneumonia there is a harsh sound, roar, or rhonchus, produced by the passage of air through the windpipe and its subdivisions. This varies in intensity in different cases, as some animals have more exudation on the mucous surface of the air passage than others, and the leathery-looking shreds of lymph adhering to the inflamed membrane vibrate as the air rushes past them, giving rise to the harsh sound which may sometimes be heard by persons standing by a sick animal. In many cases one lung alone is affected, and then the respiratory murmur is more distinct than in health wherever the lung tissue is pervious, whereas there is a total absence of sound over the consolidated organ. Occasionally an air passage remains open through a mass of hardened lung, and the air rushing through this rigid bronchial tube makes a very decided whistling noise.

In the earliest stages of pleuropneumonia the deposit of lymph on the serous covering of the ribs and lungs produces a leathery-friction sound, and as liquid accumulates in one or both cavities of the chest the respiratory murmur is lost towards the lower part of the affected side or sides, and it is alone distinct over the upper portions of pervious lung tissue.

A careful examination of the chest reveals, day by day, the progress of the disease. When one lung is affected an animal is much more likely to recover than when both are diseased. Portions of the diseased lung tissue are apt to die, and, becoming detached or softened, produce cavities in the lungs, which are indicated by a cavernous râle or sound somewhat similar to that produced by blowing air in the hollow of the hands when closed against each other.

By careful auscultation the cases that tend to convalescence may be distinguished by less marked roughness in the inspirations, and a gradual though slow return of the respiratory murmur, with increased mobility of the ribs and easier movement of the flanks.

TERMINATION.

Cases of lung diseases in cattle end in partial or complete restoration to health, or death by prostration, suffocation, purulent fever, or hectic.

As a rule, when a herd of cattle has suffered from the contagious pleuropneumonia, the surviving animals, whenever slaughtered, show old adhesions, partial collapse of the lung tissue, atrophy or wasting of the lung, thickness of the heart's covering or pericardium, and sometimes chronic abscess. Complete recovery without leaving the slightest traces of pre-existing lesion occurs. It has been noticed that cattle that have once had pleuropneumonia fatten more readily than others.

Death supervenes during the acute attacks of the disease from shock, prostration, or gradual suffocation. When animals linger on for some time in the bloodless state peculiar to this disease, and which is mainly due to the great drain on the system by the immense discharge which occurs in the substance of the lung and cavities of the chest, a permanent impairment of the functions of nutrition or assimilation occurs, and, although the appetite may be partially restored, emaciation advances, and the animal sinks. A terrible diarrhœa or dysentery usually accompanies this form of disease.

In other cases abscesses form in and around the lungs and in other parts of the body, and the animals die of purulent infection. Occasionally a cavity formed by the breaking up of diseased lung tissue communicates with the pleural sack or cavity of the chest, and a condition known to pathologists as empyema results, to the certain destruction of the animal.

DURATION OF THE DISEASE.

Affected animals usually pass through an incubative stage varying from twenty to eighty days, and usually averaging from twenty-five to forty days. The acute stage of the disorder varies from seven to twenty-one days. Convalescence extends over a period of one, two, or even three months, during the greater part of which the convalescent animal is often capable of infecting healthy cattle.

The mortality varies from one to ninety per cent. of the affected animals. When a first case is isolated early, all the remaining animals may continue to enjoy health. As a rule, in mild outbreaks, the mortality attains twenty-five per cent., and in severe cases sixty, seventy, eighty, or even one hundred per cent.

In England the lung disease has doubled the usual cattle mortality of the country, and during many years fifty per cent. of the cattle that have died of disease have died of the contagious lung disease.

LATENT FORM.

It is necessary that I should draw special attention to the large number of cases which run an insidious course and pass unobserved. These are the most dangerous, as less care is paid to their isolation.

APPEARANCES AFTER DEATH.

Animals that are slaughtered, or are permitted to die in advanced stages of the lung plague, present the following characteristics:

The internal changes are confined almost entirely to the chest. On opening this, by splitting the brisket, as the animal lies on its back, layers of yellowish, friable, false membrane, of varying tenacity, stretch across and around the sack (pericardium) containing the heart. These adhesions exist on one or both sides of the chest, but are sometimes altogether absent. They are found bathed in a yellowish, grumous fluid or serum, highly charged with albumen and shreds of solid deposit. Portions of one or both lungs are found more or less firmly adhering to the membrane (pleura) covering the ribs and diaphragm, and in passing the hands, especially round the large posterior lobes of either lung, it is difficult, in advanced stages of the disorder, to detach the diseased portions of the organ from the ribs.

The false membranes, disposed in layers which may be stripped off the pulmonary surface, are found adhering more or less closely to it, and the membrane (pleura) covering the lung, which is usually smooth and glistening, is rough, of mottled color, and with more or less marked papillary or warty-looking eminences. These are the vascular offshoots of the membrane feeding the deposit around, and in time the process of growth and formation of vascular or blood-carrying tissue may lead to as solid a connection between the lung and the sides of the chest as between healthy tissues. Such complete development is seen only in very chronic cases, or animals that have recovered from the disease.

The fluid around one or both lungs varies in amount from a few ounces to several gallons. At times it is tolerably clear when warm, and gelatinizes on cooling. At others it is difficult to separate it from the shreds of lymph and false membranes in the meshes of which it is held. Pus cells frequently abound in it, and it assumes in a few cases the character of pus. It is especially purulent when abscesses have formed in the gangrenous lung tissue, and an opening has led to communication between the lung tissue and the pleural sack. Under these circumstances, the fetor noticed on opening the chest is intolerable.

On removing the lungs, great variations in extent, but uniformity in essential appearances, of disease exist.

In recent and mild cases, one lung is found affected. Its surface may be smooth from the absence of deposit around it. Parts of the organ are collapsed, as in health, and the usual normal pink color is noticed. The affected part is swollen, hard, and mottled. On cutting into this, the older diseased portions present a very peculiar marbled or tessellated character. The substance of the lobules is solid and of a dark red color, and the tissue between the lobules is of a yellowish red, more or less spotted with red points, but sometimes of almost pure yellowish white color.

The more recent deposits are distinguished mainly by a lighter red color of the thickened lobules, and there are gradations from this condition to that in which the lobules are but slightly infiltrated with semi-liquid serum, and air still passes more or less into their air vesicles.

As the disease advances, the extent of solidified and darkened lung increases, and portions of the lung tissue lose more or less the marbled appearance, from the blood-staining of the interstitial deposit. The consolidation of structures advances so that the blood vessels are obstructed, the diseased lung loses all means of nourishment, and the older, darker, and more solid portions become detached, so that they remain as foreign bodies imbedded in cavities in the diseased tissue. The admissions of air through the air passages into these cavities by dissolution of the lung tissue, lead to the cavernous sounds which the ear can detect in the living animal, and the broken-up tissue decomposes and induces great fetor of the breath.

One lung may have several points diseased; each lobe may be affected and little or no communication between the several parts implicated. The great tenacity of a yellowish white deposit around a marked marbled center of disease has been said to indicate a certain tendency to limitation by the formation of a capsule, and several encapsulated centers may be found.

On taking a warm diseased lung, severing the still healthy portions, making incisions into the parts solidified, and suspending them so that they may drain, a large amount of yellowish serum of a translucent character, almost wholly free or more or less tinged with blood, is obtained to the extent of pounds in weight. The amount varies with weight of diseased lung drained. The quantity of this and of the solidified deposit in a diseased lung is so large, that from a normal weight of four or five pounds, a lung attains to ten, twenty, forty, and I have seen one as high as fifty-four pounds in weight.

AIR PASSAGES.

The condition of the air passages varies from one of perfect freedom in the healthy portions of the lung to a state in which the mucous surface is coated with false membrane or solid exudations of lymph in the diseased parts. By suitable means it is not difficult to isolate the solid white lymph clogging the terminal bronchial tubes and air vesicles in the consolidated tissues, but at a distance from these parts it is only in some cases that a kind of croupy complication exists. I have seen an animal gasping for breath, with its mouth open, nostrils widely expanded, eyes prominent, and visible mucous membranes of a bluish red color: on opening the air passages of this cow after death, they were found throughout their whole extent nearly filled with a deposit similar to that usually found on the surface of the diseased lung.

There is little necessity for prolonging this description of cadaveric manifestations. The heart's sack is sometimes thickened by deposits around it. Not unfrequently it contains an excess of serum. The heart itself is contracted and pale, containing a little dark blood. The organs of digestion at different stages manifest a state of dryness. The third stomach, which is so constantly packed with dry food in febrile diseases, is in the same condition in pleuropneumonia. I have known the mucous layers spotted with irregular or circular congestions or blood extravasations, and the membrane softening in these parts has become perforated. In advanced cases there is more or less diffuse redness, and even blood extravasations in the large intestine, with fluid, fetid, and sometimes slightly blood-stained, excrement, such as is discharged during life.

The anæmia—or bloodless condition of other tissues—the dark, dry look of the meat dressed by the butcher, the yellow color of the fat in some cases, and the small quantity of fat left in animals that have succumbed under a chronic attack, are all general signs of greater or less value when taken in conjunction with the changes occurring in the chest.

THE CAUSES OF THE LUNG PLAGUE.

The facts which have been adduced in the foregoing pages would seem sufficient to set at rest discussions as to the causes hitherto alleged as giving rise to the spontaneous development of contagious pleuropneumonia. Nevertheless we have seen that wherever the malady appears for the first time the relation of its undoubted cause and effect is usually overlooked. Many circumstances tend to obscure the observations even of experts, and it is more particularly in large cities, where the disease is most common and observers more numerous, that conditions mislead and have misled. With a view therefore to impede the renewal of false theories which have up to the present day insured the steady reproduction and propagation of this bovine pest, it may be well to enter into details under three heads:

1st. The alleged original causes of the lung plague.

2d. Contagion and infection.

3d. Conditions favoring or insuring communication of the disease by actual contact or approach.

THE ALLEGED ORIGINAL CAUSES OF THE LUNG PLAGUE.

Man at all times and in virtue of a strong instinct theorizes on the why and the wherefore of everything. Valentini, in his records of the lung disease, overlooking altogether many points which, with the knowledge of the present day, enable us to interpret correctly the phenomena he observed, ascribed the lung plague to atmospheric agencies and unseasonable weather. Haller, a shrewd observer and great philosopher, adopted an inductive system of research, and, arguing from his own sphere of observation, declared, in words which deserve to be written in gold, that so far as his district was concerned the disease appeared always to be imported. He did not hide the truth under a load of wild and fanciful theories in attempting to explain more than he saw and could judge of personally.

Since the establishment of veterinary colleges in France two theories have been and to a certain extent continue to be advocated. Chabert regarded the bovine pleuropneumonia so common in the dairies of Paris as contagious, whereas Huzard held the contrary opinion. The field of discussion widened, and it came to be very widely admitted that acute affections of the chest were contagious, and the chronic forms incapable of communication from the sick to the healthy. Not only was this believed of pulmonary complaints among cattle, it was also accepted with reference to glanders in the horse.

Delafond, though an able advocate of the contagious character of pleuropneumonia in 1844, had previously entertained grave doubts on the question. Even in his classical work on the disease, while advancing a large mass of invaluable information demonstrating how in truth the malady extends, his usual desire to round off and complete his works led him to theorize and err as to the origin of what he calls "spontaneous pleuropneumonia" in cattle. This expression is not applied by him to an ordinary attack of inflammation of the lungs, which no one ever ascribes to contagion, but to the lung plague. The local or determining causes of the spontaneous form of this disease he summarizes as follows:

A. Heat and impure atmosphere of stables in which cattle live for five or six months of the year, especially when this heat and impurity are combined with a very nutritive aliment that produces much blood.

B. Abundant milk secretions, required from cows in certain localities, either for the sale of milk or of butter and cheese.

C. Chills of the skin and respiration by cold, humid, misty air on pastures, either during spring or autumn; the introduction of cold air in the lungs in winter on taking animals from the stables to be watered.

D. The glacial waters which cattle are compelled to drink in winter, and the unhealthy waters of marshes which they have to take in summer.

E. The hard work to which work cattle are subjected in summer in clearing forests, &c.

F. Lastly, hereditary predisposition.

All this classified blundering might be disposed of in one sentence, by asserting the truth, that the experience of ages has shown, in many parts of the world, that all these causes, singly and combined, have failed to induce a case of pleuropneumonia. Whether we examine the agricultural annals of Scotland or Spain, of Canada or Texas, of South America or Australia, it will be found that alternations of temperature, chills, breathing the pure air of heaven as near the north pole as cattle have reached, drinking the frozen waters of North America or the stagnant pools in the swamps of the Carolinas and Louisiana during the hottest summers, the hard toils and sufferings of many a Mexican yoke of oxen, and, lastly, the greatest negligence of an agricultural people in relation to the improvements of breeds, one and all have failed ever to induce a single case of lung plague. Delafond had his theories. We have an array of facts on our side as great and as incontrovertible as any ever before adduced in support of any medical or other question.

But brevity is not always desirable when the object to be attained is the diffusion of an abundant and accurate knowledge, and interesting points may be beneficially discussed under the separate heads arranged by Delafond.

SPECIAL CAUSES FAVORING THE DEVELOPMENT OF THE DISEASE IN MOUNTAINS.

Delafond asserts that in Switzerland, Piedmont, the Juras, the Dauphiné, the Vosges, and the Pyrenees, pleuropneumonia has existed permanently. He does not ascribe this to geological formation, but he believes firmly, with almost all the veterinarians in mountainous districts, that the disposition, topographic situation of mountains and valleys, the cold temperature during six months of the year; hoar frost, heavy fogs, coldness and moisture of the nights and mornings on woodland pastures, or near lakes and rivers; frequent atmospheric currents in spring and autumn; sudden changes from hot to cold, dry to wet, or *vice versa*, &c., &c., are the local determining causes which combine, with other causes that have yet to be noticed, in inducing the lung plague. Delafond's words are that the causes enumerated concur "*à donner naissance à la péripneumonie dans la haute et dans la basse montagne.*"

Delafond erred. He had not read Haller; and had he visited any part where it was said the lung plague was a permanent infliction, he would have found, with Haller, that it was always arriving from somewhere, but never originating spontaneously. If we examine the geographical distribution of the disease we shall find the mountains of Northern Europe, of Norway, Sweden, and Denmark, free from the disease. And yet the special causes he refers to predominate there. No part of Europe has been more constantly devastated than Holland, noted for its submerged condition and the vast drainage works which render it inhabitable. In the British Isles the hills have always been most free from pleuropneumonia. It has prevailed at all altitudes, but the Scottish and Irish mountains, distant from high roads and the busy traffic in cattle, have been the healthiest parts of the country. And in America, too, the disease has traveled from the east southward along the coast, attacking cities and farms most in communication with those cities. It has not penetrated to the fine dairy farms on the hills in New York State, and is not indigenous on the Alleghanies. It were a much easier task to trace the malady to fertile valleys, where cattle are often covered, as in Holland, to be protected from cold, and to towns where animals are always in stables, than to trace the spontaneous origin of the disease to the mountains of Central and Western Europe.

FEEDING.

There are many farmers, apt to reason on insufficient data, who notice coincidences between the development of the lung disease and the great increase in some countries in the number of distilleries, and the amount of grains and distillery waste fed to cattle.

Others declare that the disease commenced with the potato disease, and may be produced by feeding cattle on diseased potatoes. The introduction of turnip husbandry, which undoubtedly first made us acquainted with a form of red water in cows, and severe apoplectic affections in sheep, has also been regarded as the cause in Great Britain of the lung disease in cattle. Delafond agrees that the foods named do not cause pleuropneumonia, and it would be easy to fill a large volume with facts in support of this assertion; and yet he goes on to say that food that is too succulent, distributed in large quantity among cattle that are being stall-fed, either for the butcher or for the production of milk, may induce (*peut occasioner*) pleuropneumonia.

We are not ignorant of the precise results which ensue when an excessive quantity, inordinate richness, or diseased condition of the alimentary matters named may operate in inducing ill-effects. Diseased potatoes induce indigestion and colic. Turnips grown on ill-drained lands give rise to hæmaturia, the red water of cows after parturition. Distillery products occasion diuresis, disturbed digestion, and, when still charged with alcoholic principles, give rise to cerebral disturbance, apoplexy, and death. These, and not pleuropneumonia, are known to us as capable of development from the abuse of otherwise useful articles of cattle-feeding.

STABLING—STALL-FEEDING.

Many have been the high-colored descriptions of the wretched stables, sheds, or what the Scotch people term "byres," in which cattle are housed. It matters not that for generations cattle were similarly housed without suffering from pleuropneumonia. There are always those ready to skim the surface for reasons, and, after noticing the closeness, filth, and torturing narrowness of cattle stalls, ascribe to that any and every plague infecting the cow shed. It is needless to walk the observer through the fetid holes in which cattle are kept for the supply of milk in Copenhagen, where pleuropneumonia has not been observed, nor to refer to the days when the London dairymen, richer in money and cows, kept the latter worse, bred from them regularly, and could maintain country farms on which to graze them while calving. It stands to reason, according to some, that such conditions must induce pleuropneumonia. In America, sensation articles and skillful illustrations have not been wanting, and no one can hesitate in declaring that the cow sheds of Brooklyn and other cities are a disgrace to a civilized people.

Huzard first described the cow houses of Paris as they were in 1793. It is needless to follow him through a long description of low sheds, in which a man could not stand erect, where cows were crippled into permanent rest, with their horns overgrown and distorted for want of regular wear and tear, and in which fowls, pigs, and rabbits shared shelter and a pestilential atmosphere. Delafond has described the wretched stabling of hill farmers. How, then, can it be said that in these sheds, where the lung plague always prevails, the conditions do not exist for its spontaneous origin?

It cannot be disputed that there are conditions—as when an animal suffers from pleuropneumonia, and has but one lung to breathe with—under which a large volume of pure air may turn the scale from death to life. It is also undoubted that the concentration of the poison so freely given off in this contagious disease must materially favor its reproduction in the systems of susceptible animals. But no one who has witnessed the slow progress of the malady in town dairies, and the rapid destruction of herds in open fields, can for a moment believe in the usual aggravation of the malady by bad stabling. Where the malady has been induced among young stock by large dairymen to prevent subsequent inconveniences, when the animals are fit to breed and yield milk, it has been found that most survived when kept warm in close sheds. Recommendations as to ventilating stables after disease had commenced have at times resulted in a much more rapid destruction of the cattle, and we are bound to admit that *a priori* reasoning has often been at fault on this subject.

ABUNDANT MILK SECRETION.

The universal prevalence of the lung plague in town dairies, where cows are kept for an abundant production of milk, has led to the theory that the drain on the system thus kept up induces the pleuropneumonia. It is asserted, and there appears to be some ground for the belief, that the human female, as well as the female among lower animals, is more susceptible to the influences of contagion than the male, but so far no facts of importance have ever been published indicating that an abundant secretion of milk induces specific disease and malignant fevers. Delafond has referred to abundant production in dairies where pleuropneumonia was always troublesome, and expresses himself as follows: "I firmly believe that cows which calve every ten or eleven months, and which are constantly yielding an abundant milk secretion, whether by being fed abundantly on rich provender, or placing them in hot, damp stables, so as to check cutaneous and pulmonary secretion, soon have their chest enfeebled, and are seized with pleuropneumonia; or, at all events, and that is incontestable, they become predisposed to the disease, which they easily get on being exposed to the breathing of a cold air, or to cold on the surface of the skin."

Here, again, it is not difficult to trace the real effects of an abundant milk secretion in stables that are close and ill-drained. Up to the time when the lung disease first appeared in London it was not uncommon for cows to be milked for several consecutive years. Large milkers were always kept on, and had a calf annually until too old or killed by disease. The disease that killed them was not pleuropneumonia, but tuberculosis. That malady, once so prevalent, is almost unknown now, inasmuch as the London cow feeders have ceased to breed from their cows, and the average duration of a cow's lifetime in a London shed does not exceed six months.

DRINKING COLD OR IMPURE WATER.

It is hardly necessary to refer at length to this reputed cause of pleuroneumonia. Not only is there an absence of fact in support of the production of the malady by cold water in winter and stagnant water in summer, but it is well known that the malady is usually most rife in many cities during the summer, when cattle are allowed to roam at pleasure during the day, coming in contact, and, therefore, infecting each other, while the supply of water is good, and indeed unexceptionable. Were it worth while, I could easily furnish many facts under this head indicating that there is no relation whatever between the condition and quantity of water cattle drink and the development of the lung disease.

CHILLS—BREATHING A COLD AIR.

East winds in Scotland were blamed by Professor Dick as the active agency inducing bovine pleuropneumonia. He overlooked the fact that the east winds prevailed before 1843, when the lung plague had not yet penetrated Scotland. I have seen on the coast of Fife a herd of cattle of all ages seized with bronchitis—a curable, benignant, and acute inflammation, presenting none of the characteristics of the lung plague; and there is no doubt that the deficient shelter, intense cold, and rapid changes of the weather may induce sporadic and non-contagious inflammations of the respiratory organs. But this is not pleuropneumonia.

It is not at all uncommon in Great Britain, Holland, and elsewhere, for farmers to ascribe the disease to chills; and its prevalence among drift cattle has been referred to transportation for long distances in open railway cars, on steamboats, and exposure in markets. But who ever heard of western cattle being struck with the lung plague in passing from Illinois to New York? Spanish cattle, reared in a country free from pleuropneumonia, suffer all the hardships of rough weather at sea, but are landed invariably sound in their lungs in Liverpool or London. Danish cattle cross the German Oçean and suffer much ill-treatment, but their dissection reveals at no time the lesions of the lung plague.

Not so with Dutch or Irish cattle. They make a short sea voyage from an infected country, and propagate pleuropneumonia wherever they come in contact with susceptible cattle.

Innumerable observations undoubtedly show that the lung plague prevails as much, and often more, during hot weather than in the winter months; it spares many cold countries into which it has no opportunity of transportation, and visits the most genial climate whither sick cattle have been taken. Italy and Australia furnish as good fields for its development as the Swiss Alps, and the colder portions of the United States.

OVERWORK.

In France and Italy it has been asserted that keeping oxen long in the yoke, exhausting them, starving, and often drenching them with rain, induce the lung disease. I know not what diseases such practices have not been said to cause. If we survey the countries where pleuropneumonia has been longest known, and where its ravages have been most intense, we shall find that, as a rule, it prevails among milk cattle that never work, steers that are grazed or stall-fed, and never broken to the plow or wagon, and herds of breeding stock, as in the Australian runs, never accustomed to restraint or punishment.

HEREDITARY PREDISPOSITION—CONGENITAL PLEUROPNEUMONIA.

It is necessary to establish clearly the difference between hereditary taint and congenital disease. A malady is termed hereditary when it is transmitted from parent to offspring by virtue of a constitutional defect, deformity, or taint. It may, but usually does not, appear at birth. The best example is furnished by cancer, which occurs frequently in the human subject, and recurs for generations. None of the specific or contagious fevers are hereditary, and although the question has been discussed in relation to pleuropneumonia, it can easily be settled. Delafond thought that the deterioration of breeds might favor its development. And why, then, has not the disease appeared in South America, while it has decimated the matchless herds of England and Australia? It may be accepted as a settled truth that the lung disease, like the rinderpest and foot and mouth disease, spreads without reference to any peculiar breed. Improved and unimproved breeds are alike susceptible of the affection.

Calves are at times, however, born of sick cows, and present unmistakable signs of the lung plague. The first observation of this sort was made by Hilfelhelseim, in the Rhine provinces, who dissected the fœtuses of cows that aborted under the disease. He found the lesions of pleuropneumonia in these animals. Delafond made similar observations, but has created some confusion by including cases of tuberculosis with others of pleuropneumonia. In 1839, a cow that had gone six months in calf was killed in Freiburg, Switzerland, while suffering from pleuropneumonia. The fœtus presented signs of the malady. It is common for calves to take the disease soon after birth, and I have shown in a government report that the contagious cattle diseases of Ireland, including pleuropneumonia, were mainly due to the active trade in sucking calves between the large towns of England and Dublin.

It has been necessary frequently to refer to animals that are susceptible and insusceptible to attacks of pleuropneumonia. This has been ascribed by some to constitutional or inbred resistance or weakness. It is due to what pathologists term, for want of a better name or explanation, idiosyncrasy. At times it appears that young animals resist the disease better than old ones; and Mr. Harvey, of Glasgow, found that by communicating the disease to yearlings and two-year-olds he had fewer deaths than when he had it among his pregnant and milch cows. But, as Sauberg has observed, outbreaks occur in which the older animals seem to bear up better than the young ones, and it is difficult, on present data, to establish any rule on the point.

It may be accepted as proved that all cattle, whatever their age, breed, sex, condition, &c., are susceptible to pleuropneumonia until they have been once seized, and then it is rare to witness a second attack. An insusceptible animal is, therefore, an animal that has once had the disease, either in a mild or latent, or severe and apparent form.

It is, however, certain that a degree of insusceptibility may be traced in animals that have never been affected, and we are quite at a loss to account for this. Similar observations are made in relation to all fevers affecting men and animals. A person has been known to nurse many during an outbreak of yellow fever, escape and live for a year, when the disease has reappeared, and the individual who has been proof against the malady one year has been among the first to die from it the next.

Not a few cases have been recorded of rinderpest—and I have witnessed a remarkable one—of a cow standing for weeks by animals that died of the malady, and which never showed signs of it. More strange than this are two observations, one in Lyons in 1853, and the other in Vienna in 1865, of dogs which could not be rendered rabid by the bites of, and inoculations from, undoubtedly rabid dogs. For the time, at all events, we must rest satisfied with the pathologist's explanation that these animals had a peculiar constitutional immunity or idiosyncrasy.

CONTAGION AND INFECTION.

Not only have theories in relation to the cause or combinations of causes which may lead to the development of pleuropneumonia been unsatisfactory, but opportunities are constantly presenting themselves to test the fact that privations, overcrowding, impure food and water, &c., singly or combined, may kill, but never induce the disease which presents the characteristics of the one referred to in this report.

The malady may be induced at will, by placing an animal suffering from it among healthy ones, and by direct inoculation. These are the only methods by which it is propagated.

Careful experiments have been instituted on this subject, and although it might be easy to refer to very numerous observations, it may suffice at present to quote from a French report, edited by Professor Bouley, and which was prepared by a committee of distinguished agriculturists, medical and veterinary professors, at the request of the minister of agriculture.

FIRST SERIES OF EXPERIMENTS.

The first series of experiments was conducted at Pomerage, in the well-known and vast domain of Rambouillet. The whole is inclosed by walls, surrounded by woods, and perfectly isolated. A stable was separated into two distinct compartments. In the first, designated A, with a southwest exposure, was a single door leading out on a sufficiently wide plot of ground, bounded by water where the cattle could be taken to drink. Every precaution was taken to prevent the cattle in A from coming within reach of those in the second stable, B. The latter was situated to the left of A, and completely separated by a solid wall.

Pleuropneumonia had never existed in the commune of Rambouillet. Messrs. Renault, Delafond, and Jouet chose the cattle and subjected them to a close examination. The herd consisted of three bulls and seventeen cows. These animals were distinguished by names and numbers, and distributed in the two stables in relation to age, breed, and sex, so as to secure an equable distribution.

Three sick cows were sent to Rambouillet on the 14th of November, 1851—one from the Département du Nord, the second from Mont Souris, and the third from Vaugirard. Three more sick cows were sent on the 2d of December, 1851. Of these six sick animals, three died and three recovered. One lived three days in stable A, a second five days and a night in the same, and the third, in stable B, survived ten days and two nights.

Of the three sick cows that recovered, one, admitted into stable A on the 10th of November, presented symptoms of the malady up to the 20th of December, viz: for thirty-four days. The second entered stable B on the 2d of December, and was sick for nineteen days. The third, also admitted in the same stable, continued ill for twenty-eight days.

Stable A.—On the 21st of November, 1851, viz: only six days after the introduction into this stable of two sick cows, a peculiar cough was shown by two cows, (La Noire, No. 16, and Norma, No. 2.) Their lungs appeared sound, and they continued to eat and ruminate.

The same symptom manifested itself successively, as follows:

First, on Coquette, (No. 3,) on the 22d of November.

Second, on Rosine, (No. 9,) on the 23d of November.

Third, on Berthe, (No. 8,) on the 25th of November.

Fourth, on Babet, (No. 7,) on the 3d of December.

Fifth, on Clara, (No. 1,) on the 5th of December.

Sixth, on Olga, (No. 6,) on the 7th of December.

Seventh, on Martin, (No. 15,) on the 10th of December.

Thus, twenty-four days after the admission of two sick cows, and eight days after the introduction of a third sick animal, out of ten healthy animals nine presented the abnormal indication of a peculiar cough. Only one cow (La Caille, No. 11) continued in perfect health.

After this first sign of sickness, the characteristic symptoms of pleuropneumonia appeared in six cows, in the following order:

First, Olga, (No. 6,) thirty-one days after first contact.

Second, La Noire, (No. 16,) thirty-two days after first contact.

Third, Clara, (No. 1,) thirty-five days after first contact.

Fourth, Rosine, (No. 9,) thirty-five days after first contact.

Fifth, Norma, (No. 2,) thirty-seven days after first contact.

Sixth, Coquette, (No. 3,) fifty-seven days after first contact.

Of these six animals only one died, viz: Olga, (No. 6,) and her carcass was removed to Alfort on the 6th of January, and there dissected by the members of the commission.

Of the five other cows in the stable, the reporters say that symptoms of variable intensity and duration appeared, and they all recovered. Certain lesions were, however, recognized some time after by dissection.

Of the three animals (Berthe, No. 8, Babet, No. 7, and Martin, No. 15) which began to cough the first day after contact with the sick cows, the only symptom which lasted, and is said to have continued for several months, was the cough.

Stable B.—On the 25th of November, 1851, viz: nine days after the introduction in stable B of the two sick cows, (Nos. 23 and 24,) the healthy cows began to cough, in the following order:

First, Suzon, (No. 13,) on the 26th of November.

Second, La Garde, (No. 20,) on the 2d of December.

Third, Marton, (No. 5,) on the 3d of December.

Fourth, Kettley, (No. 17,) on the 7th of December.

Fifth, Leduc, (No. 18,) on the 10th of December.

Sixth, Nebula, (No. 4,) on the 18th of December.

Seventh, Homard, (No. 14,) on the 28th of December.

So that, thirty-two days after the introduction of sick cows in stable B, out of ten healthy animals seven presented the peculiar cough before mentioned.

Three animals (Junon, No. 19, Bringé, No. 10, and Biche, No. 12) continued in perfect health.

Well-marked symptoms of pleuropneumonia presented themselves on four cows, in the following order:

First, La Garde, (No. 20,) sixteen days after first contact.

Second, Leduc, (No. 18,) thirty days after first contact.

Third, Marton, (No. 5,) thirty-five days after first contact.

Fourth, Homard, (No. 14,) forty days after first contact.

Two of these animals died after nine days' illness. The other two were quite convalescent in twenty-eight and thirty-five days respectively. The three other animals continued to cough for some months without manifesting more serious symptoms.

The conclusions drawn by the French commissioners from the foregoing experiments were as follows:

The epizoötic pleuropneumonia of cattle is susceptible of transmission from sick to healthy animals by cohabitation.

Twenty per cent. of the animals manifest a resistance to the contagion.

Eighty per cent. manifest various effects of the contagious influence.

Fifty per cent. are seized with decided symptoms of pleuropneumonia, and of these fifteen per cent. succumb, and thirty-five per cent. recover.

Immediate contact is not necessary for the transmission of the disease, and the first affected were among the farthest removed from the sick.

A better idea of the results of the very important experiments thus related may be formed by the subjoined tables, which show at a glance the conditions under which the disease was propagated. I have enlarged the French tables, and included all the data of importance.

SECOND SERIES OF EXPERIMENTS.

The second series of experiments was instituted with a view to learn whether the animals that had been once affected enjoyed an immunity against further attacks, and whether those that had resisted the disease were susceptible of subsequent infection.

On the 5th of March, 1852, there were placed in the stable on the farm of Charentonneau—

First. Five cows from Pomerage, viz: Bringé, (No. 10,) from stable B, which had resisted the disease; Kettley, (No. 17,) ditto; Clara, (No. 1,) from stable A, which first showed signs of pleuropneumonia on the 21st of December, 1851; Norma, (No. 2,) from the same stable, affected the 23d of December; La Coquette, ditto, date of attack 21st of January, 1852.

Second. With these five cows were placed two perfectly healthy animals, (Marion, No. 7, and Zula, No. 8.)

Third. Lastly, six cows, (Rose de Mai, No. 1, Mille Fleurs, No. 4, Jacqueline, No. 3, Blanchette, No. 8, Rosette, No. 3, and Bucheronne, No. 5,) inoculated with blood, nasal discharge, and fecal fluids, were also submitted to the influence of cohabitation.

On the 21st of January, 1852, two sick cows were placed in this stable. One of these cows was left eighteen days in the stable, and then killed to serve for the purpose of inoculation experiments. On the 27th of June another sick cow was placed in the same stable.

The result was that the five animals from Pomerage resisted the disease as well as one of the healthy ones. The second healthy cow was seized with the malady thirty-five days after cohabitation.

In order to confirm these results, the commissioners caused to be placed in stable A all that remained of the first herd. On the 6th of July, 1852, five cows were sent from Paris to Pomerage. Not one of the animals that had served in previous experiments contracted the disease.

The history of pleuropneumonia, coupled with the observations made on the supposed casual agencies capable of inducing the disease, is almost sufficient to establish the purely contagious nature of the disease, but there are several important proofs that deserve mention.

It is seen in all countries where the lung plague appears, that it spreads in proportion to the opportunities of contagion. It is worst in large cities, where cow feeders have to make frequent purchases. It is apt to diminish in severity—as, per example, in the city of Washington, in Dublin, Ireland, and elsewhere—so long as the cows are confined to stables in the winter and different herds have no chance of approach. When spring and fine weather arrive, and the cows are turned out during part of the day, or altogether, on commons, parks, or pastures, the presence of any infection results in the rapid dissemination of the disease. I had special occasion to study this among the cows turned out into the Phœnix Park, Dublin, and on the commons near Newcastle, in England.

In 1862 I chose a large estate in Perthshire, presenting the feature of being cut up into farms, on some of which cattle were wholly bred; whereas on others purchases had occasionally been made. The result was the demonstration of the fact that the disease appeared only where it was carried by diseased cattle. The estate was that of Lord Willoughby d'Eresby, comprising twenty-six farms, on eleven of which the disease was at different times imported; whereas on the fifteen other farms, interspersed between eleven, the only report to be obtained was, "Never had the disease. Breeds his own stock."

A similar inquiry relating to the parish of St. Martin, in Perthshire, showed that pleuropneumonia had appeared there in 1845. Since then ten farms have been visited by the disease, and in every case the attack has been distinctly traced to contact with diseased cattle. Nineteen farms on which cattle are bred and purchases rarely made have enjoyed a perfect immunity.

The high-prized herds of England, which have been carefully isolated by their proprietors, have always remained free from the disease, and short-horn breeders have, in many instances, exercised the greatest care not to have any admixture with strange animals, which would certainly have destroyed their stock.

It is needless to enter at length into the subject of authorities on this point. The voices of the ablest and most careful observers, who have studied pleuropneumonia practically, are unanimous on the point; and although in every country the tendency has been at first to regard this insidious disease as originating from atmospheric agencies, when the facts have been probed by skillful men the earlier opinions have been rejected. Gerlach, in 1835, Delafond, in 1844, and Sauberg, in 1846, published very abundant and conclusive testimony on this point.

THE PATHOLOGY OR NATURE OF THE LUNG PLAGUE.

There is nothing more dangerous and better calculated to retard inquiry and truth than the common practice of speculating as to the nature of specific diseases in men and animals by the analogical method. Bovine pleuropneumonia has been widely supposed to be an inflammation of the lungs, governed by the same conditions that operate in relation to ordinary inflammations of the chest in the human family, and, indeed, in all mammalia. The characteristic signs of small-pox depend on a cutaneous inflammation, but have appearances different from the results of a scald. It is as rational to define variola inflammation of the skin as it is to declare that the lung disease of cattle is an inflammation of the air passages and lungs. The local phenomena of the disease are associated with and characterized by inflammatory changes, but the cause in operation inducing all this is peculiar and specific.

The lung plague is a malignant fever, never generated *de novo*, so far as reliable observation has yet reached, dependent on the introduction of a virus or contagion into the system of a healthy animal. This principle produces a local change if inserted into any part provided with connective or fatty tissue, into which it most readily penetrates. The same local change is produced by its contact with the delicate mucous surface of the bronchial tubes. It adheres, spreads, not unlike cancer, regardless of the nature and importance of the structure it invades, and traverses the lymphatic vessels to form deposits in the neighboring lymphatic glands, but not generally throughout the lymphatic system. At first there is no great intensity of inflammation. Suppuration is only a later complication from the concomitant non-specific change in masses of areolar or connective tissue. Congestion and serous infiltration rapidly surround the spot inoculated. Heat, redness, pain, and swelling manifest themselves, and the reproduction and extension of the tissue-destroying virus may be judged by the extent of swelling; the large quantity of yellow gelatinous serosity or exudation which fills the lung tissue thickens the white fibrous structures, blocks up the adipose tissue, in which it displaces the fat corpuscles, and is limited in many cases only by the extent of connective tissue it can invade, by gravitation or otherwise, and the endurance of the animal under a process so prostrating and depletive.

That all this happens, we have tested by experiment. A susceptible animal is inoculated in the dewlap, and, at the expiration of a week or nine days, a swelling begins, infiltration extends beneath the chest and abdomen, involves both fore legs, is attended with great fever, prostration, and death. In a second case, a drop of virus is inserted in the tip of the tail. It may produce a scarcely perceptible local change, when suddenly a swelling occurs at the root of the tail. The lymphatic glands there situated enlarge, the areolar tissue is distended with a deposit, such as ordinarily occurs in this disease in the thorax, and so widely does this invade the open tissues of the pelvis as to close the rectum, sometimes to induce retention of urine, and, in the majority of instances, to kill.

As in the case of variolous inoculation, the effects often vary with the quantity of the virus introduced into a part. Many and deep punctures, especially in soft and vascular textures, will produce malignant variola in inoculating sheep. On the other hand, a single and superficial puncture results in a single pustule and imperceptible general symptoms. It is thus with the lung disease in cattle.

The slight local change produced by a small quantity of virus, even though it has been impossible to note any systemic disturbance, stands for an attack of the disease, and the animal enjoys almost a perfect immunity from further attacks.

Viewed in this light, we have to classify bovine pleuropneumonia with the contagious fevers, and we must recognize that it is peculiar and different from all other known diseases of man or beast. The ordinary phenomena of inflammations are but superadded conditions, and an animal may have the disease without indicating their presence.

5

MEDICAL TREATMENT OF THE LUNG PLAGUE.

A general and practical review of the means employed for the cure of the lung disease results in the conviction that, as a means to be relied on for the protection of the farmer's stock and the herds of a country, they are worse than useless; and it is necessary to impress this lesson on the public mind, as there are always those who base their futile efforts in this respect on the declaration that all diseases are curable if we only know the means with which to attack them and the best antidotes. When science has sufficiently advanced, it is thought disease will lose all its power; and, in accordance with extravagant views in this direction, men and beasts ought to attain a state of immortality on earth.

It is an undoubted fact that wherever rational preventive measures have been superseded by the efforts even of the most skilled veterinary practitioners, the mortality by the lung plague has always attained its highest point and continued without intermission. It must be thus to the end of time.

Nevertheless, circumstances arise when a certain relief may be afforded by remedial agents. A valuable animal or highly prized herd, so isolated from other stock as to prevent contagion, may be subjected to rational medical treatment. A survey of the means suggested in the past, of the principles which should guide us in the present state of knowledge, and of the details concerning my own practice, may, therefore, be considered important in this place.

Bourgelat, in 1769, recommended abundant blood-letting the first, second, and third day, (when the blood fails to coagulate it is a sign that this operation is useless,) emollient injections, bland or soothing beverages, (*breuvages adoucissants,*) emollient masticatories, and emollient fumigations of the nose. When the disease is far advanced blood-letting must be avoided, and reliance placed in cinchona bark and purgative injections. Bourgelat also prescribed small blood-lettings, low diet, emollient clysters, and fumigations of acetic acid in the stables.

There is little interesting on this subject up to the date of Delafond's work, 1844. He opens his chapter on the curative treatment of acute pleuropneumonia as follows: "Many persons, and some veterinarians, have sought in the arsenal of pharmacology the specific remedies for the cure of pleuropneumonia. I declare that for the cure of this disease there exists no specific, but rather rational curative means based on the nature, seat, and stage of the malady. The two great secrets, in my opinion, are, first, in recognizing pleuropneumonia at its commencement; and, second, in adopting the means that I have to describe."

I cannot, with fairness, make a very brief summary of Delafond's recommendations, and, in the main, shall give a translation of them. When pleuropneumonia, he says, affects a herd of cattle, the first animal affected must be removed and placed in an isolated spot, to be carefully examined during the entire progress of the case. Frequent examinations must be made of each animal in the herd. All that show a short, quick breathing, numbering from twenty-five to thirty respirations per minute, and an accelerated pulse, beating from sixty to sixty-five times per minute, in which the chest is evidently flattened either on one side or the other, whose respiratory murmurs are loud and associated with a friction sound, and which have their visible mucous membranes reddened, must be regarded as subjects which, notwithstanding that they continue to eat and drink, ruminate, and give milk as in health, will in three or four days cease to eat, ruminate, and give milk. They will moan and indicate all the signs of pleuropneumonia at a period when it is severe and often incurable.

An animal chosen with care in the earliest stage, and isolated, must be placed on low diet, and allowed only a little green grass or hay. Six to eight pounds of blood must be drawn, and this repeated eight or ten hours later. As soon as the blood has ceased to flow the body and limbs must be rubbed for half an hour with hay or straw wisps, and a good covering must be thrown over the body. Three hours after the first bleeding, and every two hours afterward for sixteen hours, a draught must be given, consisting of one drachm of tartar emetic in a quart of river or spring water. For animals under two years of age the dose of the tartrate of antimony should be half a drachm, and for animals from three to eight years of age a drachm and a half each time.

After the second bleeding the draughts are continued, and if, after twelve hours, the respirations have not been lowered to twenty or three-and-twenty per minute, a third abstraction of the same quantity of blood must be made. If the pulse becomes strong and full, the breathing less frequent, the mucous membranes paler, and especially if the respiratory murmurs are less loud, it may be considered that the animal is saved, and that its convalescence will be short.

Independently of the bleedings and the administration of emetic tartar, about fifteen liters* of water, with three liters of barley, may be boiled, throwing off the first water and adding thirty liters more. Two pounds of sulphate of soda are added to this barley tea, and one liter of this mixture is given, alternately with the emetic, every three hours.

Marshmallow, linseed, or coarse bran, is to be made into a decoction, and administered in the form of four injections daily. This same material may be used warm to steam the animal's nostrils, by placing it in a stable pail and covering the animal's head and the pail with a large cloth.

These measures, says Delafond, must be continued for three or four days—indeed, during the entire first period of the disease; and it is rare that the respiratory movements do not return to their normal condition. If the patient purges, injections of bran decoction are recommended.

Animals that present a yellow or pale and infiltrated aspect of the conjunctivæ must be bled to the extent of one liter or a liter and a half daily only, as heavy blood-lettings are prejudicial in such cases.

When pleuropneumonia begins by an inflammation of the pleura, the animal must be bled to the extent of two to four pounds two or three times daily. The emetic draughts are to be persevered in, the body well rubbed and clothed, and the sides of the chest must be rubbed with hot vinegar, or with a mixture of three ounces of ammonia to one ounce of vinegar. An infusion, in two liters of hot vinegar, of a pound of white or black hellebore, or of the large horse-radish sage, may be found economical in some parts. If these cannot be had, a blistering tincture may be prepared, as follows: Powdered cantharides, two ounces; powdered euphorbium, one drachm; alcohol, one-half pound. The three substances must be left in a bottle for some days, and then filtered.

If the symptoms subside, the animal is to be kept under shelter and on moderate diet. If, on the contrary, the pleurisy terminates in effusion, and the lung tissue is engorged and hepatized, no hopes can be entertained of the animal's recovery.

* Liter=2.113 pints.

When the lung disease commences by an active inflammation of the bronchial tubes, the jugular vein must be freely opened and six to ten pounds of blood abstracted; other emissions, from four to eight pounds each, must be repeated daily for two or three days. If the inflammation continues and spreads to the lung tissue, the dry rubbing, emollient fumigations, and injections of marshmallow or bran decoctions, containing three ounces of sulphate of soda, must be persisted in. This treatment must be continued four or five days; but if the cough continues, a seton must be inserted in the dewlap, and the seton medicated with the vinegar infusion of the white or black hellebore. When the inflammation subsides, the sternutatory vinegar prescribed by Mathieu renders good service. It is compounded as follows: Alum, sulphate of zinc, Spanish pepper, turpentine, one ounce each; camphor, two drachms, strong Burgundy vinegar, one pint. The solid substances are to be powdered and mixed with the vinegar and turpentine. They are to be macerated for eight hours, placed in a well-corked bottle, and well shaken before being given to the animal. Three times a day, and when the animal is fasting, a small teaspoonful of vinegar is poured into one or the other of the nostrils. The animals that have once had this operation performed can with difficulty be induced to submit to it again. Immediately after the administration, big tears drop from the eyes, and violent sneezing tends to discharge mucosities and the false membranes which obstruct the bronchial tubes and nasal cavities. Should the bronchitis terminate in inflammation of the pulmonary tissue, and this pass rapidly into a state of hepatization, further measures must be resorted to.

When pleuropneumonia is simple or complicated by pleurisy or bronchitis, and terminates in gangrene, the case may be regarded as irremediable. The same is true if there is an abundant effusion in the pleura. The animal soon dies asphyxiated.

The symptoms of a severe and desperate case are suspension of feeding and rumination, tympanitis, or distension of the paunch by gas immediately after feeding, pulse from sixty to seventy and small, tenderness on pressure of the sides of the chest, absence of respiratory murmur and friction sound, short and moaning expiration, violent heart-beats, driveling at the mouth, and the obstinate maintenance of the standing posture. It is difficult, with such symptoms, for the animal to recover, but cases of slow restoration to health have occurred.

At this stage the animal is to be bled daily to the extent of two to four pounds for two or three days. The emetic drinks must not be given, but the sulphate of soda should be persevered with. The injections, fumigations, and dry rubbings must be followed up; a seton and one or two rowels on the sides of the chest are to be inserted. A little easily-digested food is to be given the animal, and about an ounce of salt daily. If the mucous membrane remains pale and the animal feeble, drinks containing vegetable tonics, such as gentian, &c., must be used. Dieterichs recommends tar-water, to which two drachms of essence of turpentine are added, and which is used for fifteen or twenty days. When an animal is convalescent it may be turned out for an hour or two during fine weather. A relapse is to be treated by a slight bleeding, low diet, frictions, and sulphate of soda.

Such are the long and precise recommendations which Delafond gave, and which may be viewed, in the main, as measures from first to last to be scrupulously avoided. Delafond's belief in the treatment he recommends as benefiting sick animals is but one of innumerable instances of men being misled by nature's own recuperative powers.

Sauberg, in his prize essay published in 1846, devoted a chapter to the therapeutics of pleuropneumonia, but he is not sparing in words of caution, and in impressing on the minds of agriculturists that there is no specific against the disease.* He indorses Delafond's practice of blood-letting, and says that if this is resorted to at the right time the animal improves at once. If the patient is young, robust, in good condition; if the mucous membranes are red, the pulse small, hard, and frequent, breathing short and quick, heart-beats scarcely to be felt, then ten to fifteen or twenty pounds of blood must be abstracted. It is only by this means, says Sauberg, that the abundant exudation of plastic lymph in the lungs, as well as other evil results, can be averted. If no improvement is observed within eighteen to twenty-four hours, a second and even larger blood-letting must be performed. After the fifth day of an attack of pleuropneumonia Sauberg rarely bled, and whenever he did so he observed great prostration and often death. It is evident, he says, that, whereas an early bleeding may prevent the exudation, should this have taken place, the loss of blood may undermine the vital powers so as to prevent the possibility of recovery.

Sauberg is one of the strongest advocates of derivatives. He recommends a seton on the dewlap, or one on either side of the chest. He also advises a blister spread over a surface deprived of hair to the extent of a man's hand, behind each shoulder-blade. The vesicant he uses is a compound of potassio-tartrate of antimony, powdered cantharides, and euphorbium of each three quentchen,† lard four loth,‡ and one loth of oil of turpentine. He also suggests the application of the red-hot iron to the sides of the chest. In slight cases rowels dressed with black hellebore suffice. The quicker and more active the results of these applications, the more favorable is their operation.

The internal remedies recommended by Sauberg consist mainly of tartar emetic, which, he says, is attended with the best results. He gives it in the morning in one or two drachm doses, with two or three ounces of sulphate of soda, an ounce of nitrate of potash, and half an ounce of powdered juniper berries. This has an effect on the animal's bowels. In gastric or bilious complications he gives the emetic tartar in two to four ounces of white soap.

When the fever is slight, the cough strong, and appetite good, Sauberg advises not to bleed, and the same applies to old and weak animals, especially cows liable to abort, &c. He still persists in the tartarized antimony, and gives it with ten to sixty grains of asafetida, and an ounce of powdered juniper berries, twice daily in water. Bitter herbs, oil of turpentine, camphor, tar water, arnica, fennel, &c , are remedies suggested.

A wise precaution is insisted on by Sauberg, and that is to avoid a profuse and debilitating purgation.

The practice recommended by Delafond and Sauberg has very largely been carried out and recommended by other authors, such as Kreutzer, Röll, &c., even of late. Röll adds to the treatment by bleeding, tartar emetic, &c., the administration, in cachectic and feeble animals, of sulphate of iron with tar-water, or of alum, tannin, mineral acids, and other tonics.

---

*At page 131 of Sauberg's work, already quoted, the author says: "Wir haben kein Arcanun gegen die Lungenseuche des Rindviehes und werden auch keins finden; wenn man nur berücksichtigt wie die Krankheit bei den einzelnen Thieren so verschieden ist, und die Mittel, die bei einem Kranken mit Nutzen angewandt wurden, bei dem anderen, wenn nicht Nachtheile, doch nicht gleich günstige Erfolge zu Wege brachten, so wird man sich wohl bescheiden. Wo der Landmann die Behandlung der Kranken nicht einem Thierarzt anvertrauen kann oder will, sollte er nur nach allgemeinen Grundsätzen verfahren, eine zweckmässige Diät anordnen, und nicht sein Heil in kostbaren Mitteln suchen, der Verbreitung der Seuche möglichst vorbauen, und, wo Heilung der Erkrankten nicht möglich ist, das Schlachten vorziehen."

†Quentchen = 1 drachm. ‡Loth = one-half ounce.

In England practitioners have resorted to various methods of treatment. The practice of blood-letting has long been abandoned, but the advocates of setons, and more particularly of active blistering agents, such as croton oil, cantharides, and tartar emetic ointment, still exist. Small doses of calomel and tartar emetic, stimulating draughts containing creosote, turpentine, sulphuric ether, carbonate of ammonia, and alcohol, have been more generally employed. Mineral acids, the administration daily of dilute sulphuric acid especially, and an early resort to mineral and vegetable tonics, have found their advocates. Of late years the tincture of aconite has been in favor as a febrifuge, and largely used, and some have tried Indian hemp and other narcotics. Everything has been tried, without much reasoning or careful record of results. The important salient feature in the history of pleuropneumonia in England is that all the therapeutic skill of the veterinarian has not prevented greater and more general losses than have ever been witnessed in other countries, if we may except Holland.

For some years I have noticed that the earlier lesions of the lung disease partake, in their character and results, more of the features of hemorrhage—a prostrating discharge from the blood-vessels of a sero-albuminous product—than of inflammation. The congestion and inflammation are truly secondary, and once developed it is apparently impossible to control them, though their extent varies greatly. In some animals but a portion of one lung is involved, in others one entire organ is affected, and in others, which cases are almost without exception fatal, both lungs become hepatized, and the animal dies sooner or later of apnœa or suffocation.

Notwithstanding the well-founded objection of some distinguished veterinarians to the practice of administering mineral astringents as preservatives—an objection to which Professor Nicklas gave utterance at the first international veterinary congress held in Hamburg in 1863—it is certain that they far surpass all other means in the treatment of the early stages of the lung plague. Professor Nicklas said, with much truth, that where pleuropneumonia appeared there were often persons who prescribed the sulphate of iron to check the progress of the disease. The isolation of such cattle was not attended to, and the malady continued; whereas if the sick had been isolated, or slaughtered, and the remaining animals of a herd inoculated, there would have been an end to the outbreak.

On the other hand, if attention is paid to the segregation of the sick, and those indubitably free from the disease are inoculated, there is still a number, and often not a small number, sure to die within a month or six weeks, simply because inoculated too late. These animals, if of great value, and proper facilities are afforded for treatment without incurring the risk of extension of the malady, may often be treated with success.

Thermometer in hand, a good observer and auscultator can detect the invasion of this disease some days—and even as long as ten days or a fortnight—before marked symptoms appear. At that stage, the peculiar yellow deposit which first slowly invades the interlobular tissue of the lungs is penetrating into the organ, and its extension may, as I have noticed frequently, be checked by active internal astringents. The best of these are the sesquichloride and the sulphate of iron. But our choice extends further, since vegetable infusions or decoctions containing tannin, besides the astringent preparations of lead, may likewise retard and arrest the exudation.

I have on several occasions been called to prescribe for herds in which I have readily traced cases of pleuropneumonia in advanced stages of the disease. I have removed the marked symptoms, and still a large proportion of the animals had the peculiar cough so well described by the French commission; yet, to have neglected means to arrest the disease would have resulted in many deaths. Before I was led to approve, as I do strongly, of the practice of inoculation, and since, when there have been insuperable obstacles to its adoption, I have placed all the herd, sometimes in the stable and at other times in the open field, on regular daily doses of sulphate of iron, allowing about half a drachm or a drachm to a bullock, mixed with a similar amount of bruised coriander seeds and perhaps some bran, the better to disguise the iron. Thus mixed with fresh coriander seeds, cattle will leave grass to eat the medicine, and I have uniformly found a mitigation of the cough, a disappearance of the malady, and the herds have preserved an admirable condition.

I can confirm Sauberg's statement that it is dangerous to resort to active purgatives, and the common symptom of constipation, even in the earlier stages of pleuropneumonia, can be better corrected by diet and the administration of a stimulant, such as carbonate of ammonia, combined with warm water injections, than by any other plan. When the exudation in the lung tissue is not checked, and in all cases where it has advanced too far to admit of being checked by capillary astringents, it is, as a rule, desirable to leave animals entirely to nature.

The observation of many hundred cases within the past fifteen years has convinced me that, left entirely to themselves, when the malady has fairly developed, a considerable proportion of the cattle affected in one lung recover, whereas nearly all those affected on both sides die. The many methods of treatment recommended have not seemed to increase the average of recoveries among cases of one-sided pleuropneumonia.

It is extremely difficult to ascertain the conditions under which a small or a great mortality may be anticipated. This may be gleaned from the observations of the French commission. They found some animals which apparently resisted the disease. These were doubtless latent cases, as they afterward resisted contagion. If this be admitted, the mortality amounted to thirty per cent. of the animals affected, and this mortality is infinitely less than that observed frequently under circumstances which would appear most favorable to the health of cattle and their resistance to disease.

It has been seen that, as far back as 1769, fumigations were recommended for the treatment of pleuropneumonia. Of late years carbolic acid has been strongly recommended for this purpose, and may prove beneficial. Its internal administration failed many years ago, when, under the name of creosote—for much of our foreign creosote is carbolic acid—it was used especially by a distinguished English veterinarian, Mr. Charles Hunting, of Fence Houses, near Durham. The employment of antiseptics comes properly under the head of preventive measures, which are considered in a subsequent section of this report.

Notwithstanding the many authorities in favor of blisters, setons, rowels, and even the hot iron, I must assert, from careful observation, that, in the acute stages of the disease, they invariably aggravate the malady and sometimes kill. There are instances which indicate the contrary, for, when examining cases in Pennsylvania, I was told by a farmer that his cattle were dying, and he called in a professional man who blistered severely and cured several. They would probably have recovered if left to nature, though it is possible that in some cases counter-irritants may be useful. The difficulty is to choose those cases; and, as a rule, I am satisfied that any but the mildest stimulants applied to the skin irritate and do harm.

It is highly important that any medicines given to cattle with this disease should be given carefully, to avoid choking. Farmers are often very rough in giving drenches to cattle. They should go up to the off shoulder of the animal, pass the left hand into the angle of the mouth on the left side, draw the head around gently, without unduly elevating it, and pour the draught out of a small horn in moderate quantities, giving the animal time to swallow. I remember, as far back as 1851, being asked by a Yorkshire veterinarian to prepare a number of draughts, the active agent of which was carbonate of ammonia, for a herd of cows affected with the lung disease. The draughts were supplied to the farmer, and the very first day they were being administered by himself and servants, according to order, in gruel, a messenger summoned me to attend an animal which was killed by the medicine. On arriving at the farm, I perceived, from the animal's breathing, tremors, difficulty in standing, anxious expression of countenance, protruding and blood-shot eye-balls, that it was choking. I informed the farmer of the fact that the drench had been poured the wrong way, and, since he was indignant at the declaration, I opened the trachea with my penknife, and, in a fit of coughing, a quantity of gruel, smelling strongly of ammonia, was forcibly ejected. This alone saved the reputation of the medicine and its compounder.

INOCULATION OF THE LUNG PLAGUE.

In 1836 pleuropneumonia was imported from Flanders among cattle fed at the distillery of Messrs. Willems & Platel, at Hasselt, in Belgium. The town was rich in horned stock, and the malady formed one of its fixed stations and continued uninterruptedly from 1836 to 1852. Dr. Didot* ascertained beyond a doubt, by personal inquiries among the Hasselt distillers, that this was a fact, and that the disease had never been absent from their stables during these sixteen years. The Belgian government had adopted an imperfect system of slaughter to stamp out the disease; but the indemnity was small, and the distillers found it more profitable to sell their cattle to butchers; and the inhabitants of Hasselt, Liége, Louvain, Tirlemont, Brussels, and Antwerp were supplied with a large amount of diseased meat. Dr. Didot learned that, whereas government officials slaughtered one to two per cent. of the infected animals, the butchers purchased and disposed of fifteen, twenty, or twenty-five animals per week, according to the extent of the outbreaks. In the town of Hasselt alone it is computed by the same authority that 16,540 head of sick cattle were consumed during the above period. The government paid one-third of the value of 845 head of cattle during the same period. So late as 1851 M. Maris, one of the government veterinary surgeons at Hasselt, saw 1,300 cases of lung disease in that city alone.

From 1840 to 1850† the value of the horned stock lost by pleuropneumonia in Belgium amounted to 2,531,409 francs and 30 centimes. The sum paid by the government in indemnities amounted to 1,751,777 francs and 40 centimes. The disease continued

* Deux Jours à Hasselt. Essai sur l'Inoculation de la Pleuropneumonie Exsudative des Bêtes Bovines. Bruxelles, 1853.

† Rapport Décennal de 1840 à 1850. Résumé statistique, page 10.

unabated in 1851 and 1852. Every effort had been made by the distillers to arrest the disorder—ventilation, fumigation, whitewashing, turning the cattle out for a period, the placing of pigs in the stables, under the impression that they might destroy the putrid materials supposed to engender the disease, and so on.

It so happened that the son of the senior member of the first firm of distillers whose cattle had been affected in 1836 had devoted himself to medicine. Dr. Willems studied the lung disease with discrimination, but even so late as 1850 he had not fully made up his mind as to the essentially contagious character of pleuropneumonia. Dieterichs had attempted the inoculation of the disease in order to prove its contagious character, and had failed. Vix repeated the experiments, and obtained results in the form of pneumonia; a pneumonia, says Dr. Willems,* due, in all probability, to purulent infection. The French commission inoculated cows with the blood, nasal discharge, and excrementitious fluids, in order to test the contagious properties of pleuropneumonia. Dr. Willems had, moreover, observed that in his father's stables there had been, since 1836, over 500 animals that had suffered from pleuropneumonia, a considerable number of which had recovered, and remained ever after free from the disease. Yvart, Lafosse, Verheyen, and Pétry had made similar observations. These facts led Dr. Willems to institute a series of experiments as to the possibility of communicating the disease by inoculation, and the extent, if any, of the immunity thus secured to cattle.

Dr. Willems adopted the rational plan of performing experiments on animals of different species. His first series was as follows:

Date.	Material inoculated.	Animals inoculated.	Seat of inoculation.	Result.
Dec. 23, 1850	Pulmonary exudation	Three rabbits	Thigh	None.
			Neck	None.
			Thorax	None.
Feb. 10, 1851	Nasal discharges	Two rabbits	Nose	None.
	Intestinal tubercle squeezed in sirup	One rabbit	Thigh	None.
June 10, 1851	Pulmonary exudation	Twelve pea fowls	Thigh	None.
	Do	Several chickens	Thigh	None.
	Do	One dog	Tail	None.
	Do	Two goats	Tail	None.
	Do	One sheep	Tail	None.
	Do	One English pig	Tail	None.
	Do	Three Belgian pigs	Tail	None.
July 16, 1851	Pulmonary exudation	One sheep	Tail	None.
	Do	One ram	Tail	None.
	Do	One dog	Tail	None.
	Do	Eight pea fowls	Tail	None.
Feb. 26, 1852	Liquid from the lungs used to inoculate my cattle.	Two dogs	Tail	None.
		Three Belgian pigs	Tail	None.
		Three pea fowls	Thigh	None.
		Four hens	Thigh	None.

Dr. Willems observed that inoculations which were usually accidental in man were unattended by ill-effects.

* Mémoire sur la Péripneumonie Epizoötique du Gros Bétail, par L. Willems, Docteur en Médicine à Hasselt, 19.

A second series of experiments was performed on cattle. The first group of these was as follows:

Date.	Material inoculated.	Animals inoculated.	Seat of inoculation.	Result.
Feb. 10, 1851..	Blood from sick bullock	A small bullock....	Root of tail........	Slight inflammation.
	Mucus from mouth of sick bullock...	A bullock..........	Root of tail........	Slight inflammation.
	Intestinal tubercle broken up in sugar and water.	A bullock..........	Root of tail........	Slight inflammation.
	Pulmonary liquid	A bullock..........	Root of tail........	Slight inflammation.

The second group of observations is indicated below:

Date.	Material inoculated.	Animals inoculated.	Seat of inoculation.
March 5, 1851..	Pulmonary exudation............	Two lean bullocks.............	Root of tail.
	Pulmonary exudation............	Five lean bullocks	With two punctures on the nose.

Fifteen days after the inoculation small tumors were observed at the root of the tail, causing this organ to be slightly raised. In one the tumor speedily disappeared; in the other the swelling enlarged, became very hard, attained the size of a hen's egg, was situated between the anus and the root of the tail, and yielded gradually, without suppurating, to scarifications and a saline purgative.

Of the five other bullocks four showed no signs; the fifth, three weeks after the inoculation, manifested a swelling of the head on the operated side. Two incisions were made, emollients applied, and a purgative administered. Low diet was also prescribed. On the 20th of April the whole side of the head was swollen and almost of scirrhous hardness. Two deep incisions were made without finding pus. In the nose, at the point where the inoculation was performed, was a wound of unhealthy aspect from which a sanious pus was discharged. The ox grew lean. On the 17th of May a little pus flowed from the two incisions made on the 20th of April; afterward much pus flowed from these incisions, as well as shreds of areolar tissue and portions of dead skin. The tumor was subsiding. On the 22d of May a fluctuating tumor appeared below the jaws, from which much indolent-looking pus escaped. From that moment the ox began to thrive, notwithstanding that the suppurations continued till the 5th of June. By the 10th of June recovery was complete. Dr. Willems despaired for several days of this animal's return to health, and he resolved not to inoculate again in the same region.

THIRD GROUP OF OBSERVATIONS.

On the 10th of May Dr. Willems inoculated nine Dutch bullocks and two lean Belgian cows. He made two punctures in the tail of each, and used blood expressed from the muscles and liquid squeezed out of the lung of a cow suffering under the third stage of pleuropneumonia.

Several bullocks showed the effects of inoculation by the 19th of May; two more severely than the rest. On the 21st of May there was a decided swelling of the tail in six bullocks and one cow. Incisions were made to relieve the parts, emollients applied, and purgatives administered.

On the 26th of May seven out of the nine bullocks and one cow presented considerable tumefaction at the root of the tail; incisions and emollients were resorted to. On the 31st of May the swelling of the parts inoculated disappeared, and the animals regained their appetite and vivacity.

Two of the nine bullocks by this time suffered much; the root of the tail, the tissues around the anus, and the nates, were consolidated and enlarged by a deposit. In spite of all efforts, the free excision of the material so as to produce an artificial anus, the obstacle to defecation was so great, the straining so violent and constant, and the vital powers sunk so low, that on the 8th of June they died. Dr. Willems observed that in incising these tumors the animals suffered no pain.

On the 9th of June these animals were dissected. One presented a generally healthy condition of the internal organs. The lesions were localized in the anal region. The muscles and other tissues around were of a pale red color, interspersed with degenerated tissue. There was no suppuration. The anus and its surroundings for at least twelve inches in diameter appeared gangrenous. The lungs were of dark color, slightly congested, and presenting but the slightest trace of marbled hepatization. The gall bladder was found full of black dense bile. There was slight serous effusion in the peritoneum, and the mucous lining of the intestines presented red or brown punctiform discolorations and some patches of red injection.

In the second bullock the lesions were more extensive. The mortification of tissues extended up the rectum a distance of six inches. The peritoneum was inflamed, in some parts adherent by its opposing surfaces, and a reddish serosity was effused in its cavity. The liver was softened, degenerated, of a light yellowish color. The mucous membrane of the tongue and windpipe was of a dark brown color. The lungs were black, flaccid, and in the pleural sacks was a citrine-colored serous exudation. In the general disorganization of the organs of this animal the most interesting feature was a number of cysts, with delicate walls, distended by a dried homogeneous material similar to that inclosed in the intestinal tubercles of animals that die of pleuropneumonia. Some of these little saccules were in the folds of the peritoneum, but the majority, at least sixty, were in the thorax and on the internal surface of the ribs.

FOURTH GROUP OF OBSERVATIONS.

Alarmed by the foregoing results, Dr. Willems determined on attempting inoculation at the tip of the tail, as follows:

Date.	Material used.	Animals inoculated.	Seat of inoculation.
June 19, 1851..	Pulmonary exudation from an animal in the first stage of disease.	Five lean Belgian bullocks	Tip of tail.
	Pulmonary exudation from an animal in the first stage of disease.	One Dutch bullock....................	Tip of tail.
	Pulmonary exudation from an animal in the first stage of disease.	One calf two months old.............	Tip of tail.
	Pulmonary exudation from an animal in the first stage of disease.	One calf three months old............	Tip of tail.

On the 30th of June a slight swelling was observed in the parts inoculated, except in the cases of one bullock and two calves. The symptoms of inflammation advanced, and on the 22d of July the tips of the tails of four bullocks were completely gangrenous and detached. From that time the animals improved.

FIFTH GROUP OF OBSERVATIONS.

Date.	Material used.	Animals inoculated.	Seat of inoculation.	Result.
June 26, 1851..	Pulmonary exudation from animal in first stage of disease.	Twelve indigenous bullocks.	Tip of tail.........	Slight swelling on the 26th of July, and speedy recovery.
	Pulmonary exudation from animal in first stage of disease.	Two heifers............	Tip of tail.	

SIXTH GROUP OF OBSERVATIONS.

Date.	Material used.	Animals inoculated.	Seat of inoculation.
July 16, 1851..	Pulmonary liquid......................	Twelve lean bullocks................	Tip of tail.
	Do..............................	One heifer..........................	Tip of tail.
	Do..............................	One Dutch bull......................	Tip of tail.
	Do..............................	A calf four days old................	Tip of tail.

On the 24th of July four showed swelling of the tail; on the 29th all had the enlargement, and on the 10th of August Dr. Willems amputated the tail-tips of four.

SEVENTH GROUP OF OBSERVATIONS.

Date.	Material used.	Animals inoculated.	Seat of inoculation.
Aug. 18, 1851.	Pulmonary liquid from a bullock in third stage of disease.	Seven lean two-year old bullocks.......	Tip of tail.
	Pulmonary liquid from a bullock in third stage of disease.	One Dutch milch cow..................	Tip of tail.
	Pulmonary liquid from a bullock in third stage of disease.	Fourteen lean bullocks, from three to four years old.	Tip of tail.
	Pulmonary liquid from a bullock in third stage of disease.	One Belgian milch cow................	Tip of tail.

On the 9th of September the Dutch cow and two bullocks presented the first symptoms, and the remainder showed signs on the 14th, and afterward recovered.

EIGHTH GROUP OF OBSERVATIONS.

Date.	Material used.	Animals inoculated.	Seat of inoculation.
Nov. 16, 1851.	Pulmonary exudation from a bullock in the first stage, and kept ten days to note if it lost its properties.	Four small indigenous cows..........	Tip of tail.

Ten days after the inoculation the first symptoms of specific inflammation appeared, and all recovered.

NINTH GROUP OF OBSERVATIONS.

Date.	Material used.	Animals inoculated.	Seat of inoculation.
Jan. 19, 1852..	Pulmonary exudation from cow in third stage of the disease.	Five Belgian bullocks................	Tip of tail.
		One Dutch bullock	Tip of tail.

On the 2d of February the greater part of these animals showed signs of the inoculation, and afterward recovered.

One animal on the 3d of February had a swelling in the upper part of the right hind limb. The tumor increased, and the animal suffered intensely. Incisions, emollients, and purgatives were resorted to as usual. By the 8th of February the swelling had invaded nearly the whole of the right hip, pushed the tail to the left, and the anus was partly occluded so as to cause difficulty in defecation. The animal died on the 10th. Post-mortem appearances indicated little else beyond the thickening of the skin and subcutaneous tissues of the right hip. There was some discoloration of the intestines, flaccid appearance of muscles, and dark color of lungs, but no specific appearances in internal organs.

TENTH GROUP OF OBSERVATIONS.

Date.	Material inoculated.	Animals inoculated.	Seat of inoculation.
Jan. 30, 1852..	Pulmonary exudation in first stage of disease.	Four old, lean, but strong, Dutch bullocks.	Tip of tail.

Two presented swelling on the 12th of February, and recovered; the others showed no signs.

ELEVENTH GROUP OF OBSERVATIONS.

Date.	Material inoculated.	Animals inoculated.	Seat of inoculation.
Feb. 26, 1852..	Pulmonary exudation from bullock in first stage.	Six lean Dutch bullocks..............	Tip of tail.
	Pulmonary exudation from bullock in first stage.	Six fine Belgian steers	Tip of tail.
	Pulmonary exudation from bullock in first stage.	One Dutch heifer	Tip of tail.
	Pulmonary exudation from bullock in first stage.	One indigenous cow.	

From the 13th to the 20th of March the effects of the inoculations were developed. One animal only of the first group lost a little of its tail.

Dr. Willems proceeded further. On the 19th of June, 1851, he inoculated several cattle with the liquid expressed from healthy lungs without producing any effect. He then inoculated a bullock that had previously had the disease, and witnessed no results except a little enlargement at the seat of the puncture. On the 28th of August, 1861, he reinoculated a bullock that had been operated on six or seven months previously, and had lost his tail; and did the same with two small cows.

On the 19th of January, 1852, he reinoculated three large bullocks, and on the 26th of February three other bullocks, the whole of which had been successfully operated on before.

Fifty cattle that had not been inoculated were mixed in a stable with those referred to, and with the following result:

In the month of May, 1851, three bullocks sickened; on the 22d of June a fourth case; on the 26th a fifth; on the 26th of July a sixth; and at different dates up to the 10th of March, 1852, seventeen of the newly inoculated animals had suffered, and were sold for slaughter, whereas the other thirty-three had doubtless a latent form of the malady.

The conclusions drawn by Dr. Willems were as follows:

1. Pleuropneumonia is not contagious by inoculation of the blood or other matters taken from diseased animals and placed upon healthy ones.

2. By the method that I employed one hundred and eight beasts were preserved from pleuropneumonia, while of fifty beasts placed in the same stables and not inoculated, seventeen became diseased, and the disease is now banished from these stables, which had never been free from it since 1836.

3. The inoculation of the disease itself, performed in the manner that I have described, whether it may have occasioned apparent morbid manifestations or not, was the measure that preserved the animals from pleuropneumonia.

4. The blood and the serous and frothy liquid squeezed from the lungs of a diseased animal in the first stage of pleuropneumonia are the most suitable matter for inoculation.

5. The inoculation of the virus takes from ten days to a month before it manifests itself by sensible symptoms.

6. The matter employed for the inoculation has, in general, no effect upon an animal previously inoculated or having had the disease.

7. The inoculated animal braves the epizoötic influences with impunity, and fattens better and more rapidly than those in the same atmosphere with it that have not been inoculated.

8. The inoculation should be performed, with prudence and circumspection, upon lean animals in preference, and toward the tenth day after the operation a saline purge may be given, and repeated if necessary.

9. By inoculating pleuropneumonia a new disease is produced; the affection of the lungs, with all its peculiar characters, is localized in some sort on the exterior.

10. The virus obtained from oxen affected with pleuropneumonia is of a nature entirely specific; it does not always act as a virus; the bovine race alone is affected by its inoculation, while other animals of different races, inoculated in the same manner and with the same liquid, experience no ill-effects.

Dr. Willems accomplished much in his earlier experiments, as will be seen by comparing the knowledge of the present day with the results of his original investigations.

One cause contributed to strengthen the hands of his adversaries, and this was his attempt to prove that specific and characteristic elements distinguished the virus of pleuropneumonia.

Dr. Willems says:

I have examined various pathological specimens with the object of studying and elucidating the question of inoculation. My investigations have been principally directed to diseased lungs, and to a kind of tubercle, hitherto overlooked, but which I have, nevertheless, constantly met with upon opening the dead bodies of animals that died from pleuropneumonia. These tubercles, scattered throughout the intestines, but principally in the smaller one, are of a size varying from the head of a pin to that of a large pea, of a yellowish or greenish color. They are seated in the sub-mucous cellular tissue, and partly in the thickness of the mucous membrane of the intestine. They do not appear to have any relation to the glands of Peyer or of Brunner. Are they hypertrophied follicles? Nothing appears to prove it; no opening is perceived in them. They are formed of a homogeneous, whitish matter, more or less hard, showing under the microscope granulous kernels and an innumerable quantity of small elementary corpuscles, which enjoy a molecular motion, and which are also met with in diseased lungs. I have examined under the microscope parts of the lungs of animals diseased with pneumonia, with a power magnifying four hundred and fifty diameters, which is higher than that employed by Professor Gluge in his beautiful anatomico-pathological researches upon pleuropneumonia. The exuded matter presented no structure. I met with no other anatomical elements than granular cells and elementary corpuscles, provided with a particular motion, the whole pretty much resembling an inflammatory exudation, remarkable for its great quantity. The plastic exudation is formed in so rapid a manner, and in such considerable quantity, that anatomical elements of a superior development to that of these cells could not be produced in them; consequently no cells or globules of pus (I have never found any) or fibers are ever met with there. The energy of the cellular tissue appears to exhaust itself upon too large a quantity of exuded matter for the latter to be carried to a higher degree of organization. It is the same as is observed sometimes in the regeneration of tissues; in the section of nerves, for example, and in the fracture of bones, when the exuded liquid is in too large a quantity, or the fragments are too much separated, a part of the liquid, being beyond the circle of action of the energy of existing tissues, always remains at an inferior degree of development to that of the neighboring tissues. What is most important to be shown here, and of which no one has hitherto spoken, is the existence in diseased lungs of small corpuscles, endowed with a molecular motion, which appears sometimes to be made in a given direction. They are like corpuscles in process of formation, the motion of which resembles that of the granules of pigment, as well as those which surround the corpuscles of the tuberculous matter in man. In all my microscopical researches I have constantly found the same.

Wishing to know whether these corpuscles exist in any other substances than those already examined, I submitted to the microscope—

1. The saliva of a healthy ox under epizoötic influence.
2. The saliva of a diseased cow toward the third stage of the disease.
3. The urine of the same cow.
4. The blood of the same cow.
5. The blood of a healthy ox under epizoötic influence for five months.
6. The blood of a healthy ox not under epizoötic influence.
7. Parts of the liver and of the large right pectoral muscle from a diseased cow.

In none of these matters did I find the small corpuscles with molecular motion which I have constantly met with in the lungs and in the intestinal tubercles of animals affected with pleuropneumonia. That, then, is the principal seat of the disease. Are these corpuscles primitive or consequent on the disease? This question cannot be decided now; I only wish here to verify their presence in pleuropneumonia.

I examined with the microscope parts of the skin of an ox that died of inoculation. I there found the same microscopical elements and the same chemical characters as in the lungs diseased with pneumonia.

Professor Gluge, one of the members of the Belgian commission appointed to inquire into the efficacy of inoculation, reported, on the 10th of July, 1852, as follows:

It results, from the demonstrations made by Dr. Willems and our own researches—

1. That epizoötic pleuropneumonia has no characteristic anatomical products appreciable by the microscope.
2. That the inflammatory product is not distinguished from any other product of inflammation by anatomical character.
3. That M. Willems's assertions are not accurate.
4. That this circumstance, doubtless unfortunate, does not in any way prejudice the practical question, which it appears to me ought to be especially examined.

But Professor Verheyen, who was the president of this commission, continued until his death to throw discredit on the preservative efficacy of inoculation, and though he based most of his conclusions on hypotheses, he was ready to avail himself of everything that presented itself to strengthen his position.

Three commissions were almost simultaneously at work to ascertain the merits of Dr. Willems's discovery.

The first in Holland, appointed on the 17th of April, 1852, consisted of the director and professors of the veterinary school at Utrecht.*

From the 14th of June, 1852, to the 9th of July following, the commission inoculated for fourteen proprietors two hundred and forty-seven head of cattle of various ages and condition. In this number there were one hundred and fifty-four milch cows, six young cows that had not yet calved, thirty-two heifers, and fifty-five calves. The phenomena of the operation were not manifested at once on all the beasts that were subjected to it. The proportions between the inoculation and its consequences are nearly constant in milch cows and heifers; they are found to be about as three to two. In calves, on the contrary, the proportion is less; it is as four and a quarter to one. A great difference was observed in the effects on cattle of different proprietors. Thus, out of thirteen milch cows belonging to Degroot, four only experienced the consequences, while with the cattle belonging to Wynen it was successful in eighteen out of twenty; and yet the matter used for the inoculation at these two farms came from the same lung. Other similar variations were observed, and were not attributed exclusively by the commission to a greater or less predisposition to pleuropneumonia. They thought it a more probable explanation of the fact that the disease, raging with greater violence and upon a greater number of beasts in one stable than another, existed in germ at the time of inoculation, although there were no symptoms to indicate it. Thence it was, then, that with one exception pleuropneumonia caused the greatest losses to the proprietors on whose cattle the inoculation took least. The inoculated beasts that the commission had to report on as having been attacked by pleuropneumonia were sixteen in number. Although this figure, they say, is pretty considerable, it proves in no wise to the disadvantage of the preservative power of the inoculation; for it was to be expected that cases of pleuropneumonia, more or less numerous, would present themselves among the cattle subjected to the operation, since they had been stabled with infected animals, and at the time of performing it there were still several affected with the disease. "We cannot omit to state," adds the reporter, "that upon none of these animals was the inoculation succeeded by local phenomena." The opinion of those who thought that pleuropneumonia acquires by inoculation a milder character, and terminates more favorably, was not confirmed; the greater number of the animals attacked perished. The operation had not the least influence upon the beasts which, at the time it was performed, were evidently affected with pleuropneumonia. Several beasts that were known for some time to have been affected with pleuropneumonia experienced not the least effect from the inoculation.

The report from which the foregoing has been extracted bears the date of the 21st of September, 1852, and the results are indicated by the annexed table.

The second report, bearing date of the 28th of December, 1852, and prepared by the same commission, furnishes facts recorded in the subjoined table.

The conclusions drawn from the experiments were summarized as follows:

1. Although the inoculation of pleuropneumonia is not, in all respects, an inoffensive operation—as extensive derangements and even death may result from it—its effects are generally confined to the part where it has been applied.

* Further papers respecting pleuropneumonia in cattle, presented to the British House of Commons by command of her Majesty, December 6, 1852.

2. In order to prevent, as much as possible, its unfavorable consequences, it is necessary to use some precaution, both in the selection of the matter for inoculation and in the period of its application. The season, the atmospheric circumstances, and the state of nutrition, exert considerable influence upon the success. The autumn appears, for more than one reason, to be the most suitable time.

3. When an intense action and serious casualties appear locally and in the more distant organs, they may be attributed to exterior circumstances and to the individual constitution. This being the case, casualties cannot always be avoided.

4. If serious complications appear and affect the essential organs so as to cause the reaction of the whole organism, it is as difficult to prevent them and arrest their progress as it is to cure pleuropneumonia.

5. In the violent cases, terminating in death, lesions in the thorax or the lungs have never been met; hitherto they have always been concentrated in the abdominal cavity.

6. The inoculation produces no unfavorable effects, either upon the constitution or the yield of milk, while its action is limited to a local affection. Only in the cases where abundant deposits succeed a too intense local action do the animals continue sickly during a considerable period of time.

7. The operation has not had a determined influence on the excitement of œstrum. In proportion this has been more frequent on the inoculated than on the uninoculated cows. It is, however, to be remarked that No. 25 has not yet been in heat, although the period for it has long since passed.

8. The return of the uterine heats with the two cows Nos. 5 and 12, probably in consequence of abortion, can the less be referred to the inoculation, as these two cases are isolated and the effects were not observed in Nos. 19, 21, and 23, which were very markedly subject to sexual excitement.

9. It cannot be determined with complete certainty whether the premature parturition of a cow near her time, (No. 10,) as well as the consecutive phenomena observed in the mother and the calf, are to be attributed to the inoculation; it is the same with the cow No. 14, which calved before her time. These circumstances are, however, of a nature to discourage the inoculation of females in an advanced stage of gestation.

10. As abortion is frequent in the course of pleuropneumonia, it cannot be passed over in silence that this complication has never appeared with the beasts that have suffered so seriously from the inoculation as to sink under it. If, therefore, the operation has any influence upon gestation, it can be only in the last stage.

11. The hypothesis already proposed in our first report, that the evolution of pleuropneumonia after the inoculation ought to be attributed to the existence of the germ of the disease before the operation, notwithstanding the absence of every morbid phenomenon, acquires a higher degree of probability from our experiments.

12. The opinion of those who hold that cattle which have had pleuropneumonia and have recovered do not contract it a second time, or at least rarely, and that the inoculation is performed without success upon these individuals, is again confirmed by No. 16, which was inoculated twice, but in vain.

13. Our experiments furnish the remarkable proof that a power, at least temporary, of insuring against the contagion of pleuropneumonia cannot be denied to the inoculation; it remains uncertain, however, to what extent the predisposition to contract this disease is

destroyed, either entirely or for a limited period. Much time will be necessary, from the very nature of the question, before a positive solution of it can be arrived at.

Verheyen, as president reporter of the Belgian commission, issued a report dated Brussels, February 6, 1853. It opened in the following terms:

In a first report, embracing the period from the 24th of May to the 15th of July, 1852, it is stated that the commission had inoculated, either by the operations of its members or under its supervision, one hundred and eighty-nine beasts of the bovine race of all ages and both sexes. Eight herds, numbering one hundred and twenty-nine head, inhabited stables in which pleuropneumonia had lately raged, or was still raging at the time of the inoculation; eight other herds, composed of sixty beasts, abode in healthy localities, or such as were considered healthy, inasmuch as they had never been visited by the disease or had been spared by the scourge for at least eighteen months.

We made it appear—

1. That the operation had been followed by effects upon all the cattle inoculated.
2. That the matter remained inert upon two cows that we knew to have escaped from exudative pleuropneumonia.
3. That five cows had perished from the consequences of inoculation.
4. That two had lost the whole of their tails.
5. That six had partially lost them.
6. That four calves had been seized with an articular affection.
7. That, contrary to Mr. Willems's observations, the insertion of the matter in the tails of calves produced a local affection there.
8. That, finally, at the moment of dispatching that first report, M. Dele informed the commission that a case of pleuropneumonia had just appeared at the Abbey of La Trappe upon an inoculated cow.

The favorable situation certified on the 15th of July has been maintained, with but one exception, for the individuals of those herds which the proprietors still possess. The articular affection observed in four cows has not occurred again; therefore, a simple coincidence must be admitted, and this casualty explained independent of inoculation.

The commission resolved on extending its operations, and this they did by associating with themselves all the country veterinary practitioners, in accordance with the organization of the civil veterinary service in Belgium, and, secondly, by undertaking a series of direct experiments.

The government on its part did not remain inactive. It organized local commissions charged with the supervision of the operations; the losses occasioned by the inoculation were assimilated to those of animals slaughtered on account of public benefit; it undertook to pay the difference between the estimated price and the selling price of the inoculated beasts which, contracting exudative pleuropneumonia, should be sent by their proprietors to the shambles, and of which the officers at the latter would make declarations to the authorities.

Further on M. Verheyen says:

Wishing to free the inoculation from the numerous accessory questions which that practice occasions, the commission adopted for its experiments, and submitted to the minister of the interior for his sanction, this simple programme:

1. To purchase sound beasts; to watch them during a certain time, in order to be assured of the integrity of their pulmonary organs.
2. To request M. Willems to inoculate them.
3. Only to admit as preserved those in which that physician should have recognized the specific inflammation caused by a productive inoculation, and which he should have pronounced to be in the enjoyment of the immunity.
4. To have the beasts cohabit with animals afflicted with exudative pleuropneumonia, at the same time placing some inoculated animals in identical conditions.

A first batch of eight cows and heifers of Ardennes breed, selected in localities free from exudative pleuropneumonia, arrived at the veterinary school. M. Willems inoculated them on the 16th of August; on the 11th of September, those numbered 1, 2, 3, 5, 6, and 8 were examined by M. Willems, who declared that the inoculation had succeeded in those beasts.

On the same day he inoculated eight other beasts purchased by M. Windelincx, on account of the commission, at the fair of Tirlemont. We cannot affirm that they were, like the preceding, from a locality free from pleuropneumonia; we gained, however, by a rigorous and repeated examination, the certainty that the thoracic organs were intact. At the same sitting, M. Willems reinoculated the two Ardennes cows numbered 4 and 7.

All showing themselves still refractory on the 29th of September, M. Willems was apprised of it; the letter was unanswered.

On the 10th of October an ox—that marked No. 2—of the herd that came from Tirlemont, exhibited a swelling at the end of the tail. That portion of the caudal appendage, being seized with dry mortification, was eliminated.

On the 18th October three members of the commission proceeded to a fresh inoculation. They operated upon the Nos. 1, 3, 4, 5, 7, and 8, from Tirlemont, and upon the Ardennes cow No. 4.

The No. 7 of the latter breed and the No. 6 of the former were reserved.

Two of the Ardennes cows, Nos. 5 and 6, which were successfully inoculated, having been isolated in a stable, cohabited from the 24th of September with pneumonic beasts. When it was certain that the operation had had a negative result upon the Ardennes cow No. 7, and after the cicatrization of the puncture, the same locality was assigned to it, on the 1st of October, for abode.

The ox No. 2, from Tirlemont, entered there on the 23d of October, and the heifer No. 6 on the 25th of the same month,

A third inoculation, performed on the 18th of November upon the beasts from Tirlemont, Nos. 1, 3, 4, 5, 7, and 8. was not more efficacious than the preceding.

From the 24th of September, the date of the experiment, there has only occurred a first space of one day, and a second of eight, during which the stable has not contained pneumonic beasts; the number of the cattle has varied from one to three. Up to this day the three inoculated beasts, and the two upon which the inoculation was unsuccessful, have experienced no attack from the cohabitation with infected animals.

Two aged cows, inoculated by M. Willems, at Hasselt, entered the same locality on the 15th of November.

On the 28th of September, two of the Ardennes beasts, Nos. 3 and 8, were dispatched to Tirlemont to be placed in infected stables there, by the care and under the superintendence of M. Windelincx.

A third experiment, intrusted to M. Delo, has been organized at Deurne, in the province of Antwerp. The superior of the Abbey of La Trappe has been pleased to place at the disposal of the commission, for this purpose, two heifers belonging to the community, and which were inoculated with the least equivocal success on the 27th of May, 1852.

On the 30th of October, the Ardennes beasts Nos. 1, 2, and 4 were conducted to Huy, where a fourth experiment is being carried out under the superintendence of MM. Marcops and Guérin.

Not one of the animals inoculated, successfully or unsuccessfully, has contracted exudative pleuropneumonia.

While these experiments were going on, fifty-four veterinary surgeons, including Dr. Willems, inoculated five thousand three hundred and one head of cattle. They consisted in—

Beasts fattening	2, 732
Lean oxen or milch cows	2, 189
Calves and young cattle	380
Total	5, 301
Beasts living in healthy stables	2, 330
Beasts living in infected stables	2, 971
Total	5, 301
Beasts successfully inoculated	4, 324
In healthy stables	2, 030
In infected stables	2, 294
Total	4, 324

Eighty-six, including eleven beasts inoculated in the dewlap, died from the effects of the inoculation.

Seventy-four lost the tail up to the root.

Three hundred and four lost it in part.

Seventy-three contracted exudative pleuropneumonia after having been successfully inoculated.

After careful examination, it resulted that fifty-five cases of exudative pleuropneumonia, well attested, occurred upon beasts inoculated with unequivocal success. The space of time which elapsed with these animals between the inoculation and the first appearance of the pneumonia symptoms varies from seventeen to one hundred and thirty-six days.

After an elaborate analysis of cases in which the inoculation seems to have been effectual, of others in which the operation and immunity seemed to be coincidences, and, lastly, of those in which it was not preservative, the commission concludes:

1. That the inoculation with the liquid extracted from a lung hepatized in consequence of exudative pleuropneumonia is not an absolute preservative against that disease.

2. That the phenomena succeeding the inoculation may occur several times upon the same animal, whether it has or has not been affected with exudative pleuropneumonia, and that the two affections may go on simultaneously in one and the same individual; considerable derangements appear at the inoculated part, while the morbid action of the lungs progresses toward a fatal termination.

As to the point whether inoculation really possesses a preservative virtue, and, in that case, in what proportion and for what duration it maintains the immunity in the animals that have undergone it, this question can be resolved only by ulterior researches.

A summary of inoculations performed and results obtained is appended in a tabular form at the close of the report.

We now come to the experiments of the French commission, and it must not be forgotten that, in connection with the subject of the transmission of the lung plague by contact, this commission had resorted to inoculation independently of any suggestions on the part of Dr. Willems.

The general résumé, ably set forth by Professor Bouley, is regarded up to the present day as having done much to diffuse a rational belief in the efficacy of inoculation, and the experiments were conducted with great care and skill.

Experiments were instituted by the commission—

First. To ascertain whether pleuropneumonia is susceptible of being transmitted to healthy animals by the inoculation of blood, saliva, nasal discharge, and excrementitious matters from animals affected with the disease.

Second. Have animals thus inoculated enjoyed any immunity against the contagious influence of the lung plague?

Third. Is pleuropneumonia capable of being transmitted, in all its forms and characteristic symptoms, to healthy cattle by the inoculation of the liquid extracted from the lungs of a sick animal?

Fourth. In the case where inoculation of this liquid does not determine on healthy animals an exact repetition of the form and symptoms of the original disease, what are the local or general phenomena which result? In what proportion and to what extent do these characters, more or less severe, transmit themselves? How many animals die after inoculation? How many recover their health after having been subjected to this test, and under what conditions?

Fifth. Do the animals subjected to this proof of inoculation with pulmonary liquid acquire the power of resisting the contagion of pleuropneumonia?

The experiments made to solve the question whether pleuropneumonia is contagious by the inoculation of the blood, saliva, nasal mucus, &c., having been performed only on six animals, the commission has not deemed them sufficient in number to form the basis of any conclusion. Nevertheless, it was thought right to mention that the two cows inoculated with the nasal discharge, and subjected to the proof of contagion by cohabitation, have not been affected with pleuropneumonia.

Experiments by inoculating the liquid from the lungs of sick cattle have been performed on fifty-four healthy animals, and under conditions which indicated that these animals had never previously contracted the disease. Of these fifty-four subjects inoculated none have shown symptoms of pleuropneumonia as the result of inoculation. On twenty-three the effects of inoculation have only been indicated by a slight local and well-circumscribed inflammation. On twenty-one the inflammation has been very severe, very extensive, and complicated by gangrenous phenomena which have led to the death of six subjects. Therefore the number of animals in which inoculation has been benignant has amounted to 61.11 per cent.; the proportion of those having gangrene after the operation, which resulted in the loss of a portion of the tail, was 27.77 per cent.; lastly, the deaths attained 11.11 per cent. Thus 88.88 per cent. of the inoculated animals recovered, and 11.11 per cent. died.

Of the forty-eight subjects which came out of the inoculation safe and healthy, two died of accidents not induced by the operation, and thirty-four were exposed for a period of five or six months to the direct influence of contagion by cohabitation with twenty-four subjects that had not been inoculated, and which served as a means of comparison.

Twelve inoculated animals which had been placed in separate stables to serve for ulterior experiments were not exposed to the direct contact of such cattle, but were looked after by the same person who had charge of the sick animals.

Only one of the forty-six animals inoculated, viz., about two per cent., became affected with pleuropneumonia, whereas of the twenty-four non-inoculated animals fourteen, or fifty-eight per cent., suffered.

From these experiments the commission concludes—

1. The inoculation of the liquid extracted from the lungs of an animal affected with pleuropneumonia does not transmit to healthy animals of the same species the same disease—at all events, so far as its seat is concerned.

2. The appreciable phenomena which follow the inoculation are those of a local inflammation, which is circumscribed and slight, on a certain number of the animals inoculated; extensive and diffuse, with general reaction proportioned to the local disease, and complicated by gangrenous accidents, on another number of the inoculated animals, so that even death may result.

3. The inoculation of the liquid from the lungs of an animal affected with pleuropneumonia exerts a preservative influence, and invests the economy of the larger number of animals subjected to its influence with an immunity which protects them from the contagion of this malady during a period which has yet to be determined, but which the experiments quoted indicate, at all events, not to be less than six months.

Although, from the experiments of the commission, the losses per cent. among the animals inoculated were greater than the losses by the disease communicated by cohabitation, they ascribed this partly to the imperfect means adopted in inoculating, and they do not overlook the great deterioration of the animals which did not die after suffering from the natural disorder. They recommended further trials, and that the practice should be encouraged.

A mixed commission of the Central Society of Medicine and the Agricultural Committee of Lille instituted experiments on one thousand two hundred and forty-five animals, to determine the comparative effects of inoculation of the pulmonary liquid of pleuropneumonia and of septic matters. The inoculations with virus amounted to one thousand two hundred and sixteen; of these nine hundred and seventy-eight succeeded, and two hundred and thirty-eight showed no visible effects. One hundred and seventy-nine animals, or 14.72

per cent., lost a part of the tail; seventeen, or 1.39 per cent., died; lastly, twenty-nine animals, or 2.38 per cent., were seized with pleuropneumonia, and of these eight succumbed. Twenty-nine head of cattle were inoculated with decomposing matter, and only two without local effect resulting. Ten lost a portion of the tail, viz., 34 per cent. Of these animals three caught pleuropneumonia, and one of these died. The Lille committee regarded the process and results of inoculation as involved in doubts and uncertainties.

In England attention was directed to inoculation by consuls from abroad, and Professors Simonds and Morton were commissioned to proceed to Belgium to investigate the matter, and then to institute experiments at home. The result obtained, after much too limited observation, was pronounced against the practice. This sufficed to prevent the continuance of the operation among veterinarians, and the London cow-feeders alone resorted to the plan in a partial and very imperfect manner.

I witnessed many bad results in 1854 and 1855, and a case which came under my observation on the 4th of May, 1856, in which putrid matter that had been kept in an ink-bottle for a long time was used, led me to pronounce a somewhat cautious but adverse opinion in the Highland Society's transactions for that year.

My efforts were afterward directed to an exposure of the evils of indiscriminate sale of healthy and sick cattle in public markets, and I insisted on the slaughter and isolation of sick and infected animals. The little support I received at home led me, in 1863, to call together the first international veterinary congress, which was held in Hamburg, and there I met veterinarians from all parts of Europe who had steadily persevered in the practice of inoculation, and could furnish me with reliable data. It is impossible, and, indeed, it would be superfluous, to give a detailed account of the thousands and tens of thousands of cases which have led to the almost universal opinion that inoculation is the best means in the majority of instances to check the ravages of pleuropneumonia. The observations have been made in all countries where pleuropneumonia has appeared, though opposition to the practice is scarcely overcome to the extent that is desirable.

The efforts of Professor Verheyen in Belgium, and his many attacks on Dr. Willems's method, approved as they have been by some in that country, only illustrate once more the adage that a man is not a prophet in his own country. But Professor Thiervene, who was one of the original Belgian commissioners, and at first among the decided skeptics, delivered an address before the Royal Academy of Medicine in Brussels, in 1866, in reply to one by M. Boëns, who had attacked the practice of inoculation, in which he vindicates Dr. Willems's position. He indorses Professor Saint Cyr's remarks on the demonstration of a preservative influence by the most accurate and extensive experiments, and shows that of the well-informed in Belgium, who are acquainted with the character of the contagious pleuropneumonia, none now doubt that inoculation is a safe and certain preventive.

Medical men, no less than veterinarians, have a duty to perform in relation to this subject. Boards of health in cities and country districts should take up the subject in connection with the sale of the meat and milk of animals affected with pleuropneumonia. History shows that in those countries, such as England, where the sale of the produce of these animals has been most unrestricted, the traffic in such cattle has been so great as to cause the most severe losses by the disease, and without intermission.

An objection to inoculation, which weighs in the case of human and ovine small-pox as well as rinderpest, is that the inoculated disease is contagious, that the cohabitation of healthy with inoculated animals may lead to extensions of the infection, and that the foci whence the disease spreads are always on the increase. Such objections cannot weigh against the inoculation for the lung plague, as the inoculated malady is not communicated except by reinoculation. My observations on this point are very numerous, and I do not know of a single instance recorded, during the seventeen years that inoculation has been extensively practiced, in which contagion from inoculated animals has been witnessed.

Another objection which has led, of late years, to the practice being checked among the cow-feeders of Brooklyn, is the sloughing of the tail and the animals splashing blood and matter from their sore tails into the milk-cans. All this arises from the operation being performed by persons who know nothing of the precautions to be used, and especially of the proper selection and preservation of the virus. Accidents will happen; but out of nearly two thousand inoculations I have had a loss of less than one per cent. by death, and under five per cent. of the tails have lost their tips. This includes my earlier trials, and the results would be more favorable if I excluded them from my calculations.

PRECAUTIONS.

The prevention of pleuropneumonia by inoculation demands, therefore, special attention, first, to the condition of herds operated on; second, selection of proper virus; third, the preservation of that virus from decomposition; fourth, the proper performance of the operation.

First. As to the condition of stock, it may be said that at any season and under any system of management, whether cattle are being grazed, stall-fed, used for breeding purposes, or fattening for the butcher's stall, inoculation may be resorted to. It should be practiced as soon as there is reason to believe a herd has been in danger of infection or actually infected. The first case of well-marked lung plague on a farm or in a dairy shed should be the starting point for careful isolation, and the inoculation of all apparently healthy animals. The disease rarely manifests all its virulence until the third month after the introduction of a sick animal among a lot of cattle, but the longer the inoculation is delayed the more likely is it that the operation will be performed on animals during the stage of invasion of the natural disease, and the result is a loss which is sometimes ascribed to the inefficacy of the preventive. In cities where the lung plague has been rife for any length of time, and it is necessary to make frequent purchases, although a great deal in the way of prevention may be effected by judicious purchases of animals in healthy districts, it is best to resort regularly to inoculation. Dairymen should strive to buy more cows at a time, and at regular intervals, instead of picking up a chance bargain or making it a rule to go to the market weekly, as has been the custom in both England and America. It matters not if the cow is about to calve or has just calved; nothing should induce the dairyman or the farmer in an infected district to run a risk. It is desirable to keep animals clean and well littered on straw or sawdust, to prevent the tails that have been operated on from coming in contact with excrement and urine, which may poison the wound with decomposing matter.

Second. The selection of proper virus should be intrusted to veterinarians, who can detect the various stages of the disease. It is during the first stage of a mild case that the interlobular tissue of the lung is found distended with a yellow gelatinous serum, which is fluid so long as the lungs are hot, and is not readily contaminated by other inflammatory products and blood. When a large portion of lung has been so far consolidated as to present an almost uniform dark red or purplish color, it should be discarded, and especially in cases where a piece of the organ has become gangrenous and detached, or where liquid in the cavity of the chest and around the lungs is decidedly fetid. Microscopic examination will indicate, by the presence of movable rods and floating molecules, the putrefactive changes, and that should cause us to discard any such source of virus. A clear pleural fluid is often very useful for preservation, but perhaps greater reliance is to be placed on the exudation of a piece of lung in the first stage of the malady. The lung is placed on a tolerably wide strainer, or bits of wood, over a clean stoneware, glass, or porcelain dish or bowl; it is cut in various directions, and a stout piece of cloth or flannel is placed over the whole to confine the heat and prevent dust falling on the lung or liquid. It is better to place the dish or bowl over a warm water or sand bath at 100°, so as to prevent gelatinization. In a short time, according to the condition and quantity of lung, a sufficient quantity of clear yellow-colored liquid is obtained. Sometimes blood accidentally tinges the material, and this is not necessarily a disadvantage.

The old plan of keeping pieces of lung to inoculate with, and bottling up anything and everything to secure a fetid compound, to be kept for months, must be regarded as the most certain means to insure accidents as the results of inoculation.

Third. The preservation of the virus for periodic inoculations has certainly been a desideratum. Had farmers and dairymen had the facilities for procuring material which could be used with safety in their stock, they would long since have tried a method that, even when badly followed, is beneficial to them. Dr. Sticker, of Cologne, has preserved the virus in hermetically-closed tubes containing from one to two drachms. One of these tubes is emptied into a small glass, and one to two parts of rain water added. This is not desirable. A plan has occurred to me of utilizing the tubes referred to in the report of Drs. Billings and Curtis, which I am sure will meet the requirements of the case. Tubes about four inches in length, three-eighths of an inch in diameter, and tapering at either end, are sealed at one end in a blow-pipe flame, and then heated throughout their length to redness. The operation is concluded by closing the other end in the same way. The air in the tube is rarefied, all germs of decay destroyed, and there is no difficulty in further manipulations. When a proper quantity of liquid is obtained one point of the tube is passed into it, the tip broken off, and the virus is sucked in to fill the vacuum. A spirit lamp is held near the liquid, and the point of the tube transferred from this to the flame. By the aid of a blow-pipe the sealing is effected, and thus protected the virus will keep for months. The test for discarding tubes thus prepared is a microscopical one, and consists in the detection of bacteria or evidences of putrefaction in the liquid.

Fourth. The inoculation of cattle is most safely practiced on the tip of the tail. All parts that are loose, and from which any extensive exudation may spread over the connective tissue beneath the skin, must be avoided. The lips, dewlap, and root of the tail have proved dangerous localities. When the operation is properly and delicately performed the tip of the ear is said to be safe, but, on the whole, the end of the tail is found, after long experience, to be the best.

Dairymen have frequently resorted to the plan of making an incision of an inch or two in length, inserting in the part a piece of lung, and bandaging; swelling, inflammation, sloughing of the tail, and secondary deposits in the lymphatic glands and other parts of the organs, have frequently resulted from this rude practice.

Dr. Willems first described his mode of inoculation as follows: "I take the liquid pressed from an animal recently slaughtered, or of one that has died of the disease; I plunge into it a kind of large lancet; then I make two or three punctures at the lower extremity of the tail of the animal that I wish to preserve from the disease; *a single drop of the liquid is sufficient to make the inoculation.*"

At one time Dr. Willems adopted the plan of making two punctures, one on the upper part and the other on the lower surface of the tip of the tail, and both about the same distance from the extreme end of the organ. He found that this frequently led to a fusion of the exudation commencing around each puncture, and the result was the sloughing of the tail. He therefore resorted to the punctures disposed vertically in a line with the tail, and about three inches from each other. By this means the exudations commencing at the two spots had no tendency to coalesce and lead to untoward results.

Various instruments have been suggested for the operation. Dr. Sticker devised a hollow stylet, with a sharp, diamond-shaped point. The stylet is armed with a little india-rubber tube, and this passed into a wooden handle, with a spring, whereby the flexible tube may be squeezed for the expulsion of air, and by placing the point of the instrument in the prepared liquid, sufficient is sucked in for an inoculation. I have used this instrument as follows:

The end of the tail being firmly held in the left hand, the point of the instrument is plunged with the right hand superficially into the skin of the tip of the tail, and directed from before backwards, so that any effort to withdraw the tail would only hasten the operation. I can testify from practice to the simplicity and efficacy of Dr. Sticker's instrument as used by me. I have preferred this plan of operating to Dr. Sticker's method, which consists in charging his instrument, holding the tail firmly, and then pushing the stylet about one inch forward into the tail, and by a simultaneous pressure upon the key, and a slight winding motion, the virus is deposited beneath the skin and in the substance of the organ. Dr. Sticker proposed making a channel with the instrument—a channel downward, from which exudation might flow; but this is of no avail if septic matter is used, and untoward symptoms result. The result of Dr. Sticker's operation, according to his description, is a local swelling occurring about the eighth or ninth day, and which increases the tail from three to four lines in diameter, and extends over a length of one and a half to two inches; incisions have not been necessary after the operation, and the tails have not mortified. The inoculated cattle do not lose their appetites, and the flow of milk is not diminished. Dr. Sticker considers it important that the virus should be deposited in the connective tissue beneath the skin and not deep in the muscles of the tail.

With the tubes proposed to preserve the liquid a very simple plan consists in using a small bistoury or lancet, scarifying the upper surface of the tail an inch or so from the end, and from this part the hair may be clipped with a pair of scissors; the scarification must be superficial, and blood should not be drawn if possible; the tube is taken and both ends broken off; a little rubber ball or tube is fixed onto one end, and, by pressing this, a few drops of the liquid are dropped in the scarification. This is the safest method, as there is no doubt of the virus being applied to an absorbent surface, and the method of collection affords a guarantee of its purity; the tubes are thus kept hermetically sealed till needed, and, from the way they are used, there is no loss of material.

The results of successful inoculation are somewhat various; by some methods the swelling is considerable and many tails slough. It is not a little remarkable that cows do not often fail to enjoy immunity from the disease after sloughing of the organ; it might, *a priori*, have been supposed that the acute inflammation and gangrene would have prevented the specific action of the virus on the system, and there is reason to believe that occasionally this does occur, as I have seen more than one case of pleuropneumonia in cows that had lost their tail after inoculation.

Under favorable circumstances a slight heat and tumefaction occur around the puncture, at a period varying from a week to even sixty days. Commonly from the ninth to the fifteenth day the local eruption is visible, and, if at all marked, is attended with a little fever; a slight shiver, restlessness and some loss of appetite, slightly checked secretion of milk, and constipation may be noticed. I have repeatedly inoculated all the cows in a dairy, and the owner has not sustained the slightest loss or inconvenience from cows failing in their milk; indeed, this is the rule.

No pustule, no suppuration, forms; untoward results consist in the excessive local swelling, or, if putrid matter has been used, in secondary deposits at the root of the tail, around the anus and other parts. One of the most remarkable cases I ever witnessed was one in which, on the seventeenth day, after a carefully performed inoculation, both fore legs and brisket swelled up enormously, and the animal suffered intensely from fever and died on the fourth day.

As a rule, no after-treatment is necessary, the results being so slight that they even escape observation altogether. But, when excessive swellings occur, it is best to use cold applications, and nothing is better than a steady stream of cold water on the part at short intervals. Incisions are not always desirable, but, where it is deemed advisable to relieve great tension, they must be deep and free; the resulting wound must be washed with a solution of sesquichloride of iron or chloride of zinc of the strength of four grains to the ounce of water. When the animal has much fever and is costive, a saline purge, such as a pound of Epsom salts, affords relief.

JOAN GAMGEE, M. D.

Hon. HORACE CAPRON,
Commissioner of Agriculture.

APPENDIX No. 1.

Statement of losses by lung plague in cattle in the District of Columbia and vicinity, collected for Professor Gamgee by Mr. George Reid, Ingleside farm, Washington. D. C.

Number.	No. of cattle kept.	No. lost since commencement of disease.	No. lost in 1868.	No. lost in 1869.
1	5	1	1	....
2	5	2	....	2
3	30	21	....	....
4	18	7	....	....
5	30	15	....	2
6	30	10	....	11
7	22	41	15	....
8	40	2	....	....
9	16	....	....	....
10	12	....	....	....
11	16	....	....	....
12	12	1	1	....
13	22	17	5	....
14	20	....	5	....
15	12	10	2	2
16	16	8	....	....
17	25	....	....	....
18	2	....	....	....
19	5	....	....	....
20	5	4	4	....
21	4	....	....	....
22	25	28	....	....
23	40	....	....	....
24	35	25	....	....
25	14	6	6	....
26	10	....	....	....
Total	471	198	39	17

APPENDIX No. 2.

TABLE OF DUTCH EXPERIMENTS.

FIRST SERIES.

EXUDATIVE PLEUROPNEUMONIA.

Summary of the inoculations performed and the results obtained.

Names and places of abode of the proprietors.	Date of the inoculation.	KIND OF CATTLE INOCULATED.										Period at which the effects appeared after inoculation.		No. of animals affected with pleuropneumonia after inoculation.	Period at which pleuropneumonia appeared after inoculation.		No. of animals that died in consequence of inoculation.	Remarks.
		M'ch cows.		Cows not giv'g milk.		Heifers.		Calves.		Total.								
		Inoculated.	No. of those upon which effects were observed.	Inoculated.	No. of those upon which effects were observed.	Inoculated.	No. of those upon which effects were observed.	Inoculated.	No. of those upon which effects were observed.	Inoculated.	No. of those upon which effects were observed.	The earliest.	The latest.		Date.	Number of days.		
D. Schoemakers, Achttienhoven.	June 14	21	16	2	1	3	......	4	3	30	20	5th day	45th day	1	July 6	22	......	
Do	June 25	2	1	....	......	....	......	....	......	2	1	34th day	....	......	....	......	......	
Do	June 29	1	1	....	......	....	......	1	......	2	1	30th day	....	......	....	......	......	
J. Wynen, Achttienhoven	June 25	20	18	....	......	5	5	8	......	33	23	4th day	39th day	3	July 6 July 7 Aug. 15	11 12 51	4	
W. Degroot, Utrecht	June 25	13	4	....	......	1	......	2	......	16	4	27th day	....	2	July 1 Aug. 1	6 43	1	Inoculated with matter from the same lung.
J. Plomp, Utrecht	June 25	6	1	....	......	....	......	1	......	7	1	26th day	....	2	July 23 July 25	27 29	....	
F. Van Ingen, Houten	June 26	3	3	3	2	2	2	3	......	11	7	5th day	34th day	......	....	......	....	
Do	July 8	1	1	....	......	....	......	....	......	1	1	21st day	....	......	....	......	....	
J. Van Doorn, Westbroek	June 29	10	10	....	......	....	......	7	1	17	11	4th day	32d day	1	July 15	16	....	
J. Schaay, Westbroek	June 29	1	1	....	......	....	......	....	......	1	1	20th day	....	......	....	......	....	
A. Streefkerk, Nieuw Loosdrecht.	June 30	10	4	1	......	4	1	1	......	16	5	21st day	....	2	July 12	12	1	Inoculated with matter from the same lung. A pneumonic cow that was inoculated died.
Wid. Meyers, Nieuw Loosdrecht.	June 30	12	7	....	......	....	......	....	......	12	7	24th day	....	......	....	......	....	

M. Streefkerk, Nieuw Loosdrecht.	June 30	15	15	...	...	1	1	5	1	21	17	16th day.	24th day.	...	...	1	...	Two pneumonic cows were inoculated, one of which died.
F. Woudenberg, Vreeland.	June 30	21	4	...	...	...	...	9	2	30	6	9th day..	31st day.	2	July 30 July 7	5 7	... ...	
Do	July 9	...	...	...	...	7	6	...	...	7	6	16th day.	...	...	...	...	...	
Hagedoorn, Vreeland	July 9	4	1	...	...	...	...	1	...	5	1	16th day.	...	...	...	...	1	An inoculated cow, afflicted with pleuro-pneumonia from 5th of July, died.
Vossenstein, Maartensdyk.	July 1	...	...	...	...	2	2	5	2	7	4	15th day.	...	...	...	...	...	
G. Van Harte, Kamerick..	July 2	14	8	...	...	7	4	8	4	29	16	3d day...	33d day.	3	July 4 July 11 July 22	3 9 20	3	
Total	...	154	95	6	3	32	21	55	13	247	132	...	...	161	...	...	10	

APPENDIX No. 3.

TABLE OF DUTCH EXPERIMENTS.

SECOND SERIES.

EXUDATIVE PLEUROPNEUMONIA.

Summary of the experiments of inoculation made at the State Veterinary School, (horned cattle inoculated.)

Number.	Description of animals.	Where from.	Age.	Date of covering.	Date of calving.	Date of inoculation.	Date of the first effects.	Intensity of the effects.	Reinoculation.		Recovery.			Died in consequence of the inoculation.	Attacked by pleuro-pneumonia after the inoculation.	Remarks.
									Date.	Effects.	Date.	Without loss of the tail.	With loss of tail.			
			Yrs.													
1	White head	Woudenberg and Scherpenzeil.	4	July 2		Aug. 2	Aug. 6	Moderate			Aug. 30	1				
2	Black and white, (white face.)	do	5	Sept. 28		Aug. 2	Aug. 6	Considerable			Oct. 15		1			Loss of the tip or the tail.
3	Dun and white, (white face.)	do	4	June 24		Aug. 4	Aug. 11	Moderate			Oct. 6	1				
4	Black and white, (white face.)	do	4	Aug. 22		Aug. 4	Aug. 10	Moderate			Sept. 30	1				
5	Black and white, (white face.)	do	6	Aug. 18 Nov. 4		Aug. 4	Aug. 10	Moderate			Sept. 12	1				
6	Red and white, (white face.)	do	5		May, '52	Aug. 4	Aug. 8	Moderate			Sept. 1	1				
7	Black and white	do	8	Aug. 2		Aug. 4	Aug. 10	Moderate			Sept. 20	1				
8	Black and white, (white face.)	do	2	July 9		Aug. 4	Aug. 10	Moderate			Sept. 20	1				
9	Whitish head	do	9			Aug. 4	Aug. 12	Fatal						1		Died Aug. 13; probably calved a week before time.
10	Black and white, (star on foreh'd.)	do	5		Aug. 6	Aug. 4	Aug. 10	Considerable			Sept. 27	1				
11	Black and white	do	5	July 21		Aug. 4	Aug. 10	Slight	Oct. 14	None	Aug. 22	1				
12	Spotted white, (white face.)	do	5	July 1 Aug. 7 Dec. 14	Mar. 3	Aug. 4	Aug. 10	Slight	Oct. 14	None	Aug. 22	1				
13	White	do	4	Apr. 19		Aug. 4	Aug. 10	Slight	Oct. 14	None	Aug. 22	1				

14	Dun and white, (white face.)	...... do	4	Feb. 17	Nov. 14	Aug. 4	Aug. 10	Slight	Oct. 14	None ..	Aug. 22	1	....	......	....	
15	Black and white, (white face bull.)	...... do	2	....	....	Aug. 4	Aug. 11	Moderate	....	....	Sept. 14	1	....	......	....	
16	Dun............	Utrecht........	5	Aug. 27	....	July 23	....	None	Oct. 14	None ..	....	......	....	......	....	Had pleuropneumonia previously.
17	Spotted white, (male calf.)	...... do	1/3	....	....	July 11	July 18	Considerable .	....	....	Aug. 12	1	....	......	....	
18	Black and white .	...... do	9	Aug. 30	....	July 23	....	None	Oct. 14	None ..	....	1	....	......	....	
19	Black and white, (white head.)	D. Schoemakers, at Achttienhoven.	7	July 3	....	June 14	June 25	Great........	....	....	Aug. 2	......	1	......	....	The end of the tail.
20	Spotted white ...	J. Wynen, at Achttienhoven.	6	....	....	June 25	July 6	Fatal........	....	....	....	......	....	1	....	Died July 24.
21	Black, (white head.)	J. Van Doorn, Westbrook.	4	July 15	....	June 29	July 10	Great........	....	....	Sept. 1	......	1	......	....	The end of the tail.
22	Black and white, (star on foreh'd.)	G. Van Hare, Kamerick.	8	....	....	July 2	July 20	Fatal........	....	....	....	......	....	1	....	Died August 9.
23	Black and white .	J. Wynen, at Achttienhoven.	4	May 5	....	June 25	July 16	Great........	....	....	Aug. 20	......	1	......	....	The whole of the tail.
24	Spotted white ...	Stoutenburg and Soest.	....	....	....	June 3	June 8	Fatal	....	....	....	......	....	1	....	Died June 23.
25	Black and white, (white head.)	...... do	....	....	....	June 3	June 8	Great........	....	....	July 10	1	....	......	....	Nearly the whole of the tail.
26	Spotted white, (white face.)	Degroot, at Utrecht.	9	....	....	June 25	....	None	....	....	....	......	....	......	July 1	Died July 13.

REPORT OF DR. J. J. WOODWARD, U. S. A.,

ON

THE PATHOLOGICAL ANATOMY AND HISTOLOGY OF THE RESPIRATORY ORGANS IN THE PLEUROPNEUMONIA OF CATTLE.

WAR DEPARTMENT, SURGEON GENERAL'S OFFICE,
Washington, June 16, 1870.

SIR: I have the honor to transmit herewith a report on the Pathological Anatomy and Histology of the Respiratory Organs in the Pleuropneumonia of Cattle, prepared, in accordance with your request, by Brevet Lieutenant Colonel J. J. Woodward, Assistant Surgeon United States Army.

Very respectfully, your obedient servant,

J. K. BARNES,
Surgeon General.

Hon. HORACE CAPRON,
Commissioner of Agriculture, Washington, D. C.

ARMY MEDICAL MUSEUM,
Washington, D. C., June 15, 1870.

GENERAL: During the summer of 1869 the lungs of several cows, dead of epidemic pleuropneumonia, were brought to the Army Medical Museum by Professor John Gamgee, then engaged in preparing a report for the Commissioner of Agriculture on certain of the diseases of the cattle of the United States; and, in accordance with the wishes of the Commissioner, I undertook the histological investigation of the specimens. I examined them in the fresh condition, and superintended the preparation of a number of permanently mounted sections for microscopical examination, which are now preserved at the museum. (Microscopical Section, Nos. 2781 to 2819, inclusive.) These sections were made, under my direction, by Dr. E. Schaeffer, one of my assistants, and have served, in connection with the observations I made on the fresh specimens at the time of their arrival, as the basis of the following paper.

My attention was first drawn to the pleuropneumonia of cattle in the fall of 1860, by Dr. J. Newton Evans, of Hatboro', Montgomery County, Pennsylvania. This gentleman kindly placed at my disposal the lungs of several cattle dead of the disease during an epidemic which prevailed near Hatboro' at the time. I have since had various opportunities of examining the thoracic viscera in this complaint, and during the year 1869, besides the specimens furnished by Professor Gamgee dissected at the museum, the body of a tame deer (*Cervus virginianus*) which had died suddenly of the same disorder, and in which the pathological lesions were essentially similar to those which I had observed in cattle.

The appearances presented to the naked eye in all the cases which I had occasion to study agreed quite well with the excellent account given by Professor F. Weber, of Kiel, in 1854.* I did not, however, have any opportunity of observing the separation and encapsuling of isolated lung lobules described by that writer as occurring in chronic cases. The general aspect of the lesions may be described as follows:

The pleural cavity of the affected side contained a variable quantity of clear, opalescent, turbid, or even grumous, yellowish serum, and the parietal as well as the pulmonary pleura was plastered over, to a variable extent, with masses of opaque whitish yellow, or greenish yellow, fatty-looking lymph, flakes of which frequently floated in the serum. Not unfrequently both sides were similarly affected. In some cases the pericardium contained serum of the same character, with adherent lymph coating its inner surface and covering the heart. The adipose tissue about the pericardium often exhibited a peculiar transformation, which caused its appearance to the naked eye to approximate closely to that of the adjacent lymph masses

A section of the lung most generally showed its apex nearly healthy; further down the parenchyma was congested and œdematous; still lower the connective tissue septa between the lung lobules were progressively thickened, until finally they were converted into whitish, yellowish, or greenish opaque layers, which in sections of the organ appeared to map out the congested and œdematous lung tissue into angular territories, readily recognized as lung lobules. Still further toward the diaphragm the lung parenchyma between the opaque yellowish septa exhibited various degrees of red hepatization, while in the most inferior portions of the organ the lung tissue, having passed into the stage of gray hepatization, could not readily be distinguished by the naked eye from the tissue of the diseased interlobular septa, and the surface of these portions of the section appeared of a mottled reddish yellow or yellowish gray hue.

An examination of the pleural surface, after sections of the lung were made, showed, as a rule, that the adherent lymph masses on the *pleura pulmonalis* corresponded chiefly to those portions of the lung which were more or less completely hepatized.

Very great variation in the extent of the disease was noted in different cases. Sometimes one lung only was affected, sometimes both. Some animals died before any portion of the lung had passed into the stage of gray hepatization; others survived till abscess formation, or even gangrene of portions of the lung tissue supervened. Sometimes at least one of the lungs was hepatized, more or less completely, throughout its whole extent, but generally the upper lobes were nearly healthy, or at most had not progressed beyond the stage of congestion or œdema. When sections of the diseased lung were laid on a suitable perforated plate considerable quantities of bloody serum drained from them.

The peculiar appearance produced by the yellowish thickening of the interlobular septa, combined with œdema and congestion, or red hepatization of the parenchyma of the lobules involved, was seldom absent from some portion of the affected lung. This is the phenomenon most likely to arrest the attention of observers familiar with the post mortem appearances of pleuropneumonia in the human subject, when their attention is

* Die interlobuläre Pneumonie. Virchow's Archiv., Bd. vi, S. 89.

for the first time directed to the disease in cattle. It is conditioned by the peculiar anatomical arrangement of the lungs of these animals, in which the lobules are separated from each other, by processes of the pleura or by septa of loose connective tissue, to an extent which has no parallel in the human subject. The inflammation of the pleura speedily extends to these loose interlobular septa, in which a rapid lymph formation takes place, resulting in the production of the thick yellowish layers above described. Very often these thickened septa are softened in their central portions, where they frequently present irregular cavities containing a turbid serum or a puriform fluid, while the lymph next the surfaces of the adjacent lobules is much denser and more consistent.

Amidst these extensive changes of the lung tissue, the larger air passages usually remain singularly free from disease. Those which actually ramify in the diseased portions of the lung present more or less congestion of their mucous membrane and generally contain a variable quantity of puruloid mucus, or of yellow lymph, not unlike that seen in the pleural cavity; but the bronchial inflammation which exists in these situations does not generally extend to the other bronchial tubes or the trachea.

In considering the general character of the lesions briefly sketched in the foregoing paragraphs, it appeared to me that the following points were especially deserving of microscopical investigation: the alterations in the lung parenchyma; those in the connective tissue of the pleura, pericardium, and interlobular septa; the structure of the lymph masses adherent to the pleura and pericardium, and the peculiar transformation of portions of the adipose tissue in the vicinity of the heart.

For the purposes of this investigation I not merely examined the elements obtained by tearing and scraping the tissues to be studied, and observed fragments or sections immersed simply in the serum which drained from the œdematous organ, but I made use of the well-known glycerine method, and, above all, caused my assistant, Dr. Schaeffer, to prepare the thin section to which I have already alluded. For this purpose, the process most generally employed at the museum for the preparation of thin sections of pathologica tissues was resorted to, a process which I have described in full elsewhere.* Its general features are as follows:

Small portions of the parts intended for investigation are hardened and gradually robbed of their moisture by soaking them for a few days in alcohol of moderate strength, replacing this by alcohol of 95 per cent., in which they remain a few days longer, when they are immersed in absolute alcohol until they are hard enough to cut into thin sections by means of a razor and one of the ordinary cutting machines. The nuclei are then stained with Thiersch's carmine fluid, or with carmine dissolved in a saturated solution of borax, after which they are again placed a few days in absolute alcohol, and finally mounted in a solution of Canada balsam in chloroform or benzole. When the solution of carmine and borax was employed the sections were subsequently treated with oxalic acid, to give brilliancy to the carmine staining.

Instead of the above, some of the sections after staining were immersed for some time in glycerine and finally mounted in a jelly of glycerine and gum arabic. These preparations were at first quite as beautiful as those mounted in Canada balsam, but, though less

---

* American Journal of Medical Sciences, Januury, 1869, page 277; see, also, Instructions to Medical Officers to whom a Microscope is furnished, Surgeon General's Office, July 1, 1868.

than a year has elapsed since they were made, they are already considerably altered, and have long been far inferior in distinctness and beauty to those preserved in balsam.

My experience at the museum has led me to give preference to the method described over any other which I have tried for the purpose of making sections of pathological tissue. The preparations which result closely resemble in appearance those obtained when successfully-made fresh sections are stained with carmine and mounted in glycerine, after Beale's method, and they not merely present the arrangement of the parts with much less displacement of the elements, but are better suited for study with high powers, and it is possible to prepare satisfactorily much larger and thinner sections. They possess, moreover, the incontestable advantage of being capable of indefinite preservation, and hence I am able to state that those which have served for the following description can be seen at the museum by any microscopist desirous of studying them.

To illustrate the descriptions here offered, I have prepared a series of photo-micrographs, representing characteristic portions of certain of the sections. The objects photographed are shown with a magnifying power of four hundred diameters, linear. The objective used was the $\frac{1}{8}$th of William Wales, of Fort Lee, New Jersey, which is specially corrected for photography. No eye-piece was employed. The source of illumination in most cases was the oxycalcium light. The process resorted to has been published in full in my recent reports to the Surgeon General on the electric, magnesium, and calcium lights as sources of illumination in photo-micrography, and need not, therefore, be described in this place.*

The minute structure of the parts selected for study will now be briefly described in the order already indicated:

1. *The alterations in the parenchyma of the lung* will be best understood after a brief sketch of the appearances presented by sections made through normal or nearly normal portions. Such sections, prepared as already described, and mounted in balsam, afforded quite satisfactory objects for study. Since the morsels of lung selected were not inflated before immersing them into the alcohol, the air vesicles on the periphery of the pieces, of course, collapsed more or less completely. Those in the central portions, however, retained their shape to a tolerable extent, and from such portions, therefore, the sections were prepared. The air vesicles, as seen in these sections, were irregularly polygonal, approaching a rounded or oval form, and averaged about $\frac{1}{200}$th of an inch in their long diameter. Their walls, when cut transversely in the sections, appeared to be composed largely of capillary blood-vessels, the contours of which could readily be observed. The numerous nuclei of the walls of these capillaries averaged $\frac{1}{3500}$th of an inch in long diameter. In places where larger vessels came into view, the elements of their walls could usually be well made out, and were generally surrounded by more or less connective tissue, in which elastic fibers were often prominent. In all the sections there were numerous air vesicles so divided by the knife that, in certain positions of the fine adjustment of the microscope, a view of the inner surface of one of the walls of the vesicle was obtained. This always presented numerous oval nuclei arranged at regular intervals, and delicate contours could generally be traced between them, which, it seemed to me, could be best interpreted, in many cases, by supposing them to be portions of the boundaries of flat, polygonal, nucleated cells, corresponding to the epithelium of the air vesicles described by some authors. The appearances might also, perhaps, be interpreted by the supposition that the nuclei

* See also American Journal of Arts and Sciences, May, 1870, the National Medical Journal, April, 1870, and the London Monthly Microscopical Journal for June and August, 1870.

belonged to the capillaries of the wall in view, and the delicate contours might be referred to the limiting membrane of these vessels, but it seemed to me that neither the relative position of the nuclei, nor the direction of the contours, corresponded so well with this view as with that first mentioned. The nuclei, moreover, were somewhat broader than those of the undoubted capillaries in other portions of the section, though of the same average length. The epithelial cells, if such they were, averaged $\frac{1}{1200}$th of an inch in long diameter.

The first of the photo-micrographs appended, represents a portion of one of these sections, (No. 2801, Microscopical Section,) and exhibits the appearance described, as seen with 400 diameters. In arranging the focal adjustment of the microscope so as to bring into view that portion of the wall of the air vesicle which displays the epithelium-like appearance, the rest of the section is necessarily thrown out of focus, and is so represented in the photograph.

When, now, sections of the diseased portions of the lung were compared with the above, the most noteworthy alteration observed was in the contents of the air vesicles. These, which had been quite empty in the healthy lung, were in the diseased portion found to contain pus corpuscles in variable numbers. All possible transitions could be seen between vesicles containing a few scattered corpuscles and those in which the whole cavity was filled with them. Where the pus corpuscles were not numerous enough to obscure the view, delicate fibrin filaments could generally be made out between them, so that the contents of the air vesicles were, in fact, quite similar in composition to the lymph masses on the surface of the pleura and in the interlobular trabeculæ, which will be presently described. The sections containing but a few scattered pus corpuscles were from the reddened and œdematous portions of the lung, which, however, still contained enough air to enable them to float on water; those containing numerous pus corpuscles, with fibrin filaments between, were from portions of the lung which had entered, more or less completely, into the stage of red hepatization, while those which were stuffed so full of pus corpuscles that the shape of the air vesicle and its relations to neighboring parts were quite obscured, were from the most completely hepatized portions, or from those which had passed into the condition of gray hepatization.

With these changes in the contents of the air vesicles of the diseased lung, alterations undoubtedly occurred in the walls of the air vesicles. In the sections they appeared thicker than normal, they took up carmine more abundantly when stained, and their texture became more and more granular in the more completely hepatized portions of the parenchyma, so that it was difficult to make out their structure and to trace the precise changes which they had undergone. With these changes there was associated a notable diminution in the cohesiveness of the tissue, which became friable and easily torn, as has long been observed in the case of pneumonic lungs in the human subject. I regret greatly that the time at my disposal did not permit more elaborate research with regard to these changes, yet cannot avoid the opinion that the difficulties to be encountered in this direction are so great as materially to diminish the probability that more protracted efforts would have proved fruitful in the present incomplete state of our knowledge of the histology of the lung. I append two photo-micrographs taken from one of these sections, (No. 2808, Microscopical Section,) each magnified 400 diameters. They exhibit partially hepatized portions of the lung in which the air vesicles contain the pus corpuscles and fibrin filaments above described. The second photograph represents a rather more advanced stage than the first.

2. *The alterations in the connective tissue of the pleura, pericardium, and interlobular septa* have next to be described. The connective tissue of the inflamed pleura or pericardium was more or less thickened in accordance with the stage of the disease. In fresh sections it was whitish or yellowish white, sometimes lardaceous, sometimes opaque and yellow. Where lymph masses were adherent the epithelium could no longer be made out, even when the superimposed lymph was so loosely attached as to permit it to be readily stripped off. Every transition existed between this condition and that in which the diseased membrane and the adjacent lymph mass appeared to pass into each other by insensible gradations. In the microscopical examination of sections the most notable alteration observed was the great increase in the number of cellular elements. The character and distribution of these could generally be inferred from the distribution of the oval carmine-stained nuclei, $\frac{1}{3300}$th to $\frac{1}{3500}$th of an inch in length, but in many parts of the sections the elongated or even spindle-formed cells in which the nuclei were contained could be plainly distinguished. They were imbedded in a delicately fibrillated matrix, and were very generally grouped together in rows. Such rows of elements, it is well known, have, until recently, been interpreted as the progeny of the connective tissue corpuscles, from which they were supposed to be derived by the process of cell multiplication. The recent investigations of Cohnheim, which have found very general acceptance in Germany, would appear, however, to throw doubts on this view. I shall return to the subject in the sequel.

The conditions to be observed in the thickened connective tissue septa between the lobules were essentially similar to the above. The fourth photograph appended is intended to illustrate these changes in the inflamed connective tissue. It is taken from No. 2817, Microscopical Section, which is a portion of inflamed pericardium, and is magnified 400 diameters. The arrangement of the numerous nuclei, and the fibrillated character of the matrix in which they are imbedded, are well displayed.

3. *The lymph masses adherent to the pleura and pericardium*, and the flakes of lymph which floated in the serum contained in the thoracic cavities, were composed of coagulated fibrin with a variable number of pus corpuscles imbedded. The fibrin was sometimes merely granular, but very often distinctly filamentous. The serum itself usually contained floating pus corpuscles; their number being proportioned to the degree of turbidity observed in the fluid. The fifth photograph appended, taken from a portion of No. 2817, Microscopical Section, represents a portion of the lymph mass adherent to the pericardium, magnified 400 diameters. It will be seen that the pus corpuscles are quite abundant.

4. *The transformed adipose tissue about the pericardium* remains now to be briefly described. Sections showed that the fat vesicles retained their shape, and generally their fatty contents, but the delicate transparent connective tissue by which they are held together in the normal condition was greatly thickened, and in its more or less distinctly fibrillated substance numbers of new elements could be observed, as in the case of the connective tissue of the diseased pleura. In the balsam-mounted sections, these appearances are well preserved with the exception that the contents of the fat vesicles have been dissolved by the reagents used. The last of the appended photographs represents a portion of one of these sections magnified 400 diameters. It is taken from No. 2794, Microscopical Section.

Although the foregoing observations were very carefully made, they are far from being as complete as I could have wished, and many important points connected with the histology of the diseased parts, remain untouched. Still I entertain the hope that what I have been enabled to accomplish with the opportunities at my disposal, will possess some real value, particularly as the course pursued of preserving sections in a permanent form will permit these to serve for further study in the future, in connection with any similar investigations that may hereafter be undertaken in this country.

It will be observed, from the descriptions I have offered, that the disease is one of those intense and rapidly spreading inflammatory affections characterized by the development of what Rokitansky formerly described as croupous exudates, on the surface of the affected serous membrane, and in the parenchyma of the organs involved. The examination of specimens taken from animals dead at different periods during the course of the disease, and the study of different portions of the same lung when a part is comparatively healthy and a part diseased, would seem to indicate the correctness of the opinion of Professor Weber* that the pleura is primarily involved, and that the parenchyma of the lung is only affected secondarily, after the pleura coating the lobules, and the connective tissue trabeculæ connected with it, have become involved. The comparatively healthy condition of the air passages, or at least of those portions of them which are not imbedded in the hepatized parts of the lung, is particularly worthy of note.

In its histological relations, it will be perceived that the disorder is characterized by the appearance of immense numbers of pathological elementary forms in the parts involved. These appear in the air vesicles of the lungs, in the lymph masses adherent to the pleura and the pericardium, and in the abundant serous fluid which accumulates in the thoracic cavities, under the well-known form of pus cells. In the sections of the inflamed connective tissue of the pleura and pericardium, the connective tissue of the interlobular trabeculæ, and of the adipose tissue about the pericardium, the new elements do not, however, sufficiently resemble pus cells to permit me to assume them to be such without hesitation.

In describing the sections of the inflamed pericardium and pleura, I have already mentioned that the nuclei were oval in form, $\frac{1}{3300}$th to $\frac{1}{3500}$th of an inch in long diameter, and generally grouped together in rows of two, three, or more elements; and I mentioned that the views of Virchow, by which these rows were interpreted as the progeny of the proliferation of the normal connective tissue corpuscles of the part, were assailed by the recent investigations of Cohnheim. According to this observer they are, in fact, rows of white blood corpuscles, which have made their way through the walls of the blood vessels during the inflammatory process, and which are found in longer or shorter rows simply because in their "wandering" they are obliged to follow the course of the natural channels which exist in the tissues. Now, the pus corpuscles above described in the lymph masses, and in the cavities of the air vesicles, can readily be understood to have, perhaps, had this origin; certainly none of the lung sections I have preserved exhibit any appearances which would indicate that their pus corpuscles were genetically connected with any process of proliferation going on in the normal anatomical elements of the lung. But with the new elements observed in the inflamed connective tissue, this explanation is not so satisfactory. Take, for example, the sections of the inflamed pericardium. Here the nuclei of the numerous new cells, seen in the sections, resemble the nuclei of embryonic connective tissue corpuscles, and not those of pus. And where it is possible, as

* Loc. cit.

it is in many places, to distinguish the cell forms in which they lie, these are seen to have the character of young connective tissue cells. If, indeed, they are white blood corpuscles, they have then already been transformed to the similitude of the elements characteristic of the tissue in which they have imbedded themselves, and it appears to me that in the present state of our knowledge we are not yet justified in assuming such a transformation to be more than a bare possibility. In his criticism of the observations of His on the inflamed cornea, Cohnheim has, as I think, correctly attempted to show that the rows of cells supposed by that author to have proceeded from the proliferation of the cornea corpuscles are in fact rows of white corpuscles crowded into the channels which normally exist in the corneal tissue, and explains that His was misled by the transformations effected in the corpuscles by the reagents he employed. This criticism, however, will not apply with any force to the sections under consideration, for these were all prepared in precisely the same manner, and those of the lung tissue and of the lymph masses present the pus corpuscles in some places almost quite unaltered, in all readily recognizable in spite of any transformation they may have undergone, while the new cells, crowded into the connective tissue, have the characters which I have described.

I invite attention to this subject the more particularly because my study of the essays of Cohnheim lead me to regard his opinion with very great respect. His generalizations and theories are deduced from new observations made by himself and others, very many of which have been confirmed by several careful histologists. A number of them have been satisfactorily repeated under my direction at the Army Medical Museum with similar results. Among these I may particularly specify the new developments with regard to the structure of the blood-vessels resulting from the use of a solution of nitrate of silver as an injecting and staining fluid; the wandering of the white corpuscles through the vascular walls in the mesentery of wourarized frogs, when that membrane is inflamed by drawing out a knuckle of intestine through an opening in the abdominal parietes; the new observations on the structure of the cornea, particularly those resulting from its treatment with nitrate of silver, chloride of gold, and its examination while fresh in the moist chamber, and from the study by these processes of the inflamed cornea of the frog.

The results of the investigations on these subjects, conducted by myself and my assistants, have accorded so well with the descriptions of Cohnheim as to incline me to regard with much favor those of his statements which I have not yet had an opportunity of submitting to investigation, but I am not prepared to accept without reserve the ingenious argument by which he attempts to generalize from the facts acquired to the complete interpretation of the process of inflammation, and am of the opinion that much yet remains to be done before we shall be prepared to define with precision the part taken by the migration of the white corpuscles in the inflammatory process.

In conclusion, I may remark that the future success of investigations into the pathological histology of the disease under consideration must depend to a great extent upon the progress made in our knowledge of the minute anatomy of the healthy lung. At the present time the methods of research at our disposal are not such as to overcome completely the difficulties offered by the complex structure of this organ. Observers have not even agreed as to the solution of such apparently simple questions as the existence of an epithelium in the air vesicles. More intricate problems, such as the minute relations of the lymphatics, for example, lie still in utter darkness. Future success in these imperfectly explored fields may be expected in proportion as observers resort more and more to the practice of preserving in a permanent way the type specimens which serve as a basis for their descriptions, and in proportion as photographs are substituted for those half-schematic or diagramatic drawings, which represent rather the interpretation of the investigator than the objects as they exist in nature. But perhaps even more is to be anticipated from the application of new reagents, and of improved modes of preparing the tissues for microscopic examination. When we reflect on the extent of the additions which have been made to our knowledge of minute anatomy by processes quite recently introduced, such as imbibition with nitrate of silver, chloride of gold and osmic acid, the preparation of thin sections of frozen tissues and the use of the moist chamber, it is impossible to resist the conclusion that it is from future improvements in this direction that solid progress in the normal and pathological histology of the lung is chiefly to be expected.

Very respectfully, your obedient servant,

J. J. WOODWARD,

Assistant Surgeon and Brevet Lieutenant Colonel United States Army,
in charge of the Medical and Microscopical Sections of the Museum.

Brevet Major General J. K. Barnes,
Surgeon General U. S. Army.

ARMY MEDICAL MUSEUM.

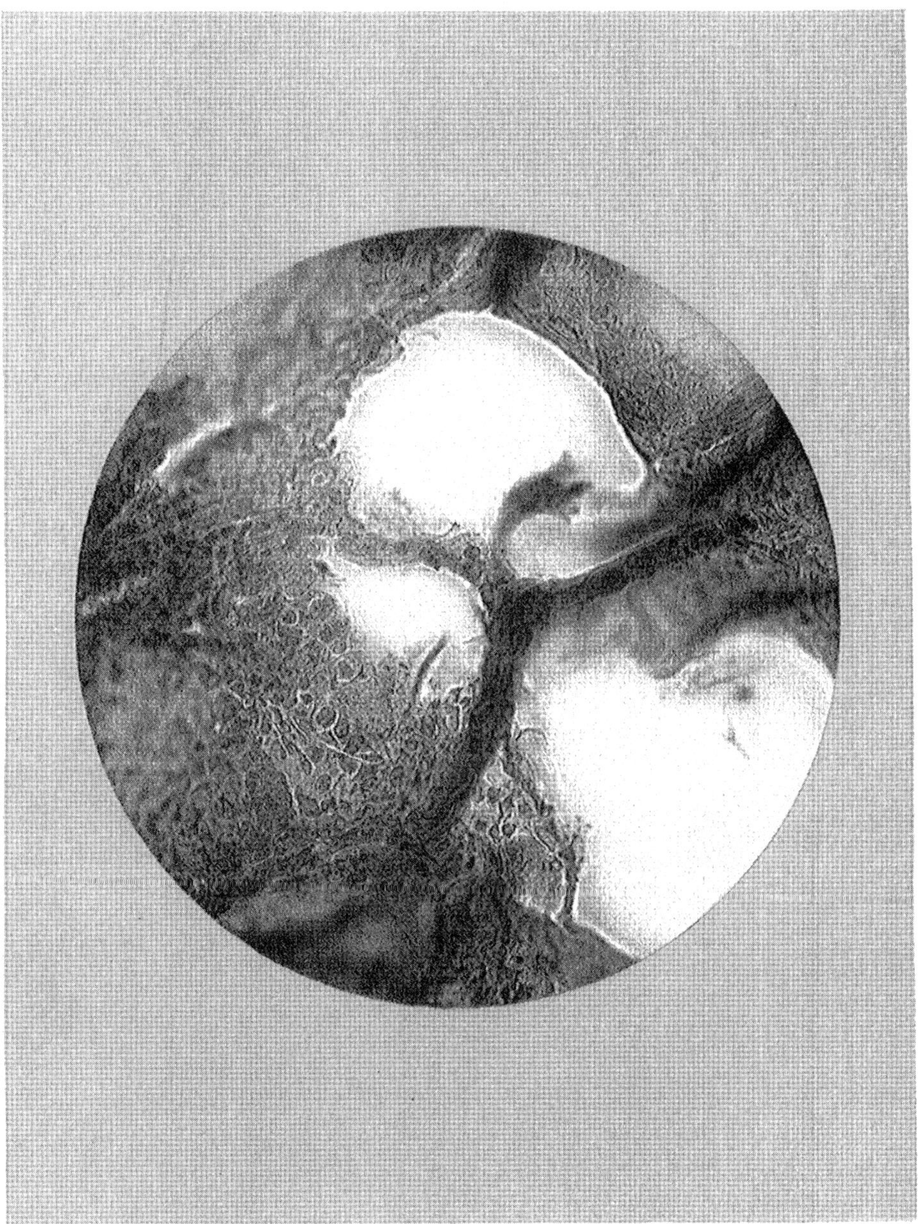

A. Hoen & Co. chromolith. Baltimore.

Nº 1. SECTION OF HEALTHY PORTION OF LUNG,

showing Epithelium (?). From a Cow dead of Epidemic Pleuro-pneumonia.

Magnified 400 diameters. Photographed by the Calcium light. By Brt. Lt. Col. J. J. Woodward Asst. Surgeon U.S. Army.

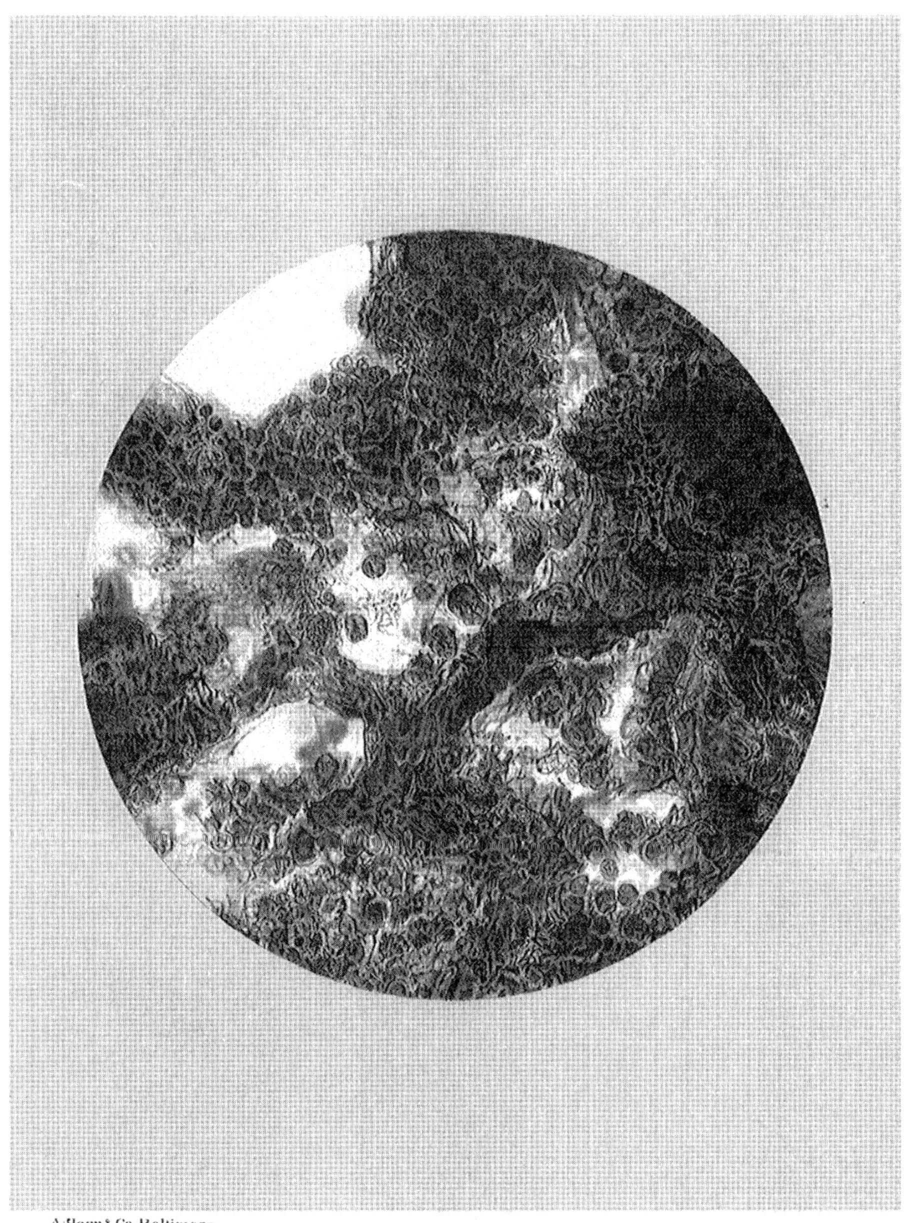

A. Hoen & Co. Baltimore.

Nº 2. SECTION OF INFLAMED PORTION OF LUNG,

showing pus corpuscles in the air-vesicles. From a Cow dead of Epidemic Pleuro-pneumonia.

Magnified 400 diameters. Photographed by the Calcium light. By Brt. Lt. Col. J. J. Woodward Asst. Surgeon U.S. Army.

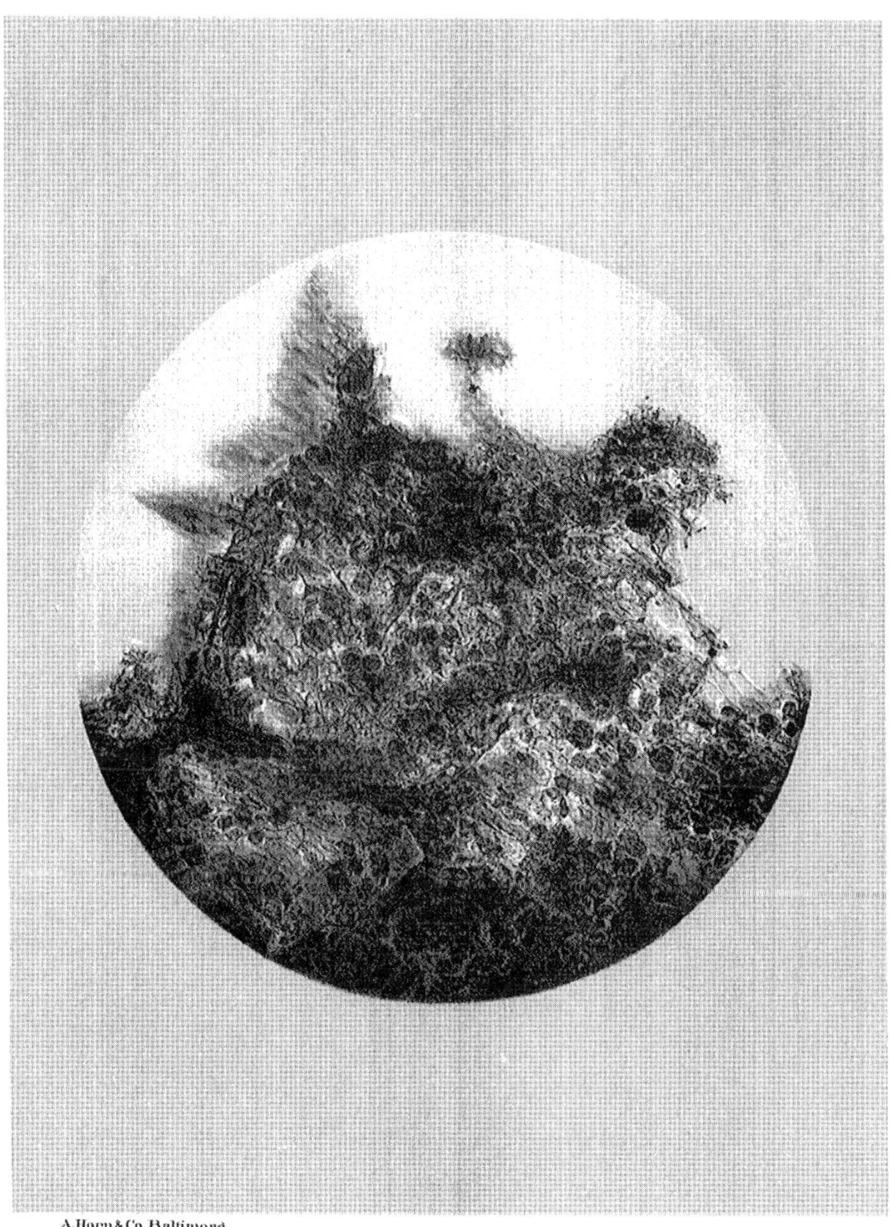

A. Hoen & Co. Baltimore.

Nº 3. SECTION OF INFLAMED PORTION OF LUNG,
showing pus corpuscles in the air-vesicles. From a Cow dead of Epidemic Pleuro-pneumonia.
Magnified 400 diameters. Photographed by the Calcium light By Brt. Lt. Col. J. J. Woodward Asst. Surgeon U.S. Army.

A. Hoen & Co. Baltimore.

Nº 4. SECTION OF INFLAMED PORTION OF PERICARDIUM,
showing numerous new elements. From a Cow dead of Epidemic Pleuro-pneumonia.
Magnified 400 diameters. Photographed by the Calcium light By Brt. Lt. Col. J. J. Woodward Asst. Surgeon U.S. Army.

ARMY MEDICAL MUSEUM.

A. Hoen & Co. chromolith. Baltimore.

Nº 5. PORTION OF THE EXUDATION IN THE PERICARDIUM,

showing pus cells. From a Cow dead of Epidemic Pleuro-pneumonia.

Magnified 400 diameters. Photographed by the Calcium light. By Brt. Lt. Col. J. J. Woodward Asst. Surgeon U.S. Army.

ARMY MEDICAL MUSEUM.

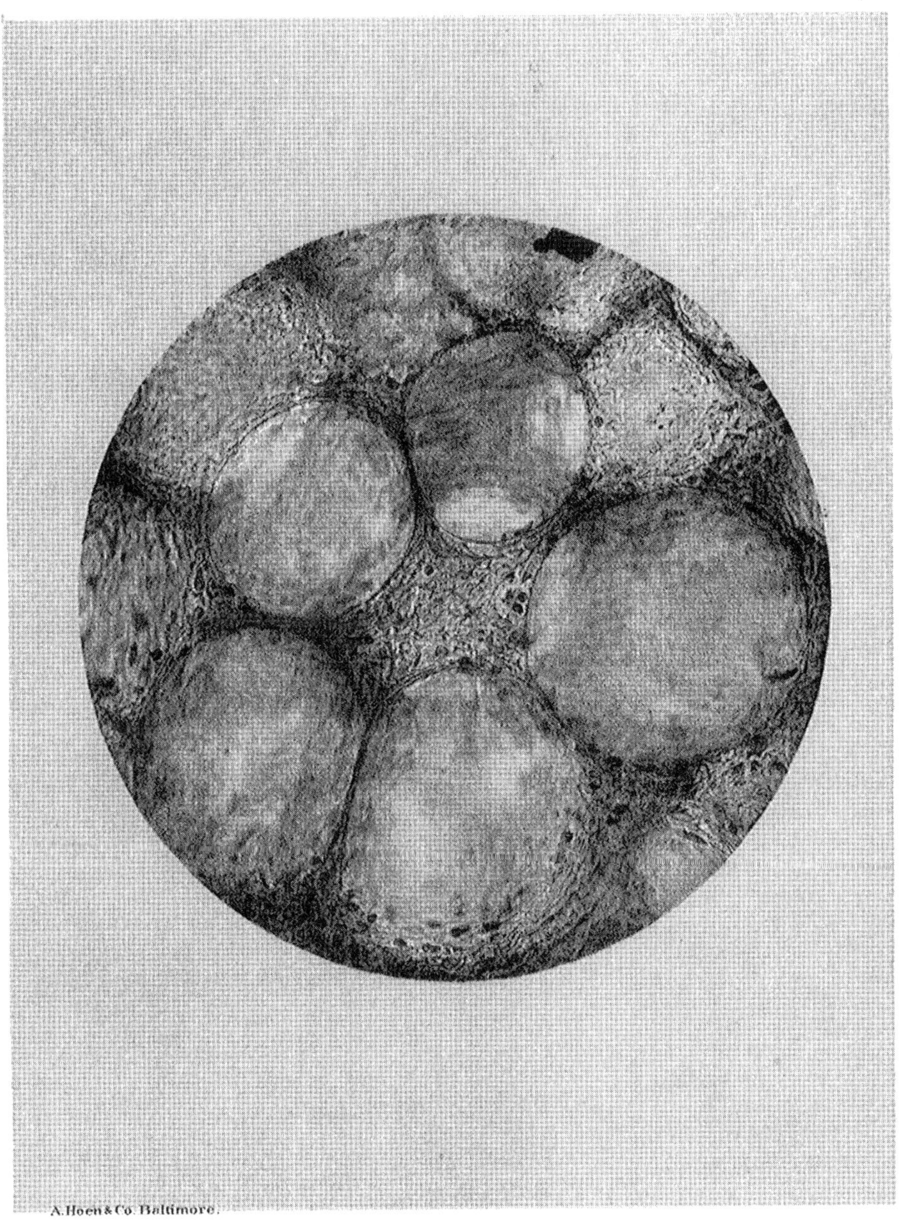

A. Hoen & Co. Baltimore.

Nº 6. SECTION OF INFLAMED FAT,

showing inflammatory products between the Fat cells. From the Fat about the Pericardium of a Cow dead of Epidemic Pleuro pneumonia.

Magnified 400 diameters. Photographed by the Calcium light By Brt. Lt. Col. J. J. Woodward Asst. Surgeon U.S. Army.

REPORT

OF

PROF. GAMGEE ON THE ILL EFFECTS OF SMUT IN FEED OF FARM ANIMALS.

SIR: The opportunity presented itself last fall for an inquiry as to the manner in which the smuts which attack plants may affect animals. The latter part of 1868 was, throughout America, very wet; a large amount of corn became smutty, that is to say, was attacked to a serious extent by *Ustilago maidis*, and reports reached me from the West and South that cattle were dying in large numbers from a mysterious malady, the origin of which was unknown. From Mills County, Iowa, I was informed, late in November, that about the 12th of the month there was a fall of snow six inches deep, and that the cattle, which usually roam at large on the prairies, were taken in by all the better farmers who had their corn gathered, and turned into the stalk fields. In about eight days the cattle began to die, all presenting the same symptoms. My informant, Mr. James Hull, of Plattsmouth, Nebraska, lost four out of nineteen head in fourteen days. This gentleman, alarmed at the number of deaths, turned his cattle out of the stalk field and gave them all the salt they would eat, mixed with copperas and sulphur. As soon as the bowels were moved the symptoms disappeared. Mr. Hull also gave the cattle asafœtida by "driving it into the cob of the corn."

Personal inquiries among gentlemen from different parts of the United States, in Washington, enabled me to trace the malady in Western Virginia, Illinois, and the Carolinas. It is much to be regretted that accurate information as to the extent of losses, and the localities affected, cannot be secured.

There are other circumstances under which cattle die from eating corn. The stalks, very late in the season, are apt to become very hard and indigestible, and without a free admixture of grass, which the early frosts kill, or other food, they produce severe indigestion and death. This is an observation that has often been made in America. Moreover, cattle die sometimes if freely fed on corn that has been badly stored, and is musty. The same results follow the use of other deteriorated foods, and a brief reference to records on this subject may be found interesting and instructive.

The facts published with regard to the prevalence of a malady among cattle in America, caused by eating smutty corn, are very few. If, however, the real cause of many cases of so-called dry murrain had been recorded correctly, there would be no difficulty in demonstrating that the condition of the corn-fields has had much to do in developing this disorder.

The Department of Agriculture has received information of the death of cattle from eating smutty corn, in Hampshire County, Massachusetts. Also from Whitley County, Indiana, where seven head of cattle, out of fifty, died, "probably from smut in the corn-field in which the herd ranged."

From Story County, Iowa, it is reported that "last November a disease appeared among herds recently turned into corn-stalk fields. The disease is evidently the dry murrain. A post-mortem examination showed the mucous membrane of the stomach to be highly inflamed, with symptoms of poisoning. It is evident that the disease is generated in the stalk fields, and probable that it is produced by gorging the stomach when first turned into the stalks, after being confined on the wild, frost-bitten, prairie grass, and lack of sufficient water." A few cattle died of dry murrain in Audubon County, in the same State, "supposed by some to be caused by smut in corn-stalks." A few head were lost from the same cause in Calhoun County, and many are reported to have died in Marshall County. We are, however, informed from Sac County that many cattle died in December—cause unknown; "some supposed from eating smutty corn, but that has been disproved." It is to be regretted that more is not stated with regard to the reasons which led persons to doubt the effects of the smutty corn. Even in New York State little credence was given to the action of smutty corn at first; but careful inquiry proved that after all it was the cause of the dry murrain of the fall of 1868. From Dakota County, Nebraska, we learn of dry murrain from this cause; whereas from Shawnee County it is reported, and no doubt correctly, that the same disease has been noticed among cattle "fed on prairie hay, cut after frost."

In Scotland the clovers are apt to induce a similar condition at times, and the malady is there called "grass disease." It is not a specific affection, but arises from a dryness and indigestibility of one kind of food, animals being debarred by circumstances from a salutary admixture of different kinds of feed.

The cultivation of maize or Indian corn is already ancient in America; and the introduction of this important grain into Spain, and as far back as 1560 into Italy, should have resulted in the knowledge of its effects on man and animals, under the many conditions in which it is found. Indeed, we are not without some knowledge of the subject, though it is to be regretted that accurate information can be gleaned from the writings of few who have referred to it. Both in its effects on men and animals, the consumption of Indian corn should be studied in localities where at times it constitutes the main article of diet, and where it is used at all times with other kinds of food.

Among men in America, from time immemorial, its use could be diversified by that of game, whereas in some parts of Italy, remarkable for the prevalence of *pellagra* among the inhabitants, people often live exclusively on corn bread, or the corn pudding they call *polenta*. The excess of starchy constituents, and scantiness of nitrogenous materials in corn as compared with the other grains from which flour and bread are manufactured, have been considered the causes of a cachectic and ill-nourished condition said to prevail wherever maize is the staple article of diet among a people.

Mazzari,* Nardi,† and Letti have described the pellagra of Italy, which I witnessed some years ago in a bad form in the hospital of Ferrara, as due to diseased or smutty corn.

The extensive cultivation of maize in Italy dates from the eighteenth century, and it is recorded by the celebrated Monati and others that before that period pellagra was unknown. Balardini experimented with a view to demonstrate that the smut on corn is poisonous, and he records deleterious effects on fowls and even dogs.

* Saggio medico-politico sulla pellagra, Milano, 1836.

† Causa e cura della pellagra, Milano, 1836.

Although this does not exactly correspond with one result I have obtained, and recorded below, it is most desirable that experiments should be continued on the subject. Balardini confirms the observation of Vallenzosca della Falcadina, that the pellagra recorded by Odoardo as prevailing in the Alps of Bellano in 1776 completely disappeared on the introduction of the potato as the basis of the food of the poor.

M. Signad, in his Diseases of Brazil, attributes the chlorosis or intertropical anæmia among the black slaves and the inhabitants on the western side of the Sierra dos Organos to the exclusive use of Indian corn.

The symptoms recorded by Jubins are, pallor of the face and body, yellowish, somewhat transparent, and sometimes greenish tint of the skin. The blacks that become affected lose their color.

M. Ruldin records, in the fifth volume of the Journal de Chimie Médicale, some observations on what he calls ergot of maize, but which Heusinger believes is the ordinary charbon, or smut. Roulin saw this diseased grain in the southern parts of Colombia, where it is called *maiz peladera*. Its use causes people to lose their hair, and this is very remarkable in a country where baldheadedness is almost unknown, even among old people.

Sometimes it causes looseness and the loss of teeth, but never gangrene of the limbs nor convulsive maladies. Pigs at first dislike this diseased corn, but soon acquire a taste for it, and after eating it for a few days their bristles drop out, and subsequently there is an awkwardness in the movements of their hind legs, and atrophy of those limbs. Eating the pigs produces no ill effects on man. Mules eat the *maiz peladera*, lose their hair, and suffer from engorgements of the limbs; they are tied in distant pastures, and with the change of diet some recover. Hens fed on the material lay eggs without shells. In the corn fields where the disease prevails it is not uncommon to see monkeys and parrots fall unable to rise again. The indigenous dogs and deer that enter the corn fields at night suffer in the same way.

It is asserted that across the Paramos, in the colder parts of Colombia, these accidents are not seen; and Dr. Roulin has indeed witnessed them only in the provinces of Neyra and Mariquita.

Dulong* has analyzed corn smut, and although his analysis cannot at the present day be considered satisfactory, it is the only one on record. He found it to contain a material similar to fungine, a material allied to osmazone, a nitrogenous substance, a fatty matter, a waxy matter, acids, a brown coloring matter, a free organic acid, and combinations of this acid with magnesia and potash; lastly, he found phosphate, muriate, and sulphate of potash, subphosphate of lime, sal ammoniac, and oxide of iron; it contained no starch.

Anxious to try some experiments on the action of pure smut on cattle, I employed a negro in January, 1869, to go into the country and collect for me a large quantity of pure smut.

It was rather late, and the rains had washed most of it off the still standing stalks; but I obtained forty-two pounds of excellent smut, free from adventitious matters. On the 26th day of February, Mr. George Reid, of Ingleside farm, near Washington, D. C., purchased two cows, in good health, and aged respectively about seven years. One cow was fed thrice daily one and one-half pound of corn-meal and three ounces of smut, mixed with as much cut hay as she would eat. The second had the same allowance, but wet.

* Journal de Pharmacie, vol. xiv.

On the 7th of March the amount of smut given in each feed was increased to six ounces. The cow fed on dry food lost flesh. On the 15th of March the dose of smut was increased to twelve ounces three times a day. The cow on the wet food gained in condition. The other one lost. In three weeks the two cows consumed the forty-two pounds of smut; they had a voracious appetite the whole time, and the only indication of a peculiar diet was a very black color of the excrement, and the loss of flesh by one animal although fed liberally on nutritious diet, which, however, was given in a dry state.

On the 12th of March the temperature of both cows was tested, and found 102°.2 and 102°.4 Fahrenheit.

No conclusions of importance can be drawn from a single experiment; but it is evident that smut is not a very active poison in combination with wholesome food, and especially if the animal is allowed moist food and plenty of water to drink. Cattle will eat the smut greedily, and possibly a morbid taste for it is acquired, as has been observed in pigs. It is evident that cornstalks, when starch and other nutritive elements have gone to build up the large quantities of smut investing them, are essentially dry, indigestible material for any animal to live on, and especially when excluded from other food. That is quite sufficient to account for the development of the dry murrain that so commonly attacks cattle in the United States, and was more frequent than usual last winter.

Diversifying and multiplying experiments on this question will undoubtedly result in some interesting information, and I am quite confident that it will be fully demonstrated that smutty corn cannot be used safely, and certainly not economically, as a food for cattle, and should not be allowed them without a great admixture of hay and other nutritious food. The more water and succulent food cattle are allowed while eating cornstalks, the less liable they will be to a deadly constipation and gastric impaction. Numerous and even angry discussions have in times past been carried on in different parts of Europe in relation to the action of mouldy, musty, or otherwise damaged fodder on the lower animals, and a few observations on the results of feeding horses, &c., on hay and grain tainted by fungi may be regarded as of importance here, if only as a means of comparison.

The evident tendency is to derange the alimentary canal in the first place, then to disturb the process of nutrition or assimilation, and lastly to excite the emunctories for the discharge of noxious principles, more particularly by inducing an excessive secretion of uiine, or diarrhoea.

MUSTY HAY.

It has frequently been observed that the imperfect curing of hay, especially during wet seasons, is followed by serious derangements among horses, mules, and other animals, which suffer from severe indigestion, impaction of the stomach accompanied by vertigo, or the profuse discharge of clear-colored urine, with intolerable thirst, emaciation, weakness, and death. It is said that the Hungarian hay, in different parts of America, and especially in parts of Kentucky, Missouri, and Kansas, is apt to cause considerable losses, if cut after full inflorescence and late in the season. I have been told by Kansas farmers that great attention has to be paid to a sufficiently early hay-making in order to avoid accidents.

In 1855 I witnessed in Lyons, France, many cases of disease and numerous deaths among horses, from the great abundance of musty hay, gathered during an unusually wet season. Scarcely a day passed but one or more cart horses were literally dragged to the veterinary college. They moved along with hanging head, sunken eye, dependent lip, and tottering gait, suffering from pains in the abdomen, and considerable tympanitis; partial sweats bedewed the body, the visible mucous membranes were of an intensely yellow color, and the urine dark. On reaching a loose box, the patients were tied to a center post, which turned as they moved round, and prevented them from dashing their heads against the wall. The muscles twitched, the horses writhed in pain, and dashed about in fits of delirium. Two hundred and forty-nine cases of this kind were admitted into the infirmary from August, 1854, to August, 1855. The disease raged almost as an epizoötic from the month of September, 1854; and not only in the neighborhood of Lyons, but in many departments of France.

In the month of November, 1856, I was requested to see a Clydesdale stallion, near Kirkcaldy, in Fife. This horse had, as is very usual on Scotch farms, been turned into a large shed, and allowed as much hay as he would eat, and a couple of feeds of oats. On moving the animal out of the stable, he nearly fell, and had evidently lost much of his natural control over the movements of his hinder limbs. It was no new form of disease, but one of those singular forms of paraplegia so commonly observed in herbivorous animals, as the result of improper feeding and acute indigestion. The owner thought the animal had seriously injured his spine. A cathartic dose of aloes, the discontinuance of the use of hay which was musty, and a few doses of tonic medicine, restored the horse. From that time I was consulted frequently, and in different parts, especially around Edinburgh and on the border counties of Scotland, regarding this disease. A large number of animals died, from ignorance of the nature and treatment of the disease, which disappeared with the close of the season during which the bad crop of hay was being consumed. These observations are recorded as mere instances of frequently recurring accidents, resulting from the feeding of horses on musty hay.

MUSTY OATS.

Among the numerous sources of inconvenience and loss to owners of horses in Europe and America, few are more troublesome than the results of feeding on musty oats. I have known a large establishment, with nearly five hundred horses, the entire stock of which was simultaneously affected. Attention was first directed to the unusual wetness of the litter in the morning, and a great craving for water. The animals were weak, dull in harness, and hollow-flanked. The wasting of tissues progressed rapidly; and in all that had any considerable exertion to undergo, the unthrifty look of their skin, well defined muscles from wasting of the fat around them, and the leanness of the upper part of the neck, where the great ligament suspending the head could be felt, like a rigid cord, constituted very decided and alarming symptoms. Persistence in work resulted in a form of albuminuria; sometimes diarrhoea was readily induced, and a purgative would so contribute to increase the weakness and prostration that the animal would die or fall in a state of hectic. All this disturbance in the functions of nutrition, assimilation, and secretion ceased on changing the diet, administering astringents or drachm doses of iodide of potassium for a few days, and following up with a course of sulphate of iron, as a tonic, in very moderate quantities, not exceeding half a drachm or a drachm to each horse per day.

Several epizoötic attacks have been attributed to rust or mildew in plants. Fromment looked upon it as causing great loss among sheep in Franconia, during the years 1663, '64, and '65. Ramazini, professor of medicine at Modena and Parma, speaks of a contagious malady affecting men, cattle, and even the silk-worm, which broke out in 1690. The preceding four or five years had been very hot, and during 1689 and 1690, much rain having fallen, the country was inundated, and the grasses, fruits, and leguminous plants became affected with rust. Plagues which raged among animals in Hesse in 1693, in Hungary in 1712, and in Saxony in 1746, occurred with, and apparently as a result of, mildew affecting vegetables. Gerlach asserts that this will produce abortion and inflammation of the womb in ewes. Numann, Masseband, and Niemann have also written on the noxious properties of plants affected with rust.

RUSTY STRAW.

In 1804 Gohier, afterward director of the Lyons Veterinary College, but then veterinary surgeon to the 20th light dragoons, published an interesting monograph entitled "Des effets des pailles rouillées." The depot of Gohier's regiment was established at Arras on the 7th of June, with about two hundred horses. For a month they continued healthy, being supplied with good forage; some of the straw, however, was rusty. The whole regiment arrived and the straw supplied was worse; several horses fell ill, being generally attacked by violent colic. In three days fourteen were affected with the disease; but, with the exception of two old horses that were ill for three days, the disease was only of a few hours' duration. The horses that partook most freely of the rusty straw were most seriously affected. In seven days thirty had suffered, and MM. Gohier and Masigny drew up a report condemning the forage. Their opinion was rejected by veterinary surgeons and others called upon to inquire into the matter, and the whole evil was attributed to some water, of which, however, the horses had always drunk while enjoying perfect health. After considerable annoyance and litigation it was recognized that the rusty straw, and even bad hay, had given rise to much disease and death among the horses of the regiment. During eight months, out of seven hundred horses, there were constantly forty-five to fifty in the infirmary, and in the month of November as many as sixty-two. The deaths were by those diseases which always prevail when animals are badly nourished, namely: stomach staggers, colic, marasmus, glanders, farcy, skin diseases, catarrhal affections, and œdematous swellings. Those horses suffering from œdema were very subject to gangrene, and if setons were applied, or a farcy-bud cauterized by fire, mortification of the wounded parts supervened, and the animals died in a few hours. Gohier says that not only the rusty straw but likewise the bad hay was a cause of the serious loss among the horses of his regiment. Gohier instituted several experiments to prove that the diseased straw was injurious, and not only was he successful with the straw, but a decoction of the same induced loss of appetite, a thin and sickly aspect, and other evidences that the animals had been poisoned.

MOULDY BREAD.

Flour is attacked by a very noxious red or orange-colored mould, (*Penicillium roseum,*) and a less poisonous greenish-blue mould, (*Penicillium glaucum.*) Bread made from flour which has been kept in a damp place, or that which is the produce of wheat grown and harvested during unfavorable weather, becomes mouldy and may be very deleterious.

Accidents have happened where horses have been fed on such bread, and I may mention that it is not uncommon in some countries for horses to be fed at times partly on bread. Eating mouldy bread has been said to induce gastro-enteritis in horses, and Professor Fuchs saw two cases of stomach staggers induced by it, which were relieved by purgatives.

SYMPTOMS OF THE ILL EFFECTS OF SMUTTY CORN.

Cattle fed on smutty cornstalks first denote ill-health by constipation. It is true that a farmer may be attracted only by an animal lying down, with an unthrifty-looking, staring coat, and dry muzzle, and perhaps trembling; or a steer may be noticed "tucked up," with hind limbs drawn under, head depressed, shivering, dullness of eyes, and anxious expression of countenance. In a third variety the animal seems excited, breathes quickly, and is apparently somewhat delirious—indeed, in the conditions described by Mr. Cumming, of Ellen, Aberdeenshire, as resulting from impactions of the third stomach, as in cases of lead poisoning, nothing is more strange than this delirium, associated as it is sometimes with blindness. A farmer writing me from the West says that when he tried to put a rope around the head of a sick cow, which he found standing with all the symptoms of sickness presented by other animals of the herd which had been with her in the corn field, she turned and fought furiously. I have seen an animal in this condition, tied up in a stall, rush forward, fall on her knees, and then, extending herself on her side, suffer from a convulsive fit. In other cases, when attempts are made to lead such animals about, they run forward, plunge, strike against any obstacle, roar, moan, grunt in breathing, and appear to suffer acutely if touched or disturbed. In other words, with the impactions of the third stomach, which is the essential lesion of the disease, whether induced by smutty stalks, old indigestible stalks that have no smut, or other kind of food or poison, there are two distinct conditions induced—the one of stupor, listlessness, vertigo, and depression of spirits, indicated by the animals standing sullenly until they drop or are relieved; the second is a state of exquisite sensitiveness, a hyperæsthesia of the skin and system generally. The animals are not only excited, but in a state of actual suffering, and die very speedily in a state of coma or in convulsions. The disease does not last long. I have seen an animal linger on four or five days, but usually the whole course of the malady is run in twenty-four to forty-eight hours.

An animal first seems to show costiveness, with a dry mucus over the scanty excrement; and although apparently undisturbed, and even feeding, may be dead in twelve to twenty-four hours.

The diagnosis of the disease at an early period of its manifestations is therefore important, and it rests on the knowledge of the manner in which animals have been treated and fed, (as the simultaneous attack of several animals shows,) and especially on the observations of a fact that I have usually noticed, that the animals which have eaten most ravenously have been the first and most severely affected. Old cattle may sometimes avoid the smutty food, and young animals eat heartily; the latter will be found the only ones to die.

POST-MORTEM APPEARANCES.

The state of torpor of the alimentary canal of animals affected with this disease is indicated on opening the belly and exposing the stomach to view. In the first stomach, or paunch, corn-husks and corn are found in a dry condition. Sometimes the rumen is very full, and gas may have become disengaged in it so as to cause a great distension, which is relieved by puncture. The contents of the second stomach, or reticulum, are in the same condition as those of the first, though sometimes mixed with some fluid. The third stomach, manyplies or omasum, is firm, distended, and on being opened the food is found caked between the folds, with marked impressions of the papillæ or little eminences which stud the mucous membrane. We find in almost all fevers a similar condition of the third stomach, and indeed in healthy animals it is that part of the digestive organs in which the food is most dry and packed preparatory for solution by the gastric juice and intestinal secretions. But there are other lesions associated with this "caking" of the food in the third stomach, in specific diseases, and its existence without these affords evidence of a primary form of impaction, which has received most remarkable names, such as "staking," "bound," "fardel-bound," &c. The fourth stomach contains but a scanty quantity of greenish, semi-digested matter, is usually reddened somewhat diffusely, and the redness increases at times toward the opening of the small intestines.

The intestine, usually replete with somewhat solid and imperfectly digested food, is usually high colored, especially in the fundus of the cæcum and in the large portion of the colon. The rectum is the seat of ramified redness, and a consistent mucus coats its contents.

Persons have reported a peculiar black color of one lung. This is due only to stagnation of blood after death, in the organ nearest the ground; and the same kind of congestion or settling of the blood is apt to pervade other tissues and organs in the side on which an animal has been lying.

TREATMENT.

I have found the accidents resulting from the feeding of smutty corn to cattle very amenable to treatment. Almost all the animals die unless relieved, but it is not difficult to treat them successfully. At first a purgative must be administered; such as a pound or a pound and a half of Epsom salts, or Glauber salts, alone, or combined with aloes, sulphur, or ginger. The following is a desirable purging drink:

Sulphate of magnesia	1 pound.
Powdered aloes	4 drachms.
Powdered ginger	2 drachms.
Water	1 quart.

This is to be given in warm linseed tea, oat-meal gruel, or pure water. A pound or two of treacle, with eight drachms of aloes or a pint of linseed or sweet oil, may be used when the salts are not at hand. Cattle should be induced to drink either plain water or linseed tea. Common salt will create thirst, and for this purpose may be given in such quantities as will not make the liquid too salt to be palatable. Warm water injections are of the highest importance, and for this purpose the enema funnel,* which can be made by any tinsmith at a charge of about fifty cents, is the best instrument yet de-

* This is an ordinary tin funnel, capable of holding one quart, with the pipe bent at right angles, about ten inches long from the bend, with the extremity rounded by a mass of soft solder to prevent the rectum from being injured by the insertion of the sharp edges of the pipe. The contents flow into the intestine by gravitation.

vised. About a quart or two of lukewarm water, without any addition but a little sweet oil to lubricate the tube of the instrument, may be poured into the rectum every half hour. On the second day it may be found that the medicine does not act very freely. The best agent to be given then is carbonate of ammonia in half-drachm doses, twice a day, largely diluted with linseed tea or gruel. Care must be taken in giving this medicine not to excoriate the mouth. As soon as the appetite returns, a succulent diet, such as grass, boiled turnips, sweet hay, &c., completes the animal's restoration.

PREVENTION.

It is evident that all such accidents as these I have described may be completely prevented by not allowing cattle to eat indigestible corn-stalks, whether their indigestibility arises from age, dryness, or smut. Mixed with an abundance of soft food such material may do no harm, and, indeed, has constantly been used with impunity; but losses are very severe if cattle are compelled either to starve or to eat what may well be compared to broomsticks.

The farmer who annually loses a large amount of the produce of lands tilled at great cost and trouble, should reflect that smut on corn is an evidence of bad farming, and, apart from the fact of danger to the lives of the animals on the farm, it is most desirable to extirpate the pest. That its eradication is possible, few will doubt who know, in case of other parasitic plants, such as the rust in wheat, how effectually the seed may be purified and a healthy plant obtained in a well-prepared soil. Having fresh land to break up or old to plow again, the farmer should plow deeply and turn over the soil effectually. He should obtain his seed from a district or farm that is high, dry, well-cultivated, and free from smut. As the spores of *Ustilago maidis* are minute and in the form of impalpable powder, thousands may be dispersed in a sample of corn, and grow with the plant. To avoid this, dipping the grain in a solution of copperas may be found of great service. The copperas, in the proportion of one pound to four bushels of corn, is to be dissolved in a little warm water, and then cold water added to make about a stable-pailful; with this the corn is simply washed, not soaked. Soaking makes the grain swell, and interferes with sowing in machines. The corn is sown as soon as dampened with the solution.

JOHN GAMGEE, M. D.

Hon. HORACE CAPRON,
Commissioner of Agriculture.

REPORT

OF

PROFESSOR GAMGEE ON THE SPLENIC OR PERIODIC FEVER OF CATTLE.

SIR: The transportation of northern cattle into Florida, Texas, parts of Mississippi, Louisiana, and South Carolina, and the traveling of southern herds across the grazing lands of States northward, result in the sickness and death of the animals which come within the range of a singular form of contamination. In Missouri, Kansas, Arkansas, Virginia, Kentucky, Carolina, and Georgia, the so-called Spanish or Texas fever has been the cause of losses prior to and since the war, and more especially during the last summer, and this fact has excited the most virulent opposition among the stock-raisers of those States to the driving of Texan steers across the prairies. The nature of this feeling is indicated by a letter from Mr. S. Morgan Welch, of Waverley, Missouri, to the Prairie Farmer of the 26th of September, 1868, in which he says: "Talk to a Missourian about moderation, when a drove of Texas cattle is coming, and he will call you a fool, while he coolly loads his gun, and joins his neighbors; and they intend no scare, either. They mean to kill, do kill, and will keep killing until the drove takes the back track; and the drovers must be careful not to get between their cattle and the citizens either, unless they are bullet-proof. No doubt this looks a good deal like border-ruffianism to you, but it is the way we keep clear of the Texas fever; and, my word for it, Illinois will have to do the same thing yet. Congress ought to do something in regard to this stock. Very stringent laws were passed in regard to the rinderpest, and yet it is scarcely more fatal than Texas fever, only the latter is not contagious among our native cattle. Texas stock should not be allowed to cross the 35th parallel of north latitude alive."

With rare exceptions the States of Illinois and Indiana were not visited with splenic fever prior to 1868, and the great reason for this is that southern stock has been slaughtered in the west by butchers and packers in the winter months, and has not been purchased in large quantities by cattle dealers and graziers, to fatten on the western prairies. But steers in Texas can be had in their prime for eight to ten dollars in gold. It has been recently computed that there are five million head in that State alone, and that the net yearly increase, after allowing a discount of twenty-five per cent. for loss by disease and casualties, amounts to seven hundred and fifty thousand head.

It is impossible to exaggerate the sufferings Texan cattle endure in being transported by steamers from the Texan coast to New Orleans, and thence to eastern or to western cities; and it is, likewise, difficult to draw too vivid a picture of the perils and anxieties of a drover's life. Energetic frontiersmen in small bands, armed to the teeth, collect a herd of cattle, varying from two to twelve hundred, and then drive at the rate of eight or ten miles a day, through unsettled lands, a distance of six to nine hundred miles; always watching lest their cattle and horses be stampeded, or their own scalps be taken by wild Indians. Storms and herds of buffaloes are minor causes tending to scatter the drover's property. It is not uncommon for a heavy percentage of animals to be lost from the several causes named.

Notwithstanding the waste in flesh and lives among stock on the New Orleans route, and the hardships to be endured by drovers in the Southwest, the prices realized for Texan steers, on reaching the great markets of America, prove, in many instances, highly remunerative.

The scarcity of cattle in the West, especially since the war; the tempting prospects of utilizing thousands and tens of thousands of acres of open and unreclaimed prairie lands; and the constitutional soundness of Texan cattle, which enables them individually to withstand influences which are destructive to other stock, are all causes which tend to favor the investment of western capital in such stock.

The current has been too strong for ordinary State legislation; and early, during the past spring, a strong tide set in, which brought large herds into the West, through New Orleans and Cairo, or, via Abilene, to St. Louis, Quincy, Chicago, Cincinnati, and to many grazing farms between those points.

The people of Illinois were warned by Mr. D. C. Emerson, of Vandalia, in a letter to the Chicago Tribune of the 26th of May. Circumstances have tended to give a historical worth to that brief communication. Mr. Emerson said:

> Having been a constant reader of your valuable paper for many years, and wishing to promote the general good and prosperity of our great and growing State, I would call the attention of farmers and cattle-growers to the following facts: While at Centralia yesterday I saw a very long train of stock cars filled with Texas and with Indiana oxen on their way to Iroquois County, there to be fattened on the rich prairies; and I learned that there were in the lot fourteen hundred head of old, worn-out oxen, bringing the Spanish fever with them. A writer in the Missouri Democrat has described this disease as contagious, and says that it causes the destruction of our home cattle wherever these Texas cattle are taken.

I arrived in Chicago on the 1st of June, the day on which Mr. Emerson's letter was published, and wrote to the Chicago Tribune, communicating information which had been furnished me by the Commissioner of Agriculture, and which indicated that, while trustworthy and appalling reports of the Spanish fever had been furnished by the people of Kansas, Missouri, Kentucky, and even Illinois, the Texas people were indignant at the imputations cast on their herds, just as the Russians were when the rinderpest was attributed to importations from their country.

Although the subject of meat preservation had brought me to America, it was only because I had for years striven, and to a certain extent striven in vain, to secure rational regulations of the cattle traffic for the prevention of contagious diseases in my own country; and it was a matter of deep interest to me to find that similar dangers threatened the stock owners of the West.

The abundant influx into Illinois of Gulf Coast cattle was soon followed by notices of ravages by disease at Cairo and elsewhere; but none were heeded, until it was reported on the 27th of July that Mr. E. Richardson, of Farina, had written to Governor Oglesby in regard to the numerous deaths among the cattle of the inhabitants of his district, and that eight to ten a day were dying. Mr. John L. Hancock, of the firm of Cragin

& Co., Chicago, at once induced the Pork Packers' Association to appoint a commission, consisting of Mr. W. E. Richardson, Dr. Blaney, and myself, to visit the localities where the disease had appeared, and report on the matter.

We accordingly started on the evening of the 29th of July, and prosecuted inquiries at Tolono, Farina, and Cairo, returning to Chicago on the 4th of August. On the 5th I was requested to continue my investigations for the Department of Agriculture, and, with the Commissioner's consent, had the advantage of continued, earnest coöperation on the part of Mr. W. E. Richardson, and Mr. H. D. Emery, editor of the Prairie Farmer. Both these gentlemen brought to bear a knowledge of the country and the cattle trade which materially aided me in my inquiries, and they have favored me with their advice and assistance up to the completion of the present report.

In accordance with the instructions received, I aimed at determining the following points:

1. The extent and nature of the Texan cattle traffic, and the state of health of the Texan cattle.
2. The circumstances under which these animals communicate disease to the stock of the West and other parts north of the Gulf States.
3. The history of the Texan fever, as it spreads over the States.
4. The symptoms, post-mortem appearances, and nature of the so-called Spanish or Texan fever.
5. The means to be adopted for the prevention of the disease, and the cure of the sick animals.

My investigations have extended over the States of Illinois, Indiana, Kentucky, Missouri, Kansas, and Texas, and these enable me to speak very positively as to the nature of the disease and the means which must be adopted to prevent it.

In the present report it is my intention to restrict myself to the annexed heads:

1. Definition of the disease.
2. Symptoms.
3. Post-mortem appearances.
4. Causes and nature of the disease.
5. Curative treatment.
6. Prevention.

DEFINITION.

The splenic or periodic fever, commonly known as Texas fever, Spanish fever, or cattle fever, and which has been observed wherever and whenever cattle from the States on the Gulf of Mexico have been driven north during the summer months, is a disease peculiar to the ox tribe, which has never been described as attacking the southern cattle, and which occurs, in a more or less latent form, among them. Its distinguishing features have been most marked in the cattle of Georgia, Tennessee, Virginia, Kentucky, Missouri, Kansas, Illinois, and Indiana, wherever these have grazed on pastures previously or simultaneously occupied by herds from Texas and Florida. It is, so far as we have yet ascertained, incapable of communication by the simple contact of sick with healthy animals; and, in the strict sense of the terms, is neither contagious nor infectious. It is an enzoötic disorder, probably due to the food on which southern cattle subsist, whereby the systems of these animals become charged with deleterious principles, that are afterward propagated and dispersed by the excreta of apparently healthy as well as of obviously sick stock. It is not one of the epizoötics proper, and in its origin and distribution differs from the plagues due to specific animal poisons which are common in various parts of the Old World and the New. The malady is probably incapable of communication by inoculation, and the flesh, blood, and secretions of such cattle have been handled and consumed by human beings without the manifestation of untoward results.

In Texas, cattle of all ages, from the time they begin to graze, are afflicted with the malady in a somewhat latent and mild form. Early in the year many animals die, especially when the wet deteriorates the grasses; and the mortality, of which any one can gain evidence in crossing Texan prairies and seeing the carcasses, is ascribed to poverty. It is, however, a feature everywhere that cattle do not attain the same weight in the South, even on the best grasses, that they do in northern latitudes; and this is, no doubt, accounted for by the uniform signs of irritation and even erosions of the stomach, enlarged spleen, fatty liver, and sometimes ecchymosis in the kidneys.

The disease in its acute form is characterized during life by a long and variable period of incubation, which is generally of five to six weeks' duration. The temperature of the body then rises, the secretions are checked, and indications of depression and listlessness are afforded by drooping head, depressed ears, arched back, approximation of limbs, and indisposition to move, or to rise when down. The fæces, usually dry, are sometimes blood-stained; and the urine almost invariably becomes of a dark port-wine color, and is retained for hours, and then evacuated in inconsiderable quantities. Frequent pulse, hurried breathing, and tremors are almost invariable symptoms; and, according to the severity of the attack, there is more or less paralysis, which partially affects the hind quarters, the fore quarters, or both. From implication of the cerebellum there is occasionally a defective coördination of movement; and, when the brain proper is involved, the animal either lies comatose, or is delirious.

In the first case there is more or less blindness, and in the second a wild, staring gaze, and the greatest restlessness. Animals recover, especially if from the South; but the communicated disorder among northern stock is extremely fatal; and, in many forms, destroys every animal exposed to its ravages. Death usually occurs about the third or the fourth day from the time the animal is very obviously sick; but probably not for ten or twelve days from the first indications to be obtained by the thermometer. The symptoms of approaching death are usually great prostration, the animal lying and refusing to rise, retention of the urine, the head occasionally drawn forcibly round, especially to the right side, and the muscles of the neck twitching without much intermission. After death there is marked cadaveric rigidity; the skin and subcutaneous tissues are usually sound; but effusions of serum, and sometimes of blood, have been witnessed under the lower jaw and sternum. The respiratory organs are commonly healthy, but in some cases the lungs are somewhat ecchymosed, and more frequently there is partial interlobular emphysema. The heart is frequently blood-stained both on the inner and the outer aspects. The peritoneum is sometimes ecchymosed, and, in one instance, was found to contain a large amount of free, coagulated blood. The digestive organs, from the mouth to the fourth stomach, are, as a rule, healthy. The fourth stomach, or abomasum, is, with rare exceptions, the seat of distinct lesions, viz., dark redness, ecchymosis, yellow granular-looking eruptions, and erosions of the cardiac end; the pyloric end is of more normal color, but frequently the seat of extensive superficial erosions, penetrating the substance of the mucous membrane, to which, wherever an abrasion exists, food usually adheres. The small intestine is generally the seat of punctiform or ramified redness throughout its whole extent; and blood extravasations are common in the cæcum, colon, and rectum. The liver is often congested, and the gall-bladder distended with viscid bile. The spleen is two, three, or even five times its natural size; and, according to the duration and severity of the attack, is more or less broken up and disintegrated in its internal structure. In one case the spleen had given way at its base, and hemorrhage had taken place into the peritoneum. The kidneys and suprarenal capsules are usually congested. The mucous membrane of the urethra, at its origin in the pelves of the renal lobules, is often the seat of extensive ecchymosis. The urinary bladder is usually very much distended with bloody urine, which never coagulates spontaneously, and only under the action of heat and nitric acid. The constant and pathognomonic lesion of this disease is the enlargement and even disintegration of the spleen, with redness and erosion of the stomach. The blood is always more or less affected, being anæmic, and the functions of nutrition are disturbed. In its course in the South, it resembles the periodic fevers of man; is usually sub-acute in form, and varies in intensity at different times.

I propose to designate this disease the Splenic Fever of Cattle, for the reason that the disease is readily distinguished, as a rule, by the enlargement of the spleen, coupled, no doubt, with other lesions. It is an enzoötic disease, allied and corresponding to the endemic periodic fevers of man, for which the Southern States are remarkable; and it may be deemed prudent to use a more general expression than splenic fever, viz., that of periodic fever of cattle. Splenic fever is readily prevented, in all cattle north of the Gulf States, by withdrawing them, during the summer months, from the pastures and roads on which southern cattle have traveled and fed. The prevention of the disease in Texas would call for a further and more extended inquiry into all the local causes in operation; but, generally speaking, the condition of soils and grasses might be altered by thorough cultivation, drainage, deep plowing, &c. In Texas I have found that feeding on corn tends to modify the conditions of cattle, and to invigorate their constitutions; and much may be expected from the corn-feeding system only recently introduced on a comprehensive scale.

No specific means of cure have been discovered for the malady; and palliative measures consist in allowing animals, which suffer from the acute form of the disease, abundant mucilaginous drinks, neutral salts, and occasional diffusible stimulants. Animals have recovered when left to nature, as, indeed, also when they have been profusely bled and purged.

SYMPTOMS.

Splenic or periodic fever evidently occurs in two forms, and its course may be subdivided into four stages.

The first form is insidious, latent, and usually the most fatal one. There are few fevers that do not, at times, attack animals in such a way as to produce so little general disturbance as to prevent their recognition in the living animal. Cases of this description occur in rinderpest. I have alluded to them in my official report on the lung plague, the contagious bovine pleuropneumonia of Europe, and have witnessed them in outbreaks of small-pox in sheep; but in enzoötic maladies, and especially in the various forms of anthrax, it is not unfrequently found in post-mortems of animals from districts where such diseases arise, that the healthiest and strongest have suffered or are suffering organic changes which a special systemic vigor or constitutional resistance hides so long as the animals are in life.

Whether we study the malady as seen by me in Texas, or on Smoky Hill, in Kansas, where a sudden shock to the system of a steer, on the occasion of its being stampeded, developed symptoms and induced death; or look to the other animals, apparently fresh and grazing, which indicated an abnormally high temperature of the body, it is evident that a large herd, traveling from the region whence splenic fever is propagated, carries not only the active cause of such propagation in the systems of animals composing it, but the evidence of specific disease induced, which remains for an indefinite time latent and unobserved.

During the early part of our investigations we could not fail to be forcibly struck by the apparently healthy condition of the vast herds of Texan steers which had scattered a most deadly poison on the pastures of Illinois and Indiana; and even our dissections, limited as they necessarily were, failed to elicit the truth. But the inspection of vast numbers of Texan cattle in Kansas and in the Chicago slaughter-houses has proved that appearances may be very deceptive; and I consider that the abnormal weight of the spleen in southern cattle, coupled, as such an indication is, with gastric redness and erosions, pale blood, and the not unfrequent presence of bloody urine in the bladder, demonstrates that splenic fever often, and indeed usually, occurs in a latent form among southern herds, which communicate the disease; and none but a trained expert, thermometer and scalpel in hand, can declare positively that any stock is in the enjoyment of perfect health.

We are almost warranted in believing that the latent causes of splenic fever are recognizable by the elevation of temperature; but this is a symptom of all fevers, and it is only by studying this condition in relation to many other circumstances—such as the source whence stock is derived, the evidence of some unusual mortality, and the post-mortem indications of certain animals in a herd, concerning which there may be suspicions—that it is possible to determine the presence of splenic fever in its occult form.

The stages into which any case of splenic fever may be subdivided, and which are readily recognizable in well-developed instances of the disease, are:

I. The incubative stage.
II. The stage of invasion.
III. The congestive or bleeding stage.
IV. Termination.

I. *The incubative stage.*—The stage of incubation has not been satisfactorily determined in individual cases; that is to say, it has been impossible, as yet, to obtain experimental facts which, as in the case of rinderpest and *variola ovina,* enable us to state positively that, from the date of contamination of an animal by the poison, so many days elapse before the manifestation of the disease, and that such period cannot be prolonged beyond a definite and ascertained limit; nevertheless there are important data which indicate that, from the period of arrival of a Texan herd on any distant or on any defined pasture, five to six weeks elapse before the disease appears in the indigenous stock, grazing with or after the southern cattle. It is proved that the animals may simply pass leisurely over a road or prairie, feeding as they move along, and, without remaining for any length of time on any portion of the ground they traverse, leave behind them sufficient poison to destroy all or nearly all the cattle which continue to feed upon it. In such cases the disease usually takes more than a month to attain its full development. There are instances on record which seem to indicate that the incubative stage may be shorter, and we have met with others where it was reported that the disease appeared in a week from the date of importation of Texan stock; but, as a rule in such reports, the whole facts are not before us, and it is not safe to draw any conclusions from exceptional cases. For instance, in the Monthly Report of the Department of Agriculture for April, 1867, it is reported from Osage County, Kansas, that about the 1st of August, 1866, the disease made its appearance at Burlingame:

The first case that occurred was that of an ox which belonged to a logging team of seven yoke. This ox, on account of his breachy propensities, was kept at night in a stable and watered from a well of pure water. When not at work in the day time he was staked out to grass, with a long rope. About two weeks before he was attacked with the disease a herd of Texas cattle came along, and were stopped and fed around him for an hour or more. Soon after, the rest of this team were attacked, and all died but one, which escaped the disease.

The reporter from Bates County, Missouri, says: "The disease is never seen until ten days to two weeks after the Texas cattle have passed through the country."

Texan cattle began to arrive at Cairo on the 23d of April, 1868, and the first case concerning which we could get reliable reports occurred on the 1st of June. At Tolono the largest body of Texan cattle arrived toward the end of May, and the disease broke out on the 27th of July. One gentleman of Tolono gave accommodations one night to three hundred Texan steers, on the 25th of June, and the disease appeared among his stock on the 28th of July. At Farina two hundred and fifty Texan cattle were placed with fifty Illinois steers on the 10th of May, and the disease appeared among the latter on or about the 15th of July. Near Sodorus, a farmer had his cattle grazing on the prairie over which Texan cattle passed on the 1st of June, and his stock commenced dying on the 28th of July. In Champaign County, Texan cattle were placed on the prairie on the 15th of June, and the indigenous stock began to die on the 3d of August, twenty out of thirty-eight head dying in four days, that is to say, by August 7th, the date of my inspection.

Our experience agrees with the cases recorded, where dates are given with some care. Thus, in the Agricultural Report for 1867, the reporter from Oldham County, Kentucky, says:

The 24th day of June, 1860, there were driven on my farm, to stay one night, about fifty head of Texas cattle. Some forty days after they left, about the 18th of August, the disease broke out among my milch cows and heifers and work cattle.

Thus we see that thirty to forty days usually elapse between the placing of Texan stock on a pasture and the manifestation of disease to the stock owners of the neighborhood.

The first indication which attracts special attention is usually the death of a cow or steer. It is evident that this very imperfectly defines the length of the incubative stage, as in all probability the native stock is not instantly poisoned, and then the disease is active some days before symptoms, such as an ordinary farmer may detect, or deaths occur. It is probable, however, that eighteen to twenty-five days are usually required for the poison to exert any marked influence on an animal's health, and then the second stage occurs.

II. *The period of invasion.*—My examination of animals in apparent health, picked out of a diseased herd, indicates that the invasion of the malady is characterized by an elevation of temperature. Here we have some similarity to rinderpest; but since there is not the same uniformity in the length of the incubative stage in splenic fever that there is in the Russian murrain, it is probably more common to find steers with a normal temperature in a herd infected with the former than when infected with the latter disease.

The first opportunity I had of testing this matter was on the 31st of July, at Tolono, where we saw the first animal of a herd, a yearling, lying dead. I began by examining a well-bred short-horn cow in blooming condition, and found her temperature to be 106° Fahrenheit; second was 106.5° F.; third 106.7° F.; fourth 106.7° F.; fifth 106.1° F.; sixth 107.2° F.; seventh 106.7° F.; eighth 107.2° F.; ninth 104.2° F.; tenth 106.7° F.

At Junction City I examined the healthiest-looking animals of an infected herd, and noted the following temperatures with one of Cassella's self-registering thermometers: First 104.6° F.; second 106.6° F.; third 102.8° F.; fourth 107.7° F.; fifth 103° F.; sixth 102.4° F.; seventh 105.8° F.; eighth 103.4° F.; ninth 107.2° F.; tenth 102.2° F.; eleventh 107.8° F.; twelfth 102.6° F.; thirteenth 103° F.; fourteenth 102.4° F.; fifteenth 102.6° F.; sixteenth 102.8° F.; seventeenth 102.6° F.

I examined three sick steers in this herd, and found their temperature to be respectively 104° F., 107.2° F., and 105.8° F. Of the apparently healthy ones no less than six indicated a temperature as high as or higher than that of the undoubtedly diseased animals, and in all the temperature was greatly exalted.

On Smoky Hill we inspected cattle in blooming health, so far as external appearances would indicate. We had found a case of splenic fever there, and determined to have some steers caught with the lasso and examined, with the following result: First 103.4° F.; second 102° F.; third 103° F.; fourth 104.2° F.; fifth 103° F.

The last temperature was that of a work ox, one which could be handled quietly, and it afforded me an opportunity of noticing that the use of the lasso did not sensibly affect the temperature. I infer, from a considerable range of observation, that animals are from four to six or seven days in the process of sickening, from the earliest indication of fever heat to the manifestations of decided symptoms of disease.

III. *The bleeding or congestive stage.* The acute or active stage of the disease is characterized by a series of well-defined symptoms which last for two, three, four, and even six days.

GENERAL APPEARANCE.

The ears of the animal droop, the gait is sluggish, and secretions are somewhat checked. In cows yielding milk there is a sudden diminution in the amount by one-half, more or less. At first the animal eats, ruminates occasionally, and its paunch appears full; but soon there is a disposition to lie down; and, wherever pools exist, the sick cattle are apt to lie in the water. It has been said that one of the surest premonitory symptoms is a cough. This does not accord with my experience. The depressed head, drooping ears, arched back, hollow flanks, tendency to draw the hind legs under the belly, and knuckling over at the fetlocks behind, are early and very marked symptoms. The skin is dry and rigid; the fæces not materially affected except in a few cases, which show early slight hemorrhage; a small, delicate blood-clot is apt to be seen on the surface of the droppings; at first the urine is clear. Many cases are, it is true, not observed till the urine is bloody; but the urine remains of its natural color in probably ten or fifteen per cent. of the cases, and is not usually one of the earliest signs which a veterinarian can detect.

The visible mucous membranes are rather pallid. I have seen a turgid appearance of the membrane of the nose, with discharge of glairy mucus; but any decided redness is usually confined to the folds of the rectal membrane, seen when animals defecate.

The pulse is frequent. In the early stages it is hard and wiry. It becomes more feeble, the artery is easily compressed, and in many instances, as death approaches, it is not possible to take the pulse at the jaw. So far as frequency is concerned, I have found it to vary from sixty to one hundred and twenty, and even more. In two cases, where the animals were lying with their heads stretched around over the right shoulder, and stupefied, the pulse was quite imperceptible at the jaw, and the heart-beats numbered one hundred and twenty.

Thermometric tests are of great value in the active stage of splenic fever. There is a considerable difference between cases; and, in all probability, this depends on the extent to which blood-extravasations occur. The temperature is high at the commencement of the attack; but, as death approaches, and bloody urine flows, it is very perceptibly reduced.

The annexed table indicates the ascertained temperature of sixty cases:

F.	F.	F.	F.	F.	F.	F.	F.	F.	F.
°	°	°	°	°	°	°	°	°	°
104.4	106.0	107.2	106.1	103.1	107.2	106.5	107.0	103.0	106.5
103.1	106.5	106.7	100.5	106.0	105.8	107.0	105.8	104.5	104.7
98.6	107.4	104.2	106.1	101.0	104.6	104.4	106.7	107.2	107.0
106.0	106.7	106.7	102.5	106.7	106.6	105.0	99.0	103.8	105.4
102.5	107.0	101.3	104.9	105.5	107.4	106.7	104.8	105.0	105.8
98.6	106.0	106.7	103.6	104.0	99.8	103.5	107.4	106.0	107.0

To the touch the temperature of the body varies much. It is not at all unusual to have great heat of the poll, of the ears, and horns, and of the extremities. At other times the limbs, and especially the hind ones, are cold; and the general surface of the body, which is hot in the earlier stages of the disease, has a tendency to cool as death approaches. The breathing is accelerated, and sometimes labored. In some animals, with great restlessness and tendency to delirium, I have found the respirations as high as one hundred per minute; whereas, in comatose animals, they have been slow, deep, and stertorous. On an average, however, the movement of the flanks has indicated simply increased frequency, reaching sixty respirations per minute in some cases.

The nervous phenomena are often very marked. In some the muscles of the flanks and thighs are seen to be constantly trembling. In others there is decided and continuous twitching of the cervical muscles. In nearly all, when an attempt is made to walk, there is evidence of feebleness in the hind limbs, which are rolled from side to side as the animal staggers along. When lying down and wishing to rise, it is found that several efforts have to be made before the hind quarters can be fairly raised from the ground; and then, in attempting to extend the fore limbs, great difficulty is experienced, and the animal often sinks to the ground. In one case, which I saw near Tolono, the animal seemed fixed to the soil, from inability to direct its muscles. With assistance it was got up, and its fore legs were propped out; but, when driven, the action of its limbs was quite irregular, and the animal faltered along, to drop again almost immediately. This inability to control the voluntary muscles, this defective coördination of movement, prevails in a less degree in a considerable number of cases. Great listlessness and even stupor are very common indications of early death. The most singular manifestations of these conditions occurred in two cows. One was lying with her head forcibly drawn upon the right shoulder, and the cervical muscles twitching as in a severe attack of chorea. In another the animal had the same position of the head and jerking of the muscles; but she was lying motionless on her belly, with all four legs sprawling, as if they had yielded and slipped out without an effort, as the body sank to the ground. The state of the secretions is usually a good index in the course of the disease. There is little tendency to free perspiration, and the only remarkable change of the skin is œdema which distends it in some cases below the jaw, or under the sternum. Hide-bound and costive, the animals indicate the febrile crisis by slight blood-staining of the fæces and by hæmaturia. The latter is commonly profuse, until the animal is so far paralyzed in its hind-quarters that there is retention.

With rare exceptions the bladder is found distended, and weighs, with its bloody contents, ten, twelve, or fourteen pounds; this, too, when the animal has urinated immediately before or in the act of death. Under the microscope the urine presents no tints, but only amorphous deposits of hæmatine and some epithelial cells. From first to last it coagulates by the aid of heat and nitric acid, except in those cases where it retains its normal color.

The milk secretion is all but entirely suspended, and the little which is drawn is dense, and mainly composed of cream. No change of a definite kind can be detected by a microscope.

IV. *Termination.* In the majority of cases depression and listlessness increase, the pulse increases in frequency, the respiration becomes labored, the animal heat reduced to 100° and to 98° F.; and the animal stretches out on the ground, on which it has been lying motionless for some time, and dies without a struggle.

In exceptional cases the febrile symptoms subside, the secretion of milk in cows is restored, the color of the urine becomes paler and paler, till it is normal, and the animal recovers in ten days or a fortnight, indicating its previous condition only by a stiffness of gait and considerable emaciation. A month or six weeks is required before evidence of thriving is obtained.

I have seen animals in apparently a convalescent state and manifesting considerable appetite; after distending their stomachs on grass, they have appeared uneasy, the fever has returned, diarrhœa set in, and death occurred within thirty-six to forty-eight hours. Such accidents are undoubtedly dependent on the lesions of the fourth stomach and intestines. They are gastro-enteric complications, and not indications of a true relapse.

POST-MORTEM APPEARANCES.

The structural lesions which occur in splenic fever are so numerous and various that I deem it advisable to transcribe the notes of a sufficient number of examinations in support of a summary, which may be considered sufficient for practical purposes by many who may refer to this report.

That form of splenic fever which is mostly latent, and seen among southern cattle, is not recognizable after death by the condition of skin, muscular system, or, in many cases, even by the mucous membrane, with the exception of that of the stomach. More or less, however, the blood extravasations, congestions, and blood-stained urine have been found; but these would very rarely have been noticed but for the plan, suggested by me,of inspecting all slaughtered cattle, and carefully weighing the spleens.

Dr. Rauch, the medical officer of the city of Chicago, no sooner ascertained my wishes than he arranged for the supervision of all slaughter-houses in Chicago, and for weighing, in the first instance, all the spleens, and, later, all the livers as well as spleens of slaughtered cattle. To Dr. Rauch's energy and care we are, therefore, indebted for facts which none but a medical health officer, armed with the necessary powers, could well have obtained. As the tables can serve only for purposes of reference, it has been thought proper to publish them in an appendix; but the facts brought to light admit of being readily stated, and it is due to Dr. Rauch that I should quote his report to the board of health of Chicago, read on the 18th of September, in demonstration of the valuable conclusions he was enabled to show very shortly after adopting this method of observation.

The weight, feel, and texture of the spleen and the condition of the urine have been found to be almost infallible in diagnosing the disease. Since the investigation commenced over two thousand spleens have been weighed. During the first few days of the investigation the spleens only were weighed, but as your committee began better to comprehend the importance of the questions involved, and the value of the facts to be learned, the livers were also ordered to be examined at the same time. Of these about five hundred have already been weighed. The committee have only had time to present the average of the three different kinds of cattle slaughtered here.

	175 native spleens.	175 Texan spleens.	175 Cherokee (?) spleens.	175 native livers.	175 Texan livers.	175 Cherokee (?) livers.
	Pounds.	*Pounds.*	*Pounds.*	*Pounds.*	*Pounds.*	*Pounds.*
Aggregate weight..............	260	441	382½	2,227¼	2,132¼	1,878¼
Average......................	1.48	2.52	2.18	12.72	12.18	10.73

The above were taken indiscriminately, and do not include any of the marked cases that have fallen under our observation. During the past week spleens have been found in Texan and in Cherokee cattle that were as much disorganized as any that were found in the native cattle that died from the disease. The important part that the spleen performs in the economy of cattle will be better appreciated when it is recollected that its enlargement and disorganization are always present in this disease, while the condition of the other organs may be regarded as concomitant. The liver was at one time supposed to show evidences of enlargement and increase of weight in this disease, but this does by no means necessarily follow, as in some of the most marked cases no change whatever in the size of the liver was perceptible. In fact, as a general rule, it has been found that, whenever the animal was in a good condition, the spleen weighed less and the liver more than when the opposite was the case. It was also noticed that in the animals which had been driven or transported a great distance the spleen weighed more in proportion than the liver. When the animal is in good condition the liver is large; when there is a depressed or lower condition of vitality the spleen is enlarged.

The annexed table gives the results of calculations based on the tables in the appendix; and it is safe to draw conclusions after the careful examination of no less than 4,739 cases. These indicate that the average weights of spleens are in excess in southern cattle over those observed among western steers, the excess amounting from a half to upward of one pound. Many of the Texan cattle had spleens weighing over three pounds. Some of the so-called Cherokee cattle might be from the Indian Nation, near the Texan frontier, but few were from the Cherokee Nation, and many, no doubt, were from Texas. This will explain the note of interrogation I have used wherever the term Cherokee has been used, in accordance with the information that has been tendered to me.

It is very important to notice that the earlier observations in August, when the spleens alone were weighed, brought out a greater indication of deviations from health in the spleens of southern cattle than those made subsequently. Thus the averages were—

	Native.	Cherokee (?)	Texan.
In August	1.38	2.36	2.83
In September	1.45	1.942	2.531

It is much to be desired that the weights of internal organs be better determined in future in all enzoötic diseases and during all seasons. This field of inquiry promises ample and valuable results.

	Native western cattle.			Cherokee (?) cattle.			Texan cattle.			General totals.			Cattle in which the spleens alone were weighed.		
	257 males.	1,012 females.	1,338 males and females.	361 males.	152 females.	441 males and females.	491 males.	29 females.	262 males and females.	2,607 native western cattle.	954 Cherokee (?) cattle.	782 Texan cattle.	132 native western cattle.	127 Cherokee (?) cattle.	137 Texan cattle.
	Lbs.	*Lbs.*	*Lbs.*	*Lbs.*	*Lbs.*	*Lbs.*	*Lbs.*	*Lbs.*	*Lbs.*	*Lbs.*	*Lbs.*	*Lbs.*	*Lbs.*	*Lbs.*	*Lbs.*
Total weight, spleens	375½	1,441½	1,963½	577¾	241	1,034½	1,109¼	69¼	701	3,780½	1,853.25	1,879½	183¾	301¾	530
Average	1.46	1.424	1.467	1.60	1.585	2.345	2.259	2.007	2.675	1.45	1.942	2.503	1.39	2.37	3.86
Total weight, livers	2,929	12,361¾	16,679½	3,731	1,611	4,702¾	6,070	360	3,139	31,970¼	10,044¾	9,569			
Average	11.39	12.215	12.466	10.335	10.6	10.66	12.36	12.413	11.98	12.263	10.529	12.236			

The examination, after death, of cattle in Illinois, Indiana, Missouri, and Kansas indicates that the usual post-mortem appearances, in well-marked cases of splenic fever, are as follows:

The skin, very often infested with ticks, is occasionally seen studded with dried drops of blood, as if the animal had sweated blood in dying. Then small blood clots have been found freely distributed over the neck, trunk, and limbs, and especially between the thighs.

On removing the skin, blood-extravasations, or serous infiltrations, are sometimes found beneath the lower jaw and brisket. The subcutaneous areolar tissue, as a rule, is pallid and not congested, as in anthrax.

The muscular system is normal, and I have not been able to distinguish any deviation from the common appearance of slaughtered cattle, if the animals are examined immediately after death.

The organs of respiration are, in many instances, healthy. The respiratory passages are always so. The lungs, sometimes the seat of cadaveric congestion, on the side on which the dead body has been lying, are occasionally ecchymosed, and the pleura is of a dark purplish color, over distinct lobules which are found intensely congested, but never hepatized throughout their substance. I have not found a single portion of lung tissue which would not float on water.

In nearly half the cases the collapse of the lungs, when the chest is opened, is imperfect; and according to the extent of interference with this collapse do we find interlobular emphysema. The areolar tissue between the lobules is blown up with air; and on the outer aspect of the lung, especially on the arteries and middle lobes, a beaded and streaked appearance, owing to the distension of the connective structure, is striking and well marked. The pleuræ are rarely found changed; but occasionally, scattered over the mediastinal reflections or on the diaphragm, are well-marked ecchymoses.

The pericardium is usually empty, but I have found it considerably distended with bloody serum. The surface of the heart is almost invariably blood-stained to a greater or less extent. The most common seat of these ecchymoses is on the apex, or the auricular appendages. In the right side a small blood clot is very commonly found in animals that have been lying dead for several hours, and the left side is found empty. Both ventricles, and sometimes even the auricles, may be found entirely ecchymosed; but, as a rule, the extravasations are most marked and extensive in the left ventricle, and especially on the fleshy pillars.

DIGESTIVE ORGANS.

The mouth, pharynx, and œsophagus are always healthy. The rumen is usually full of food, and its coats healthy. The mucous membrane alone has been found congested in two cases.

The recticulum, or second stomach, containing semi-fluid material, has been often found reddened; but especially in cows which had swallowed nails, wires, needles, or other foreign objects, that are so commonly found in the second stomach of cattle. In two cases wires had perforated the recticulum and diaphragm, and in one the pericardium was adherent to the diaphragm, and injured.

The omasum, or third stomach, is almost invariably in a normal condition; and whereas there are some instances in which it is considerably distended, and the food packed dry between the folds, there is no appreciable difference between the condition in which we have found it in our numerous dissections, and the state in which we should expect to find it in a similar number of healthy cattle.

The abomasum, or fourth stomach, is almost invariably the seat of distinct and specific changes. On opening it, throughout its whole length it is found varying from a pink to a deep blood-red color over its cardiac end. The pyloric end is more commonly of a natural color. But although there is this marked difference in the general aspect of the two sections of the abomasum, both present further and very characteristic morbid appearances. In the cardiac end, three different forms of lesion are seen, in different cases. In some the folds, and even the membrane between the folds, are studded irregularly with minute petechiæ of a dark, blood-red color. Each petechia is like a flea-bite, though somewhat smaller, and darker in color. Its center is dark, and sometimes softened or perforated. The areola around this center is well defined and regular, offering a marked contrast to the surrounding membrane, which, though usually congested and reddened, is not of the same depth of color as the petechial spot. In other cases the reddened folds are studded with minute yellowish-gray granulations, due to a change in the epithelium, which becomes swollen, and has a tendency to drop off. Each granulation does not usually exceed the size of a pin's head. This appearance is most marked where the folds are most congested; and in some cases, where the congestion is slight, it requires a somewhat careful inspection to recognize the presence of this change. Scattered throughout the folds, especially near their free edges, we find the third change, which consists of marked erosions, as if the epithelium had been peeled off with a sharp finger-nail.

The margins of the erosion are well defined, and of the color of the surrounding membrane, or they are often paler. The center of each erosion is of a blood-red or brownish color.

It is very rare to find the pyloric end, however natural its general aspect, without some well-defined patch, from which the epithelium is stripped and a dark, granular surface left, to which the green food adheres more or less firmly. On the pyloric gland this erosion, as frequently observed, is of a zigzag form, and tolerably deep fissures into the membrane give to the gland a shriveled and wrinkled appearance.

I have seen nearly the whole of the mucous surface in the pyloric antrum eroded; but more commonly there are three, four, or more isolated patches, varying from half an inch to even two inches in diameter.

The duodenum is often of a deep red color. Sometimes its mucous membrane is deeply tinged with bile. At others it is the seat of scattered ecchymoses, less numerous and regular than those on the folds of the abomasum.

The jejunum and ileum may be reddened throughout on their mucous surface. Sometimes the redness is in patches. It is punctiform; and, in parts, ecchymoses heighten the general color. In one case I found one of Peyer's glands somewhat tumefied, but free from any deposit around, and simply turgid and congested. The cæcum is often extensively ecchymosed, especially on the free margin of the effaceable mucous folds, so that, when the membrane is stretched, it has a striped appearance. The stripes may be of a bright or rusty-red color, but are often blackened, as we so commonly find, with blood extravasations in the large intestine of cattle. The ileo-colic fold is usually ecchymosed, tumefied, or of a blackish color. Scattered petechiæ are not uncommon, and the fundus of the cæcum may be found the seat of marked, ramified redness. The general appearance of the mucous lining of the colon is often the same. In the rectum the folds are commonly ecchymosed, and we have found free but delicate clots adherent to the membrane. The blackened appearance of the interstitial extravasations is nearly as common in the rectum as in the cæcum.

The liver, so often the seat of chronic lesion in cattle, such as thickening and induration of the capsule in spots, is often the seat of fatty degenerations, and is found congested and heavy in some cases; whereas the reverse holds good in others. Reference to the weights of the livers will show that there is no relation between any distinct state of the organ, as ascertained by the scales, and the existence of splenic fever.

The gall bladder is usually distended with viscid bile, and its lining membrane is at times the seat of ramified redness. The coats of the gall bladder have been found, in several cases, much thickened by interstitial, serous infiltration, which, from being retained in the areolæ of the connective tissue, had the appearance of a gelatinous mass.

The spleen is uniformly enlarged, as indicated by the many observations noted in the tables published in the appendix. The weight varies from two to ten pounds. It rarely exceeds six or seven. One of the largest Texan spleens, weighing eight pounds, and found by one of Dr. Rauch's inspectors in a slaughtered animal, measured twenty-seven inches in length, seven and one-half inches in width, and three inches in thickness at its thickest part.

The spleen is of a purplish color, its peritoneal surface sometimes ecchymosed; and on making an incision into its capsule the pulp oozes out. A section shows the complete effacement of the usual granular look, which is due to the Malpighian bodies, so well seen in the ox's spleen. The scraping with a knife readily forces out the currant-jelly-like pulp, and leaves the trabeculæ free and clear. In thirty notably diseased spleens, Dr. Mannheimes found only two in which the trabeculæ were firm and sound. They were generally destroyed and completely undistinguishable from any other part of the tissues of the organ.

URINARY ORGANS.

The kidneys may be perfectly healthy, but are most commonly of a dark brownish-red color, from intense congestion. The pelvis of each may be normal; but, in the earliest stages, I have found linear interstitial blood deposits in the mucous membrane. At first these are of a bright arterial hue, but they become more extensive and dark in color as the disease advances. Whenever there is bloody urine in the bladder, the pelvis of each kidney contains some of the same. In one case I found one of the lobes of the right kidney fluctuating on pressure, and, when opened, it was found to contain a cyst, distended by a couple of ounces of dark, bloody urine. In the majority of cases the urinary bladder is found very much distended with blood-colored urine. Its mucous surface may be normal and pallid, but is sometimes congested; and, in several cases, I have found it studded with very minute ecchymoses, which have existed either in the fundus or at the cervix, or have been thickly disseminated over the whole of the internal lining. The organs of generation are found healthy, and cows with calf have always retained the fœtus, whether it was a few days or several weeks old. In one case I found the peritoneal surface of the womb studded with ecchymoses precisely similar to those seen on the internal surface of the bladder, and in another, the broad ligaments of the uterus had a marked appearance of the same description.

NERVOUS SYSTEM.

In all the cases in which partial paralysis of the hind quarters alone was marked, we found the upper cornua of the gray matter in the lumbar region reddened; and the microscopical examination showed blood-extravasations and staining of the nerve cells. This appearance could be traced in all parts of the cord, in cases of more general paralysis; and, in one instance in which it was most general and marked, there was blood-extravasation outside the dura mater, beneath the medulla oblongata. The gray matter of the medulla was itself slightly blood-stained. On opening the cranium, in one instance, we found the inner surface of the dura mater studded with bright red spots, similar to the small ecchymoses seen in the urinary bladder; and the spots were distributed over the whole of the cranial surface. The pia mater is often congested, and the gray matter of the cerebrum and the cerebellum often reddened. The puncta vasculosa, in the oval centers, are very marked; and the lateral ventricles, in one case, contained a little reddish-colored serum. Beyond this tendency to congestion and occasional blood-extravasation, no lesion was discovered in the nervous system; and both white and gray matter were usually firm and not softened.

SPECIFIC OBSERVATIONS.

The following group of observations of post-mortem appearances, made in the West during the investigations of the summer of 1868, illustrate this branch of the subject more specifically:

Observation I, July 30, 1868.—Red cow; the property of Mr. A. J. Moore, of Tolono, killed by bleeding. Blood flowed freely, and was of a bright arterial hue. The skin was removed and the respiratory organs first examined, and found in a normal state. The pericardium was opened, and its reflected portion was sound; the heart of normal size and consistency, but studded with punctiform extravasations of blood around the apex, on the left auricular appendix. The right cavities were found empty and normal. The left were also empty, but there was extensive discoloration of the endocardium over the fleshy pillars and the septum. It was of an alternate purple and blood-red tint, and on cutting through the endocardium it was found infiltrated with blood. This infiltration extended in some parts to a sixteenth of an inch in depth beneath the serous membrane. The mouth, fauces, œsophagus, and the first three stomachs, were healthy. The fourth stomach contained a greenish liquid, and its mucous surface was intensely reddened, with the exception of the antrum pylori, which retained its normal color. The folds of the cardiac end were thickly studded with ecchymoses, which appeared to have coalesced, and the membrane had in many parts given way, so as to induce the appearance of small, irregular ulcerations. There was no thickening around the ulcers, nor evidence of progressive ulcerated change, but the solutions of continuity seemed due to the discharge of epithelium and death of the subjacent membrane in the center of the bloody extravasations. The duodenum was of a deep yellow, bile-tinged color. The jejunum and ileum were carefully examined throughout their whole extent, and found reddened. Peyer's glands were healthy. The cæcum was reddened around the ileo-colic opening, and the colon had irregular patches of congestion. In the rectum blood extravasations were found all along the free margin of the folds. The spleen was of a deep purple hue, weight seven and one-half pounds; and its structure was so disintegrated that a black mass of pulp oozed out of the incisions, and with the slightest force nothing remained intact but the trabeculæ. The liver and gall bladder weighed twenty-seven and one-half pounds. They were congested, but otherwise apparently healthy. The liver afforded indications of fatty change. The kidneys were of a dark color, and contained bloody urine in the pelves. The urinary bladder was enormously distended with dark, blood-colored urine, and weighed with its contents nineteen pounds. The uterus was healthy, and contained a fœtus about a month old. The brain and spinal cord were carefully examined. The meninges were generally congested, and the posterior part of the cord, when cut across, indicated very decided redness of the superior cornua of gray matter.

Observation II, July 30, 1868.—Cow; the property of Mr. C. B. Chamberlain, of Tolono. This animal was also bled to death and skinned. The thoracic organs were found quite healthy. The first and the second stomach were likewise normal, but the third was somewhat inordinately distended by dry food firmly impacted between its folds. The folds themselves were sound. The fourth stomach was congested throughout, but its folds, at the cardiac end, were of a deep, modena-red hue. In the vicinity of the pylorus were a couple of small patches of erosions of the mucous membrane. The small intestine was the seat of ramified redness throughout its entire length. In the large intestine, from the cæcum to the rectum, there was a dark, inky-looking deposit of blood along the free edge of the mucous folds, and between these, at points, the membrane was considerably congested. The liver was much congested, fatty, and weighed twenty-one pounds. The spleen was of a purple hue, its tissues undergoing disintegration, and it weighed two and one-half pounds. The kidneys were dark colored, and the bladder largely distended with bloody urine. The spinal cord only of this animal was examined, and the gray matter found of a dark red color in the posterior part adjoining the cauda equina.

Observation III, July 31, 1868.—Two-year-old steer; the property of Mr. Matthews, near Tolono. Examined three hours after death. Marked cadaveric rigidity. Organs of respiration healthy. The heart, of normal size and firmness, was extensively ecchymosed on its outer surface, especially down the anterior and the posterior ventricular furrows. The right cavities contained a small amount of blood; the left were empty, but the fleshy pillars were of a deep purplish tint from extensive ecchymosis. The mouth, pharynx, œsophagus, the first and the second stomach, were healthy. The third stomach was considerably distended by dry food. The fourth stomach was the seat of diffuse redness over its entire mucous surface, but the depth of color was greatest at the cardiac end. Freely dispersed over the surface were small, circumscribed erosions with red areolæ round them; and these evidently resulted from ecchymotic patches, which sloughed in their centers. In the pyloric end were several irregular patches of cuticular degenerations. The green contents of the stomach adhered to the denuded surfaces. The jejunum was the seat of ramified redness over its mucous surface, and a similar congestion partially affected the ileum and large intestine. The liver was normal in size and general aspect. The spleen was of a dark purple tint, about three times its natural size, and its pulp softened. The kidneys were turgid with blood, and the urinary bladder was much distended with bloody urine.

Observation IV, August 1, 1868.—Seven-year-old steer; the property of Mr L. D. Ayers, of Farina. This animal was first seen ill on Thursday, the 30th of July, and died at noon on the 1st of August. Respiratory passages healthy. On opening the chest it was noticed that the lungs were only partially collapsed. They had rather a blanched appearance, and, on removal from the chest, it was found that through the posterior lobes, and all along the upper aspect to the anterior lobes of the lungs, there was well-marked interlobular emphysema. Incisions in various parts of the emphysematous tissue presented the normal aspect of the lobules, with free extravasation of air in the connective tissue around them. The lungs weighed fifteen pounds. The mediastinal reflections of the pleura were closely studded with ecchymoses, and the same appearance pervaded the pleural portions of the same membrane. The pericardial sac contained a little yellow serum; and the heart, of normal size, was extensively ecchymosed around the base of both ventricles. The right side contained a small quantity of partially clotted blood; and the left ventricle, also containing a little dark blood, was the seat of extensive ecchymoses over nearly the whole of its inner aspect. The alimentary canal, from the mouth to the third stomach, was in a normal state. The contents of the third stomach were soft and moderate in quantity. The cardiac end of the fourth stomach was of a dark red color, and its folds thickly studded with small yellowish elevations, having the appearance of vesicles, but solid, and apparently consisting of opaque epithelial enlargements. The pyloric end was of normal color and free from erosions or other signs of disease. The small intestines, of a pinkish hue externally, were intensely reddened on their mucous surface. There was general capillary congestion, and the ramified character of the red tinge was most marked. One of Peyer's glands had an elevated and somewhat thickened appearance. The color was rather less deep than that of the adjacent membrane, and on making an incision into it there was no evidence of deposit beneath it, or noteworthy change in structure. In the cæcum a very marked ecchymosis surrounded the ileo-colic opening, and several blood extravasations, well circumscribed and limited in extent, existed in the colon and rectum. The liver and gall bladder weighed twenty-nine pounds. The tissue of the liver was congested, and betokened active changes in the shape of fatty degeneration. The spleen was dark, friable, and weighed eight pounds. The two kidneys weighed four and one-quarter pounds, and were of a dark red color. The bladder was much distended with bloody urine. Its mucous membrane was congested at the fundus. The cranium was opened and its entire contents found abnormally vascular. On removing the brain the dura mater was found studded with bright vermilion blood spots, about the size of an ordinary pin's head. The medulla oblongata was healthy The gray matter in the cerebellum was of a very decided reddish hue; but the consistence of both white and gray matter appeared normal. The cerebrum showed very marked puncta vasculosa on making horizontal sections of its hemispheres.

Observation V, August 1, 1868.—Red cow; the property of S. F. Randolph, of Farina. Died at 2 p. m., and examined at 5 p. m. Cadaveric rigidity marked. Respiratory passages healthy. On opening the chest it was found that the right lung collapsed imperfectly; it was palish, and the seat of interlobular emphysema on its upper border, and between the middle and inferior lobe. The left lung was somewhat ecchymosed. On the surface of half a dozen lobules there was a dark, flea-bitten appearance, which corresponded with considerable congestion of the lung tissue within. The structure floated on water, and was certainly free from inflammatory deposit. The lungs weighed twelve pounds. The heart, of normal size and consistence, was freely ecchymosed over its entire outer surface. The right ventricle contained a little frothy blood, but was not blood-stained. The left ventricle also contained a little dark fluid blood, and was free from ecchymoses. On opening the left auricular appendix, it was found studded with punctiform petechiæ. Of the alimentary canal, all anterior to the fourth stomach, was healthy, but this organ was of a deep red color over the mucous folds of the cardiac end. The antrum pylori was studded over its entire surface with irregular erosions, exceeding twenty in number. None of these had the granular surface or peculiar edges of true ulcers, but looked like abrasions, the epithelium having been removed and the reddened mucous surface more or less discolored by adherent vegetable matter, constituting the base of the solutions of continuity. The duodenum was of a dark yellow color, and the areolar tissue around it was œdematous; while the whole internal surface of the small intestines was the seat of ramified redness, with marked ecchymoses scattered in large numbers throughout. Some of the blood-stained spots had sloughed in their centers. The ileo-colic fold was blackened and tumefied, and the longitudinal mucous folds in the colon and rectum were stained with blackened blood extravasations. The liver and gall bladder, to all appearances in a healthy state, weighed nineteen pounds. The spleen, of a dark color, with a deep red pulp which oozed out of incisions made through the capsule, weighed five pounds and four ounces. The kidneys weighed two pounds, but, with the exception of urine of a port-wine color in the pelvis of each, appeared sound. The bladder was distended with bloody urine, but its coats were of a healthy color. The cranial contents appeared unusually vascular, but otherwise healthy. The spinal cord was not examined.

Observation VI, August 6, 1868.—Three-year-old cow; the property of G. F. Byers, of Sodorus. Died the night previous to the examination. No cadaveric rigidity. Decomposition commenced. On removing the skin it was found that effusion had taken place under the sternum. The organs of respiration were found healthy. The heart was somewhat softened from incipient decay; both outer and inner surface were the seat of cadaveric blood-staining. The entire alimentary canal was found normal, and free from congestion, ecchymoses, or erosions. The liver also was sound. The spleen, much enlarged, probably four times its natural size, was softened at its base, and blood had flowed freely out during the life of the animal, as clots and liquid blood dropped out of the peritoneum when it was first opened. The kidneys were normal, and the bladder wonderfully distended by clear-colored urine. It is worthy of note that this cow had been noticed to be sick for two days, but discharged clear urine on the evening of the 5th, and did not then appear in a dying state. She succumbed suddenly and unexpectedly during the night; and, as the post-mortem indicated, from hemorrhage from the spleen.

Observation VII, August 7, 1868.—Steer; the property of Mr. P. Harris, of Champaign. Organs of respiration healthy. General aspect of heart normal. Right cavities containing a little blood, and free from ecchymoses. On the fleshy pillars of the left ventricle there were marked and diffused extravasations of blood. The anterior part of the alimentary canal, as far down as the third stomach, was quite normal. The fourth stomach was slightly reddened; and, at the cardiac end, the folds were studded with small, yellowish eminences, as described in a previous case. The pyloric end was the seat of marked and numerous erosions. The intestinal tract was quite healthy, with the exception of slight redness of the mucous surface of the small intestine. The liver and gall bladder were normal. The spleen was at least twice its natural size, of a dark color, and softened structure. The kidneys were dark-colored from congestion, and the bladder was very much distended with urine of port-wine color. On severing the head from the neck, it was found that around the dura mater, in the foramen magnum, there was an exudation of yellowish lymph, studded with numerous confluent petechiæ of a very dark color. On removing the brain it was found of normal consistence. The spinal cord in the dorsal and the lumbar region was reddened, especially in the posterior horns of its gray matter.

Observation VIII, August 7, 1868.—Steer; also the property of Mr. P. Harris, of Champaign. Killed for the purpose of dissection. Organs of respiration healthy throughout. Heart slightly ecchymosed on the outer surface of the ventricles. The right side contained a small quantity of fluid blood, with slender clots somewhat adherent to the auriculo-ventricular valves. Left ventricle empty and healthy. Pharynx, gullet, the first and the second stomach, healthy. The third stomach impacted with dry food. The fourth stomach of a deep red color over its cardiac folds, and studded somewhat with small, grayish eminences of the size of ordinary pins' heads. The mucous surface of the pyloric end, wherever it was whole, was of normal color; but it was freely spotted with very distinct erosions of irregular shape, dark in the center; and the largest of these was on the pyloric gland, and extending on the transverse fold at the pyloric opening. The duodenum, and indeed the entire small intestine, was found with the mucous surface congested. The cæcum, colon, and rectum, throughout their entire length, were reddened within, and ecchymoses were freely distributed over their whole interior. The liver and gall bladder were normal. The spleen was dark colored, soft, and thrice its natural size. The kidneys were somewhat congested, and the urinary bladder, though presenting no abnormal appearance of its coats, was distended with bloody urine.

Observation IX, August 8, 1868.—Small two-year-old steer; the property of Mr. Frank Peters, Scott Township, six miles west of Champaign; had died the previous night, and presented the somewhat unusual appearance of dried, clotted drops of blood, each about the size of an ordinary drop of water, freely distributed over the neck, flanks, body, and limbs. Organs of respiration healthy. Heart beginning to decompose, but showing no signs of disease. First three stomachs healthy. The fourth stomach was slightly reddened at its cardiac end; but its folds were thickly studded with small, grayish eminences, having the general appearance of a vesicular eruption. The color of the mucous surface of the pyloric antrum was healthy, with the exception of two small, irregular erosions. The small and the large intestine were entirely free from congestion or other indications of disease. The liver and gall bladder were sound, and weighed eleven pounds. The spleen was freely ecchymosed on its surface, soft and enlarged, weighing three and a half pounds. The kidneys were dark colored, and beginning to decompose. The bladder was healthy and much distended with bloody urine. The brain and spinal cord were healthy.

Observation X, August 8, 1868.—Four-year-old cow, belonging to the same proprietor as the last steer. On opening the chest it was found that the lungs collapsed imperfectly; and that on their dorsal aspect, especially of their posterior lobes, there was very marked interlobular emphysema. The external aspect of the heart was normal. The right cavities were full of dark blood, and indicated cadaveric blood-staining of the endocardium. The left ventricle, also, contained much dark blood; and its free wall, as well as the columnæ carneæ, was extensively ecchymosed. The first three stomachs were healthy. The fourth was the seat of ramified redness on the mucous folds, at the cardiac end; and numerous punctiform eminences of yellowish color gave the eruptive appearance noticed in previous post-mortem examinations. The pyloric end was normal, and free from erosions. Both the large and the small intestine were quite normal. The liver was swollen as the result of decomposition, and the gall bladder was distended with normal bile. The spleen, of a dark purplish tint and friable structure, weighed five pounds. The kidneys were congested, and the urinary bladder distended with bloody urine. On severing the head from the neck, a considerable quantity of bloody serum flowed out of the meninges. The cranial contents were somewhat congested, but otherwise healthy.

Observation XI, August 8, 1868.—Three-year-old steer; the property of Mr. ———, of Champaign. Killed by division of spinal cord. Organs of respiration healthy. Heart of normal appearance, with the exception of slight ecchymoses in the left ventricle. Mouth, fauces, gullet, and first three stomachs healthy. Fourth stomach of a dark red color over the folds at the cardiac end, which were thickly studded with small, circular ecchymoses; and, wherever these congregated, the epithelium was detached, and the membrane exposed of a brownish color. Many of the isolated ecchymoses had abrasions in their centers; and the red areolæ around the erosions sometimes spread out irregularly. The abraded surface, in various parts, had the green contents of the stomach firmly adhering to them. The pyloric end was, to great extent, free from congestion, but was studded with erosions and zigzag fissures. Three of the abraded spots were much larger than the rest, extending from an inch and a half to three inches in length, by an inch to an inch and a half in breadth. Over the larger abrasions a scab had formed, to which the food was adherent. The irregular ulcers of the edges were red, but flat, and without tending to thickening or erosions. The small intestine was congested throughout the fundus of the cæcum, of a deep red color, and over the whole mucous surface of the colon there was ramified redness. In the rectum there was blood extravasation in the substance of the mucous membrane, along the margin of the longitudinal folds. The liver and gall bladder weighed twenty-one and a half pounds, but offered no sign of morbid lesion, beyond fatty change in the gland. The spleen, of a dark color, with softened pulp, weighed five and a half pounds. The kidneys were turgid with blood, and the urinary bladder was much distended by bloody urine. The cerebro-spinal centers were healthy.

Observation XII, August 11, 1868.—Red cow; the property of L. R. Hastings, Chicago. This cow had been sick about a week, and was killed, by bleeding, for the purpose of dissection. The organs of respiration, the organs of deglutition, and the first stomach were healthy. The second stomach contained many foreign objects, such as nails and wires, and one considerable piece of iron wire perforated the fundus. The mucous membrane was of a dull, dirty-red color over its whole surface. The third stomach was healthy. The fourth stomach, reddened at its cardiac end, was studded, over the whole of its transverse folds, with grayish-yellow eminences of the size of an ordinary pin's head, as previously described. The pyloric end was also somewhat congested, but studded throughout with irregular ulcers, four of which were of considerable size, and near the intestinal opening. There was ramified redness throughout the whole of the mucous membrane of the small intestine. The ileo-colic valve was ecchymosed, and ecchymoses were scattered over the whole fundus of the cæcum. The inner lining of the colon and rectum was congested. The liver and gall bladder appeared generally healthy, with the exception of some congestion of the gland and fatty degeneration. The spleen was much enlarged and thicker in the center than in any previously examined case. It weighed seven and one-half pounds. Organs of respiration healthy. The heart was slightly ecchymosed on its outer surface. The right cavities were full of frothy blood, and ecchymosed on the free wall. The left ventricle was empty, and infiltrations of blood in and beneath the endocardium existed on the fleshy pillars and the septum. The kidneys were much congested. On cutting into the pelvis of each kidney, the mucous lining was found densely studded with ecchymoses, as seen in the illustration. The bladder was filled with dark urine. The mucous lining was dotted all over with small, vermilion, punctiform ecchymoses, as delineated in plate. The uterus was studded over its horns with small ecchymotic spots, similar to those on the inner surface of the bladder, as indicated by plate. The cerebral meninges were slightly congested, and the arachnoid sac contained an excess of serum. The gray matter of the medulla oblongata was reddened. On cutting into the cerebellum its gray centers were found ecchymosed, and similar well-marked extravasations of blood existed in the gray matter of the crura cerebri. In other respects the brain appeared healthy.

Observation XIII, August 12, 1868.—Red and white cow; the property of Mr. King, of Bridgeport; was killed by effusion of blood. The organs of respiration were found healthy. The heart was of normal size, but slightly ecchymosed at the apex, and the outer surface of the left auricular appendix was of a uniform dark blood color, as seen in plate. The organs of deglutition and the rumen were healthy. The mucous membrane of the reticulum was throughout of a dull, port-wine color. The third stomach was normal. The fourth stomach was the seat of diffuse redness throughout, with an irregular abrasion near the pylorus. The small intestine was reddened in every part, and the large intestine ecchymosed in the cæcum, and toward the end of the rectum. The liver and gall bladder were healthy. The spleen was at least four times its natural size, of a dark purplish tint, and its structure disintegrated. The kidneys were dark colored and congested. The bladder was enormously distended with bloody urine. The brain and its meninges gave signs of intense congestion, and the puncta vasculosa of the cerebrum were very marked.

Observation XIV, August 13, 1868.—Red steer; the property of Mr. Joseph Heath, near Oxford; killed for dissection. Organs of respiration healthy. Heart healthy and free from petechiæ. The mouth, pharynx, œsophagus, and first three stomachs were found healthy. The cardiac end of the fourth stomach was of a deep red color, some of the folds ecchymosed, and some of the dark centers of the ecchymoses had sloughed. The pyloric end was much less congested, but its entire surface more or less abraded. The exposed vascular membrane was of a dark red color, and the food firmly adhered to it. Both small and large intestines indicated some congestion of the mucous lining. The liver was considerably enlarged, much engorged with blood, and was fatty. The spleen weighed five and a half pounds, was dark in color, and friable in consistence. The kidneys were congested, and the bladder was largely distended with bloody urine.

Observation XV, August 14, 1868.—Red steer; the property of same owner; also killed for dissection. With the exception of slight ecchymoses of the pleura on the anterior lobe of the left lung, the organs of respiration offered no indications of disease. The heart was of normal size, but appeared more flabby than in health. The right cavities contained a little fluid blood, and the columnæ carneæ of the ventricle were slightly ecchymosed. The blood-staining of the endocardium was much marked on the fleshy pillars of the left ventricle. The organs of deglutition, the first, the second, and the third stomach, were quite healthy. The fourth stomach not quite so much congested as usual, but its cardiac folds were studded with very numerous ecchymoses, many of which were perforated in their centers. The pyloric end was also somewhat congested, but the erosions were more marked and extensive than on the transverse folds of the cardiac end. Near the pyloric opening were several small ulcers, to the surface of which the gastric contents had adhered. In the intestines, the only lesions discovered were a number of punctiform ecchymoses in the rectum, especially near the anus. The liver was fatty, much engorged with blood, and appeared greatly increased in size. The spleen weighed four and a half pounds, was of a dark color, and its structure softened. The kidneys were of a deep red color, and the bladder much distended by bloody urine. The mucous surface of the bladder was studded all over with small petechiæ of a vermilion hue, as seen in other cases.

Observation XVI, August 20, 1868.—Red steer; at slaughter-house in Bridgeport. Organs of respiration healthy. Heart firm and of normal size, was slightly ecchymosed at the apex, and on the fleshy pillars of the left ventricle. Organs of deglutition and the first stomach sound. The fourth stomach was slightly reddened at the cardiac end; two small erosions, about one-third of an inch in length, existed near the pylorus, where the membrane generally was of normal color. The intestines were healthy. The liver and gall bladder, to all appearance, normal. The spleen, of a dark color, weighed four and a half pounds; but its structure had undergone little change, was firm, and of a brighter red than any previously examined in cases of splenic fever. The appearance of this spleen is shown in plate. The kidneys were slightly congested, and, on cutting into the pelvis, some bright ecchymoses were found, as if in the earliest stage of blood extravasation in these structures. The bladder contained a moderate quantity of clear-colored urine, but was slightly ecchymosed near its neck. The cerebro-spinal centers were healthy.

Observation XVII, August 21, 1868.—Red cow; examined at St. Louis. Killed by effusion of blood. Respiratory passages healthy. On opening the thorax the lungs were found pale, and only partially collapsed. The posterior lobe of the right lung was the seat of extensive interlobular emphysema. On the anterior and the middle lobes were several scattered patches of congestion, corresponding to congested lobules, within which were simple reddened, not solidified, globules, and they floated on water. The heart, of normal size and consistence, was slightly ecchymosed on the anterior and the posterior ventricular furrows. Internally the right cavities, containing a little fluid blood, were healthy; but the left was tinged by ecchymotic spots on the fleshy pillars of ventricle. The mouth, pharynx, gullet, and first three stomachs, were healthy. The fourth stomach was reddened at its cardiac end, and its folds studded all over with ecchymoses. The small intestine was the seat of ramified redness throughout. In the cæcum, in a line with the mucous folds, the blood extravasations which had occurred were of a dark rusty color; and similar changes were seen in the rectum. The liver and gall bladder, much congested, weighed twenty-five pounds. In the liver were old adhesions, and some deposits of yellow granular lymph, near the surface, extending in one instance to half an inch in depth. There was also marked evidence of fatty degeneration. The gall bladder was the seat of extensive, ramified redness on its inner surface. The spleen, of a dark purplish tint, weighed six and a half pounds. Wherever an incision was made, its softened pulp exuded without pressure. The kidneys, paler than usual in this disease, weighed three and one-quarter pounds. They were free from ecchymoses. The urinary bladder was much distended with bloody urine. The cerebro-spinal meninges were intensely congested. The gray matter of the brain was reddened, and the puncta vasculosa in the oval centers very marked.

Observation XVIII, August 24, 1868.—Black steer; the property of Messrs. Palmer and Perry. Died during the day. Post-mortem examination at 6 p. m. Respiratory passages normal; cadaveric congestion of left lung. On opening the pericardium, the heart was found extensively ecchymosed at the base of the right ventricle, and over the origin of the pulmonary artery. The right cavities contained a little dark, semi-fluid blood. The left side was nearly empty, but on the columnæ carneæ of the ventricle there was a dark purplish tint of the endocardium from extensive extravasations of blood in and beneath its structure. The digestive organs anterior to the true stomach were sound. The cardiac end of the abomasum was of a diffuse red color. The mucous membrane of the pyloric end was of normal color wherever it was not eroded, but it was studded with twenty to thirty abrasions of the epithelium, exposing the vascular membrane in patches varying from one-fourth to one and one-half inch in length, and usually longer than broad. The duodenum was turgid with bile. The jejunum was extensively ecchymosed on its inner surface. The large intestine was healthy, except some extravasations on the rectal folds. The liver and gall bladder, of general normal look, but congested, weighed twenty-seven pounds. The gall bladder was distended by inspissated bile. The gland itself was softened by fatty change. The spleen, dark and softened, weighed seven and one-fourth pounds. The kidneys were intensely congested, but not ecchymosed. The bladder was full to repletion of bloody urine, but its coats were normal. Darkness precluded the examination of the brain and spinal cord.

Observation XIX, August 26, 1868.—Two-year-old roan steer; the property of Mr. Richard Callahan, near Abilene. Organs of respiration healthy. Heart flabby and blood-stained on the posterior ventricular furrow. Interior of right side unchanged, but on the septum, and fleshy pillars in the left ventricle, were extensive ecchymoses. On opening the abdomen the peritoneum was found studded with punctiform ecchymoses. Organs of deglutition and first three stomachs normal. The cardiac end of the fourth stomach was intensely reddened, and its folds marked by zigzag fissures or ulcerations, in the center of which were black scabs, with adherent food. The pyloric end was of more normal color, but four ulcers, about one-half inch broad, and of irregular shape, existed in its middle; and at the pyloric end was a larger spot of ulceration, about one inch in length. The duodenum was much congested on its minor surface, and diffuse redness pervaded the mucous membrane of the jejunum and ileum. In various parts of the latter were small, dark petechiæ. The mucous membrane of the whole of the large intestine was of a dark red color, and the excrement in the rectum was tinged with blood. Through the whole of the longitudinal mucous folds extravasations of blood had occurred. The liver and gall bladder weighed seventeen and one-half pounds, and appeared healthy. The bile in the gall bladder was thick. The spleen was very dark in color, its pulp soft, and its weight was five and one-half pounds. The kidneys were much congested, and the mucous membrane of each pelvis was spotted with dark ecchymoses. In the peritoneal cul de sac, around the bladder and rectum, were numerous bright ecchymoses. The bladder was full of bloody urine, and its mucous lining extensively dotted with small blood spots, of a vermilion hue. On severing the head from the neck, a large quantity of serum flowed from the meninges. The meninges were dark, and of the general color of the gray matter of the cord, and the brain was much redder than in health.

Observation XX, September 5, 1868.—Three-year-old red-and-white cow; the property of Dennis Doran, Brighton, near Chicago. This cow had died during the preceding night, and was dissected at 3 p. m. on the 5th. There was no sign of decomposition, and the internal organs were still warm. The organs of respiration were healthy. Heart and pericardium sound, and free from ecchymoses. Organs of deglutition and first stomach healthy. Second stomach of a dull red hue in its inner lining. Third stomach normal. Fourth stomach of a dark red color at its cardiac end, with various ecchymoses, and half a dozen small circumscribed spots where the epithelium had been thrown off, and the dark red vascular membrane exposed. The general color of the lining in the antrum pylori was much less intensely red than in the transverse folds, but was the seat of several erosions. The pyloric gland had a zigzag ulcer on its summit. The small intestine was the seat of ramified redness. In the large intestine the longitudinal mucous folds were all reddened along their free margins by blood extravasation. The liver was sound, but the gall bladder was thickened by serous infiltration, and its mucous lining indicated the ramifications of the lesser arteries and veins, which were gorged with blood. The spleen weighed six and a third pounds, was of a dark purplish tint, and its pulp softened. The kidneys were congested, but not ecchymosed. The urinary bladder was distended by bloody urine. The broad ligaments of the uterus were thickly studded with ecchymoses of a bright arterial hue; cerebro-spinal centers not examined.

CAUSES AND NATURE OF THE DISEASE.

In those parts where the splenic or periodic fever of cattle is enzoötic, the prevailing influences are such as favor the development of intermittent disease in man. There are parts more healthy than others; and the beneficial effects of constant winds, a dry soil, adequate elevation, and the introduction of good systems of culture, tend to make many regions in the vast countries over which malarious conditions prevail favorable for the health and prosperity of man. In the more swampy parts those diseases which characterize low and unhealthy lands in all parts of the world annually recur with the intense heat of summer, and often extend into the winter season. The bilious remittent and intermittent fevers in man are represented in animals by the deadly charbon or anthrax, the black tongue of domestic and wild ruminants, as also by a marked form of the splenic fever which I am describing.

Texas and Florida have been chosen as resorts for invalids—for consumptive people during the winter; and to cast a doubt over the salubrity of Texas might lead any one into difficulties in that State. It is not too much to say of the State that its acclimatized inhabitants prefer to live there rather than to choose what might be viewed as a healthier climate further north; but it is impossible for an unprejudiced stranger traveling through the State not to observe the usual spare habit of body, the sallow, yellowish complexion, and the want of activity prevailing among the inhabitants. There are exceptions and exceptional spots; but it is evident that there exists some condition, either of soil or climate, unfavorable to the health of man.

I had not anticipated witnessing universal indications of a low standard of health in animals. Texans pride themselves on their herds of beeves, on the size cattle often attain, on the masses of fat rolling over the bones and muscles of steers fed only on mesquit, and they look upon Texas as a center whence the world may be supplied with beeves.

There is every reason for believing that Texas must remain one of the greatest, if not the greatest, cattle-growing State of the Union; but its progress and prosperity demand that farmers should be informed of the conditions which are ever in operation against them, and they will doubtless bring their intelligence and industry to bear in correcting evils that are far from imaginary.

Inquiries as to the diseases of Texan cattle in Texas are almost always met by people of that State by the declaration that cattle are never sick there; yet a "norther" may sweep down and drive the cattle upon a narrow neck of land, where they starve at times for want of food; drought, as in 1864, sometimes destroys thousands; while in the winter excessive wet destroys the grasses, favors diarrhœa, and unless the cattle can get in the woods and eat some swamp moss, wild onions, or other products of the river bottoms, they must occasionally succumb.

The close of 1868 and beginning of 1869 have been remarkable for an excessive amount of rain. Cattle have suffered greatly, and on all the sedge grass lands along the Brazos starvation has not been uncommon. Further west, on the mesquit, not far from Corpus Christi, cattle have been in fair condition; but some idea of the scarcity of really fat cattle during the winter months may be obtained from the fact that, at Indianola, cattle for New Orleans market could not be had under twenty dollars in gold. We hear so much of cattle being worth only a few dollars a head in summer, and people killing them by the thousand for their hides and tallow, that the only reason to be given for heavy winter prices is the scarcity of really fat stock, and the great distance it has to be driven, even to such a port as Indianola.

I have seen many large herds of Texan cattle that had been wintered in Illinois, Indiana, or Missouri, and have made myself acquainted with the average weight of cattle in Texas, and one most important fact appears, viz., that a Texan steer will increase in twelve months on the grasses of a more northern latitude than that of his native State, by one, two, or three hundred pounds over and above the highest weight he will ever attain in Texas. Let us take the cattle fed on the mesquit, said to be fat all the year round—and where, therefore, an animal has not to make up for lost condition—and age for age, it will take three of them to weigh down the Illinois steer, and probably four. I take the best and the average, and it will be found, on careful examination, that the cattle on the noted grasses of Texas, whether from the soil, heat, water, or other cause, do not attain the weight and condition that the same cattle do if removed to the north, nor that northern or western cattle do on their native prairies.

Texans are finding this out, and, much to their credit, they are introducing a system of corn-feeding that gives them cattle that can compete in western markets with other corn-fed cattle. They can, it is true, show us some prodigies from mesquit grounds, but the average run of grass-fed cattle in Texas might be greatly improved by attention to the subjects of breeding, shelter, artificial feeding, &c.

What are the active causes in operation which tend to influence prejudicially the stamina of southern herds? Traveling over the prairies, no one can fail to be struck by the large number of dead animals to be met with. The dissection of these, or the slaughter and dissection of the first animal met with, reveals three distinct and unfavorable manifestations. The spleen is enlarged; the animals have, without exception, the "ague cake"—the stamp of a malarious district; the liver is fatty, and this is a lesion that might be anticipated in so warm a country; the true stomach is reddened at its left end, the membrane is eroded, or appears as if scratched with a sharp nail on its folds, and although there may be only a single and small erosion, nevertheless the trace of gastric disorder is there. I have not failed in a single instance in Texas to trace this, and I have opened as many as twenty-six animals per day, weighing their organs carefully, and watching closely for these signs. Sometimes the scars of old ulcers are more marked than the erosions on the mucous folds, and it is not uncommon to find there traces of ancient lesions about the pylorus, or intestinal opening.

My observations extend further. From the earliest age that the calf feeds on grass, to the oldest that a bullock attains, the morbid lesions alluded to are found. They grow better and worse, and, in dissecting a dozen animals, one or two will be found to have blood extravasations, of a very limited and delicate character, in the pelvis of the kidney, in the urinary bladder, and in the intestinal mucous membrane. During the summer, so far as I can learn, more than at any other season, a few bullocks in a herd may be seen to droop behind, and void bloody urine. Mr. Louis Brandt, now a practicing veterinarian in New York, who lived twelve years in Texas, often witnessed these symptoms; and persons engaged in shipping large quantities of cattle throughout the year have told me that they have at times seen the symptoms.

It is difficult to get at the truth; but from personal observation, and very careful and numerous inquiries, I am in a position to state that almost if not quite universally, in the States bordering on the Gulf of Mexico, and for a distance of at least two or three hundred miles inland, the cattle do not attain the full weight they can and do reach elsewhere; that they very commonly appear in blooming health, and are usually free from acute and marked symptoms of any disease; that, nevertheless, these animals are usually more anæmic and less firm than northern cattle, and that, without exception, all of them that I have dissected have shown the spleen enlarged to twice or thrice its usual weight, the liver slightly or very fatty, and the true stomach reddened and eroded. The removal of these animals to a northern State results, especially as winter approaches, in a diminished size of spleen, a great deposit of fat, and development of blood and muscle, and the cicatrization of the gastric lesions.

Side by side with observations made by me in Texas on the bodies of animals that had died, and on others slaughtered in apparent health, must be placed Mr. Ravenel's researches in relation to the cryptogamic origin of the disease. I do not wish to forestall his observations, or the report of Doctors Billings and Curtis, but certainly it appeared that the grasses which the animals ate had a healthy aspect, were not infected by parasitic plants, and could not, on a casual observation, be recognized as presenting any peculiar character that might account for the ill health of animals eating them.

Conjecture is not always profitable, and as yet it is impossible to say more with certainty than that, in a warm country, where a rich and retentive soil is ever charged with considerable moisture, and where artificial systems of culture are in their infancy, a general low tone of system prevails, which manifests itself in the shape of an imperfect development of blood, an enlargement of blood glands, and very significant lesions of the stomach and liver.

Descriptions of the Texan fever, which have been published for years past, all agree that the Texan and also Florida cattle, which have caused so much mischief, appear themselves to be in perfect health; and the thriving condition of many herds in Indiana, Illinois, Missouri, and Kansas tended, at first, to convince us that whatever injured the improved breeds indigenous to these States had no effect on the long-horned Texan cattle. It is true that at Cairo we were informed, by a gentleman whose statement we had no reason to doubt, that he had seen many Texan cattle die in the railway pens; and as many as nine or ten in one morning had been found dead, having, in his opinion, succumbed to the same disease as that destroying the cows of the inhabitants of Cairo. He supplied the hay for all the cattle landed there, and the first few lots, landed in April, appeared sound; but he afterward saw three or four lots, numbering from two hundred and fifty to five hundred head, which were affected by the prevailing disease. He distinctly avers that six, eight, and even ten head of dead cattle were hauled off the boats when they arrived laden with stock, and the men in charge got medicine for the disease. One lot of two hundred and fifty animals, referred to by this informant, was taken off the cars at Farina, after leaving Cairo for the North, simply because they were suffering severely, and it was supposed that this arose from the journey; but they communicated disease to all the cattle that fed in their path, and killed forty-seven out of fifty Illinois cattle with which they grazed, from the 10th of May to the middle of June.

In opposition to hearsay evidence, it was my duty to examine cattle alive and those which were dead. I saw sixty-four Texan steers, fresh from New Orleans, which were unloaded at Cairo on the 1st of August. They all appeared healthy. We had previously seen a considerable number of the same kind of stock without being able to detect the slightest evidence of disease, and were happy to receive an invitation to visit Mr. Alexander's farm, at Broadlands, near Homer, where there were four thousand five hundred and twenty-seven Texan steers, which had been driven to Broadlands, and had communicated disease not only to the cattle feeding on their trail, but also to a herd of Illinois cattle with which they were mixed in reaching their destination.

The numbers and dates relating to the several importations at Broadlands are as follows:

Purchased at—	Date of arrival at Broadlands.	No.
Tolono	May 31, 1868	499
Tolono	June 2, 1868	228
Tolono	June 18, 1868	496
Tolono	June 20, 1868	349
Abilene	June 25, 1868	537
Tolono	June 26, 1868	140
Tolono	June 30, 1868	107
Abilene	July 2, 1868	248
Abilene	July 3, 1868	241
Chicago	July 4, 1868	195
Tolono	July 22, 1868	362
Tolono	July 25, 1868	611
Tolono	July 28, 1868	514
	Total	4,527

Up to the 12th of September, the date of a letter from Broadlands, thirty-one of the animals had died, "most if not all of them from injuries received in transit." Of four thousand five hundred and twenty-seven animals driven or transported in steamers and on railroads, it is not surprising that some should die, considering the great distances they had to travel; but all which we examined alive appeared healthy and thriving. That they communicated disease to a very serious extent is proved beyond doubt; and it would have been important to determine, by the slaughter of many, their real condition.

On the 6th of August I visited Broadlands a second time, for the purpose of dissecting a Texan steer which the people of the neighborhood believed would show signs of the disease. We inspected the herds generally, which still looked in perfect health, but one of the imported cattle was reported ill and dying. He had. reached the farm about the middle of July, and had not thriven well. It was, as usual, supposed that he had sustained injuries on the journey. When I saw this animal alive, he was lying down, with his head stretched on the ground; imperceptible pulse at the jaw, great listlessness and prostration, but presenting no distinctive symptoms of splenic fever. After death I found that there was an effusion of bloody serum under the jaw. The organs of respiration were healthy, and the heart sound. The whole of the stomach and the intestines were normal, as also the liver, gall bladder, and spleen. The kidneys and bladder exhibited no signs of blood extravasations, or alteration in the urine, such as is seen in splenic fever. From the general emaciation of the body, and the absence of any lesion of disease, it was evident to me that this animal had died of hectic; or, in other words, of the ill effects of prolonged starvation and ill usage, which had permanently arrested the functions of assimilation. The Texan cattle were intermixed in the pastures of Broadlands with about six hundred native animals. All but two hundred and eighty of these were soon sent to eastern markets, and those which remained with them began to die on the 26th of July. They were then placed on green corn; but they continued to sicken and succumb to the disease until one hundred and ninety-eight of all kinds, including a yoke of old Texan steers, which had been some time on the farm, had been buried. At the time of my visit the mortality was raging at its highest point, and men were busy, from sunrise to sunset, skinning, digging graves, and burying. Information afterward received was that one hundred and fifty of the cattle sent to New York died before they arrived there, and the rest were sent to the rendering tanks.

Colonel Sullivan, of Twin Grove, Vermillion County, Illinois, purchased five hundred Texan steers at Cairo, on the 24th of May. They remained healthy, but communicated the disease to forty Illinois steers and twenty heifers and cows. The disease appeared at Twin Grove on Tuesday, the 28th of July. Of the Texan steers three have died as the result of accident. The next group of southern cattle which come under special observation was that of J. A. Harris, near Champaign. He had eighty-five head of southern cattle, purchased last fall. There were with them thirty-eight Illinois steers, and this herd of one hundred and twenty-three had grazed together the entire season. On the 15th of July they were placed on pasture over which a herd of Texans had been driven on the 15th of June. On the 3d of August the Illinois cattle began to die; and, in four days, twenty out of the thirty-eight were buried. The eighty-five southern cattle remained in perfect health.

This special immunity of the cattle imported from the South indicated that they had overcome the influences which operate, however mildly, to the prejudice of their health in the South.

On the 13th of August we visited Hickory Grove, near Oxford, Indiana. There were at that place one thousand animals, which had been imported in the fall of 1867, and had caused no disease either in transit or on the farm. On the 1st of June, 1868, two hundred and sixteen head were purchased, which came from New Orleans and Memphis; and, on the 12th of July and the 8th of August, two separate droves of one thousand head were taken on the farm from Tolono. The condition of the whole of this stock was as perfect as any grazier could desire. Many of them were quite fit for the butcher; and those purchased last were in a thriving condition. The last two droves communicated disease on their trail; but, being by themselves at Hickory Grove, had no opportunity of inflicting any damage.

At Parish Grove, adjoining the last-named farm, a herd of about five hundred Texan cattle had just been imported from Tolono. It was said that the cattle, on their way from Paxton to Hickory Grove, in July, referred to above, had crossed the prairie in which the Parish Grove, Illinois, cattle, numbering five hundred, had grazed. Within seven or eight days after the last herd of five hundred cattle had reached Parish Grove from Tolono, the Illinois cattle began to die. Fifteen car loads of these had just been sent by rail to Chicago; and, of the remaining number, few survived. I inspected four sick steers, and it was evident that the malady would destroy nearly all the Illinois stock. On an adjoining farm Mr. Edward Sumner had nearly one thousand head of northern cattle, among which the disease had appeared.

On the 14th of August we visited Mr. Joseph Heath's farm, near Oxford, Indiana, and found there one thousand one hundred Texan cattle which had been purchased at New Orleans and Tolono. These had communicated disease over the road they had passed, and Mr. Heath's native stock, numbering seventy or eighty, were dying fast. We examined three alive, and dissected two, showing all the indications of splenic fever.

On the next day, at Reynolds, we visited a herd of over two hundred Texan steers, which had arrived on the 27th of May; and disease appeared at Reynolds the beginning of June. One car load of the animals was unloaded at Chalmers, and driven upon J. M. Bunnell's pasture, at Reynolds. They remained there only two days; but, five weeks afterward, the disease appeared, and killed the whole of Mr. Bunnell's stock, amounting to about eighteen hundred head. The bulk of the Texan cattle were sent to Kenton's pasture, three miles from Reynolds, where they were mixed with seventy-three head of native cattle. Of these, at the time of our visit, from fifty-five to sixty had already died, and others were sick. Cattle on the west side of the track at Reynolds were safe; but cattle east, between the station and Kenton's pasture, had died.

It is worthy of special mention here that, for the first time, the transportation of Texan cattle was established in 1868 from New Orleans, by steamboats up the Mississippi to Cairo; and thence, via the Illinois Central road, to the pastures of Illinois and Indiana, having heretofore been sent, since the war, from New Orleans up the Mississippi to Louisville, Kentucky, with the same results as at Cairo. The first lot of Texan cattle was landed at Cairo on the 23d day of April; and between that time and the 1st of August, when the railway peremptorily refused to transport any more stock, about sixteen thousand animals passed from the South on that route. At Cairo the splenic fever appeared about the end of May, or beginning of June; at Farina early in July; at Tolono on the 20th of July; and thence, at later periods, usually dating five weeks from the time the Texan cattle were driven upon the roads and pastures, where disease afterward appeared. The majority of the cattle, amounting probably to ten thousand, were handled by the railroad people at Tolono; and Mr. Charles Troyford, of that place, who had lost forty-eight out of ninety-eight Illinois cattle by the disease, at the time of our visit, informed me that he had not seen a single Texan steer diseased, out of the whole ten thousand, the feeding, driving, and delivering of which he had personally superintended.

From the commencement of my inquiries I had considered it highly probable that cases of splenic fever would be found even among southern stock; and rewards were offered, at Tolono and elsewhere, to any one who would indicate cases alive or dead. Considering that, wherever we traveled, the people whose stock had been destroyed were anxious to furnish us the positive proof, if such could be obtained, it is remarkable that not a single case was brought to our notice.

I returned to Chicago, and again had occasion to inspect both Texan and Illinois cattle in the slaughter-houses; and having, by that time, ascertained the means whereby even the latent forms of the disease might be discovered after death, I had no difficulty in tracing lesions in steers reputed healthy, and slaughtered for human food. This information I communicated at once to Dr. Rauch, medical officer of health of the city of Chicago, who invited me to address a meeting of the board of health, on Tuesday, the 18th of August; and, as what I then stated is of material moment in the history of developments made by me on this subject, I do not hesitate to transcribe, from the short-hand writer's notes, the following passages:

I was called upon, a fortnight ago, to reply to the question whether, if any of the flesh of the sick animals happened to be sold, it was probable that human beings might suffer? I unhesitatingly asserted then what I repeat now that the meat is not poisonous, and is incapable of injuring human beings. To that opinion I adhere.

If I should be asked what regulations should be made by city authorities, in relation to the traffic in diseased meat, I have simply to declare what I have said for many years past, viz., that it is impossible to draw a line between health and disease, except as the two conditions are known to medical men; and, notwithstanding the apparent disadvantages of condemning more meat than there is any necessity for, it is essential that a sanitary officer should be supported, on the broad general principle that a diseased animal is an animal unfit for human consumption.

The danger of an abundant supply of animal food, the produce of animals affected with Texan fever, has almost passed. Some farmers and shippers have learned that it is not safe to send stock to such markets as these, and the action of this, as of other boards of health, has no doubt been already beneficial.

But any system of inspection now to be adopted must almost inevitably fail, if directed mainly to the condition of live stock at the Union stock yards.

It is in the slaughter-houses that a ready means of ascertaining the real condition of cattle can be secured; and the recognition of the Texan fever rests in the examination specially of the spleen, which is much increased in size, sometimes before animals show any external signs of sickness. A medical inspector would likewise detect blood extravasations in the internal organs, ulcerations of the stomach, and, as the disease advanced, bloody urine; but the most satisfactory sign, for the purpose of meat inspections, is the condition of the spleen. The flesh of animals slaughtered, when affected, shows no signs of morbid change, so that it is essential to examine the internal organs in order to draw conclusions as to the condition of any carcass.

On the 20th of August we left for St. Louis, Kansas City, and Abilene. We met with cases of splenic fever in the first-named city; but, from the manner in which the Texan droves are segregated while awaiting their transfer to the cars at Kansas City, the indigenous stock in that district was found healthy. At Junction City we found a herd of sick cattle which had crossed the Texan trails at Salina, having been used in the West for draught purposes. We proceeded to Abilene, the center of the shipment of Texan steers.

It had been confidently asserted that the stock, driven by easy stages from Texas through the Indian Territory and unsettled lands of Kansas, had communicated no disease ; but this we found erroneous, as the indigenous stock around Abilene had suffered, and herds had just been seized, from which we had ample opportunities for examining such cattle, both alive and dead.

We learned at the Drover's Cottage that, scattered along the creeks at intervals of four or five miles, large herds of Texan cattle could be seen over a distance of forty or fifty miles. This led us to undertake a journey across the prairie, as far down as Big Turkey Creek, near the Little Arkansas River ; and it is but just that publicity be given to the anxiety manifested, and assistance tendered us in our investigations, on the part of the gentlemen engaged in the southern trade. Major Call, who owned two of the largest herds, zealously undertook the necessary arrangements for our journey ; and, by this means, we had an opportunity of examining carefully over fifteen thousand head of cattle, which had arrived at their destination during the months of July and August.

In general terms, it may be said that the whole stock indicated how much better it is for cattle to be driven slowly, where there is an ample supply of food and water, than it is to transport them, even for two or three days, in railway cars. There was a difference in the herds according to the speed they had maintained on the journey, and it appears that an average walk of eight miles daily, over the whole journey, is as much as the cattle should be subjected to in order to secure improvement rather than deterioration in their condition. The best drovers avoid shouting and the stock-whip; and much depends on the intelligence of the person who superintends a herd as to the selection of the best grazing ground and searching for a sufficient supply of water. The creeks, scattered throughout the whole of the prairie lands of Kansas, dry up in summer, and cattle must sometimes be driven thirty or thirty-five miles before water can be found. This is rare; but, under the most careful management, the driving of cattle from Texas to any point on the eastern division of the Union Pacific road at or west of Abilene is attended with some such inconvenience. Nevertheless, wherever proper supervision is exercised that the animals may never be overheated, it is found that they improve in condition, grow stout and hardy, and are in a fit state for slaughter at the end of their journey on foot.

Of the stock we examined, two hundred head of Indian cattle, from the Chickasaw nation, were in pasture five miles from Abilene, and all appeared in very fine condition. The greater part of the remaining stock we inspected was from Northwestern, from Central, and from Eastern Texas.

The only evidence of suffering was, at first, lameness, which in some cases was due to injuries from animals fighting or spraining themselves in getting through difficult places. At times a steer gets lame from the long sharp grass, wounding the skin between the hoof; and at other points, as on Smoky Hill, the stony surface, with angular fragments of iron-stone and other hard and sharp bits of flint, wounds the feet and disables a considerable number of cattle.

On Smoky Hill we found, on the 27th of August, a herd which had been collected, from forty to two hundred miles from the coast, in Southern Texas, between the 1st and the 18th of May. It arrived at Smoky Hill on the 22d of August. Two animals had died on the route; one died after getting lame, and the other refused to eat, was depressed, languid, and passed blood with the excreta. At the time of our visit there were twenty or thirty animals which looked gaunt and weak, but we were told that they were work-oxen in poor condition. One animal was lame and stiff, but was reported as improving in condition. Another had died during the night, and we proceeded to examine its internal organs. It was a dun Texan steer, four years old, that had been stampeded with others the day before, and shortly afterward had succumbed. The body was still warm, and free from all trace of decomposition. The skin and subcutaneous tissues presented no mark of injury or disease. The organs of respiration were healthy. The heart, of normal volume and consistency, was ecchymosed at its apex, and circumscribed blood extravasations dotted the reflection of the pericardium over and around the pulmonary artery. The right cavities of the heart contained a small clot of blood, and the left were empty. The endocardium was of normal color and thickness throughout. The mouth, fauces, pharynx, esophagus, and the first three stomachs were healthy. The fourth, or true stomach, was reddened over its entire mucous surface. The folds at the cardiac end were of a deep red, with numerous petechiæ scattered irregularly over their surface. The petechiæ were usually dark in the center, where the membrane was softening, and of a lighter crimson hue on their circumferences. Many were round, and others of irregular shapes, either from coalescence of several extravasations or the irregular spreading of one original bleeding spot.

The small intestine, of a reddish or purplish hue externally, was the seat of ramified redness, with some petechiæ scattered throughout its whole extent. Peyer's glands were healthy. The ileum was, however, more congested than the duodenum or jejunum. The cæcum, somewhat reddened on its entire mucous surface, was striped with blood extravasations which had occurred along the prominent edges of the mucous folds at its fundus, and there were several well-defined ecchymoses scattered irregularly over the whole lining. The colon was more or less reddened throughout, until near its termination, where it had a natural color. The rectum was not discolored, but near the anus there was a small patch with a thin film of coagulated blood on its unabraded surface, and, when the membrane wrinkled by the action of the sphincter, the free margin of the folds was streaked with interstitial deposit of blood. The spleen, of a dark purplish color, weighed three and a half pounds, and its structure was soft and friable.

The liver was of normal size and color, but the gall bladder appeared thickened from an exudation of yellow serum in the substance of its coats. These appeared three or four times their normal thickness. The small arteries and veins of the mucous membrane were much distended with dark blood, and there was also some capillary congestion. The kidneys were healthy. The bladder was moderately distended by clear-colored urine, but its mucous surface, reddened at the fundus, was dotted with small petechiæ of a vermilion hue at and around the neck of the organ.

Failing to obtain further evidence of splenic fever in this and an adjoining herd from a careful inspection of the animals, I determined on having some of them caught and examined with a self-registering thermometer. Four steers, caught with a lasso, indicated a temperature of 103.4°, 102.4°, 103°, and 104.2°. This indicated a somewhat exalted temperature for animals which to all appearances were in health; and I was fortunate in getting an animal that had been used in a wagon, driven quietly to camp, and then examined. This indicated a temperature of 103° Fahrenheit. My conviction that the lasso would not vary the temperature was thus confirmed, and it is hard to reconcile the observations made with perfect freedom from disease.

The inspections of herds grazed on and near the Santa Fé road, and inquiries among drovers and herders, failed to bring to light any other cases of sickness or death; and the evidence of the suffering of Texan cattle from splenic fever, so far as our observations in Kansas go, rested on the very marked case examined at Smoky Hill, on the high temperature manifested by animals in the undoubtedly infected herd, and on the observations as to the relative weights of spleens in healthy and sick cattle, reported in the foregoing pages.

Notwithstanding, however, the favorable report which can be made regarding the general appearance of southern herds, it is proved by the experiences of past years, and of this, that they disseminate disease among cattle north or west of the Gulf States. The impression was left on my mind, after the first observations of the malady, that the Texan steers might be found to communicate the disease only for a limited time after leaving Texas. There is reason to believe that such is the case, though we found that two months' journey, from Texas to the Union Pacific road, had not sufficed to effect this object. Experiments on this point would be desirable, though expensive, and demanding much time and attention. We were told, however, that the cattle which had induced so much disease at Farina, on being removed to Loda, were placed on lands which brought them in contact with Illinois cattle, and no bad results ensued. Mr. Robert Clark, of Indianola, who has had great experience in driving cattle through Missouri into Illinois, states it as his decided opinion, from repeated observation and inquiries among drovers, that the Texan steers are most dangerous immediately after leaving Texas—and hence the great opposition to their importation into Missouri—but that after they have traveled a long distance they are far less liable to do any mischief. This point is of great importance in relation to means which might be suggested for the prevention of the disease, and it is worthy of note that, without doubt, cattle driven into Kansas, Missouri, or other States, in the summer or autumn of one year, and grazed in such State during the winter, fail to retain any deleterious principle, and can readily be intermixed with any stock during the winter and spring. Texan herds, therefore, do purify themselves; and the point of greatest importance in relation to the traffic in such stock is to establish, without doubt, what length of time is required for such purification, and if means can be adopted to accelerate so desirable a result.

NON-TRANSMISSION OF THE DISEASE BY NORTHERN OR BY WESTERN STOCK.

During the three months last summer many well-marked cases have been seen of communication of splenic fever to Illinois and to Indiana cattle. At first these animals were allowed to die; but, as soon as large herds of grazing stock were attacked, an effort was made to save what could be saved by shipping and sending to eastern markets. Cattle trucks have thus been filled in large numbers with infected steers, which died or were slaughtered and committed to the rendering tanks. But not a single case has transpired to show that these animals have induced, directly or indirectly, any disease in the stock of Eastern States. How different from this is the working of a contagious disease! Had any malady of the nature of rinderpest or lung plague been favored in its transmission as this one has been, the farmers of Ohio, Pennsylvania, and New York would have bitter experiences to record, similar to those of the much-injured Illinois farmers. That which is obvious in relation to the progress of the disease through the country is also apparent in any district invaded by the disease. None but southern cattle communicate disease, and they rarely, if ever, do any mischief through stock yards and cattle cars, and only by feeding on pastures over which other stock afterward roams and feeds. No case has been brought forward to show that a railway car loaded with Texan cattle will communicate disease to other stock afterward placed in such car. Numerous instances of this description would have come to light had we been dealing with what is commonly understood as a contagious plague.

COMMUNICATION IN STOCK YARDS.

The earlier reports from Cairo stated that the cows in that city had caught the disease from the Texan cattle in steamboat and railway pens; indeed we were informed that many of the Cairo cows had been in the habit of wandering not only near, but into the cattle pens, and eating the hay the Texan cattle left behind them. This is the only observation that would give color to the view that hay might be a means of propagating the disorder. But we learned at Cairo that Texan cattle had been loose on the common within the levee, and some stray animals had remained for some days on the very prairie which is the only pasture for the cattle of the town. It was impossible to find a single case which afforded reliable grounds for supposing that the only chance for contamination was in the cattle pens of Cairo.

It may be suggested that eating hay which has been poisoned must be as bad as eating prairie grass over which Texan steers have wandered. But there is this difference, that cattle are not apt to eat hay on which the excretions of other cattle have been deposited, and would attempt to pick up only the clean fodder. On grass lands the growth of grass and the washings of the pasture by rains clear off the filth, though they may often leave adhering deleterious principles, which are swallowed. A good illustration of this is afforded by the dissemination of the tapeworm, the ova of which are distributed with the excrement of dogs and other carnivora; and, while the fæces are washed away, the ova adhere to blades of grass, and develop in the systems of cattle and sheep.

I would not wish it to be understood that I consider it improbable that hay may, under some circumstances, be poisoned by Texan steers, and afterward give disease to other stock; but, as yet, no facts prove that such has been the case. On the contrary, the most reliable, though accidental, experiment is afforded by cattle fed by Mr. Sherman, of the Union stock yards, Chicago. He has thirty-five cows which have grazed all summer close up to the cattle pens where thousands of southern steers have been inclosed, without intermission. Of these cows the majority have been purchased out of the yards at different times, some last spring, and some have been in the cattle pens with Texan droves. On the occasion of my visit to the yards I have also seen a Texan calf placed with the cows; and yet no animals could be in better health than those in Mr. Sherman's dairy.

This suggestive case proves, in the most incontrovertible manner, that western cattle can be mingled with Texans in stock yards, can graze side by side with them if separated by a fence, and that cows can suckle the Texan calves, without becoming affected with splenic fever. I am not prepared to say that any of the cows purchased by Mr. Sherman were fed on hay in the yards while they were in the same pen with the Texan cattle, but in all probability they were.

This point has acquired some importance since the British government prohibited the importation of hay from the United States. Acting on the side of prudence, with the necessarily limited information that could have been at its disposal when that order was issued, and in view of the losses by contagious diseases which have become chronic in the British Isles, it was in all probability the only course that could have been adopted. But it may be well to state, for future guidance, that it is not possible for bales of hay shipped to Europe to carry the splenic fever. For years to come the open prairie lands on which we have witnessed the dissemination of the disease cannot yield hay for the markets of America; that hay is produced in the Eastern and the Western States, in localities where Texan cattle never have been and probably never will be grazed; and, moreover, in the fields mown for hay cattle are not pastured.

The larger tracts of country on which southern droves feed are likely to remain unsettled for years to come, and neither scythe nor sickle has ever reached them. England is as likely to get rinderpest as splenic fever from America; and the only way in which it might see the latter would be by transporting herds of Gulf-coast cattle across the Atlantic, to feed on British pasture lands, side by side with British stock.

SEASONS.

The influence of seasons on the development of splenic fever is most marked. A few nipping frosts check its ravages anywhere and everywhere. In Missouri and Kansas it has broken out as late as October and December. Thus, in the report of the Department of Agriculture for 1867, it was stated from Christian County, Missouri, that, in 1866, "Spanish fever was introduced into the western part of this county by droves of Texas cattle, passing in October." From Woodson County, Kansas, it was reported that the "Spanish fever broke out in December, and raged until the 1st of January, *when the cold weather set in and checked it.*" The droves of Texan cattle, which communicate the disease during the summer, leave Texas by the close of winter; so that the Texan winter in no way interferes with the development of that state of system which renders Texan herds so dangerous.

In a case reported, too vaguely to be of real value, in the report of the Department of Agriculture for 1867, we are informed that, in Douglas County, Kansas, "the Spanish fever, or *something similar*, made its appearance about the 1st of February, among a few cattle that were driven from the South." In all probability this was not splenic fever; and the reporter adds: "I think the severity of the winter caused the greatest loss; about one-third of all the cattle brought from the south have died." It is certain that, in States north of Missouri and Kansas, splenic fever prevails in the months of June, July, August, and September. Straggling cases may occur in May and in October; but the great losses are observed during the four months just named.

Does this depend on the influence of heat and drought, or on the accidental circumstances that Texan cattle have been mainly distributed over the country during these months? The second is the main reason; but it is impossible for me to reconcile many observations which I have made with the idea that heat does not favor the development of the disorder. It is not sufficient to name it, but it is asserted by practical men that Texan cattle can be handled most safely when the summers are wet and cool. The wet may wash the grasses, but the cold seems to favor a constitutional resistance to the attacks of the disease. A record of the cases which demonstrate that Texan cattle can be freely placed with western stock in winter would fill a volume. At Broadlands, Hickory Grove, near Champaign, and in a host of other places, southern cattle, purchased last fall, were placed with indigenous stock, have remained with them ever since, and have induced no disease. This is very generally known and admitted. A reporter from Cedar County, Missouri, writing in 1866, said: "It is thought that our cattle would not take the disease in the winter season, but this may be only conjecture, as no large droves have yet been driven here from the South in the winter." Of late years, however, there has been an effort to drive from Texas for the October and November markets, and we have not heard of a single case where stock-drivers, up at that time, had done any mischief in Illinois or Indiana. Nipping frosts may and do kill the disease, by destroying the pasture, and compelling people to feed their cattle. This completely arrests that method of transmission, which I believe to be the main or only one. As soon as western stock is removed from the pasture on which Texan cattle have been fed, it is safe; and this is an unanswerable argument in favor of the views I have promulgated since the time of my first observations. It is not the breath, nor the saliva, nor cutaneous emanations which are charged with the poisonous principle, but the fæces and the urine.

It has, however, been very generally remarked that Texan cattle are covered with the tick. I owe to the kindness of C. V. Riley, esq., State entomologist of Missouri, a drawing of the tick as found on Texan cattle. In the annexed engravings are an upper and an under view. As the legs do not alter in size in proportion to the body, a view has been given of a smaller specimen between the two. This tick belongs to the Class *Arachnidæ*, Order *Trachearicæ*, and Family *Ixodidæ*. It has eight fine, jointed legs. It is not confined to cattle in the South, and is seen in many woodland pastures of the United States. For convenience, and to distinguish this species from *Ixodes reticulatus*, I propose to call it *Ixodes indentatus*, from the peculiar indentations on the body and absence of stripes. These ticks fasten on the bodies of native cattle, and breed. The young ticks are distributed in myriads on the grasses, and it has been supposed that the grasses are thus poisoned.*

NAT. SIZE

The "tick theory" has acquired quite a renown during the past summer; but a little thought should have satisfied any one of the absurdity of the idea.

1st. Ticks are not easily fenced on a piece of land by a wood fence, as cattle are. A wood fence sufficiently isolates cattle to prevent splenic fever.

2d. We have seen Texan cattle both alive and dead, and also dead western, quite free from these parasites. There has been no relation whatever between the abundance

---

* The following remarks on the *Ixodes bovis* are from C. V. Riley, St. Louis, Missouri:

Ixodes bovis, (Riley.)—A reddish, coriaceous, flattened species, with the body oblong-oval, contracted just behind the middle, and with two longitudinal impressions above this contraction, and three below it, more especially visible in the dried specimen. Head short and broad, not spined behind, with two deep, round pits. Palpi and beak together unusually short, the palpi being slender. Labium short and broad, densely spined beneath. Mandibles smooth above, with terminal hooks. Thoracic shield distinct, one-third longer than wide, smooth and polished; convex, with the lyrate medial convexity very distinct. Legs long and slender, pale testaceous red; coxæ not spined. Length of body, .15 of an inch; width, .09 of an inch. Missouri Coll., C. V. Riley.

This is the cattle tick of the Western States. Several hundred specimens, in different stages of growth, have also been received from Pulvon, west coast of Nicaragua, taken from the horned cattle, and on a species of *Dasyprocta*, by Mr. J. McNeil. They preserve the elongated flattened form, with the body contracted behind the middle, by which this species may be easily identified. The largest specimens measure .50 by .30 of an inch. When gorged with blood they are nearly as thick through as they are broad. In the freshly-hatched hexapodous young, and the young in the next stage of growth, the thoracic shield is one-third the size of the whole body, which is pale yellowish, with very distinct crenulations on the hinder edge. The fourth pair of legs is added apparently at the first moult. It is called "*garapata*" by the inhabitants of Nicaragua.

of ticks and the severity of the disorder. The malady has been quite as malignant where few or no ticks occurred.

3d. We have been asked to watch for the irritating parasites in the stomach and intestines, and it was believed that they acted mechanically; but we have never seen a tick during any stage of its development in the alimentary canal.

4th. The tick is not confined to Gulf-coast cattle, which we know communicate this disease; but it is met with in various parts of the States where cattle are reared that never cause splenic fever. Why should the ticks not communicate the malady from western cattle to other cattle, if they can induce it by crawling from the Texan to western stock? Many erroneous views as to the origin and propagation of the Texan fever may be set at rest by showing what it is not; and for this reason I shall proceed to discuss the analogies and differences between splenic fever and other disorders afflicting cattle, and even the human species.

THE NATURE OF SPLENIC FEVER.

The history of splenic fever would seem to indicate its complete isolation from every disease, and especially every form of plague hitherto described. But a careful study of its progress and development, with the light afforded by a knowledge of other cattle diseases, enables us to demonstrate points of great resemblance, and indeed of identity with maladies which annually recur in various parts of the world. It is, moreover, important, in a practical point of view, to show how it differs from maladies which spread from country to country, and from the east westward, devastating broad tracts of land, and calling for the most decisive and energetic means for their suppression.

Splenic fever is not an epizoötic, properly so called. It is not propagated through time and space by contagion. The true plague of animals, or epizoötics, such as the Russian murrain or rinderpest, the lung plague or contagious pleuropneumonia of cattle, the foot and the mouth diseases of all warm-blooded animals, variolous fevers, hydrophobia, and the like, spread by direct or indirect transference of an animal poison, a virus, from sick to healthy animals; and in the Old World the sick, as a rule, indicate, by very manifest outward symptoms, the disease under which they are laboring. The poisons take effect without regard to seasons, and are alike developed in the systems of sick animals. It is not contact between Texan and southern or western cattle that induces the malady; and, so far as recorded observations and my own inquiries at present extend, the animals contaminated by feeding on Texan trails have not in a single instance propagated the disease to other animals. Indeed, I have not met with one instance where sucking calves have caught the affection from their dams, or from other cows which they have been made to suck. Many cases have come under my observation of cattle in Illinois, Indiana, and elsewhere, coming in contact with Texan cattle through a fence, by drinking of the same water, and even being housed in sheds with sick natives, and yet escaping the disease. We must, therefore, distinguish it from the contagious maladies alluded to, and refer it to another group.

Splenic fever is an enzoötic. It originates in various parts of the Gulf States. Florida cattle driven north are as dangerous as Texans, deriving the same deleterious properties from the soil on which they are reared, and in all probability the vegetation on which they feed. In the South, splenic fever is distinctly indigenous, and, so far as

Texas is concerned, I have satisfied myself that the disease is universally prevalent in that State.

Its complete manifestation is readily witnessed in States north of 34° north latitude. Here the malady can no longer be declared indigenous; but there are numerous instances which can be cited of purely enzoötic diseases spreading a certain distance by contagion. Two of the most marked instances are furnished us by the malignant anthrax of Russia, better known as the Siberian boil plague, and the milk-sickness, or trembles, of the United States.

The milk-sickness is due to cattle feeding on low woodland pastures, where certain poisonous plants abound. It originates only in a very limited area of country; but the animals may travel, and their flesh and milk will communicate the disease when eaten by other animals, and even by human beings. Trembles is, therefore, an enzoötic disorder, capable of being primarily produced only in definite localities; but the poison which contaminates the food is capable, through that food, of attacking a second and a third animal, or as many as partake of it. There is another striking similarity between the course of milk-sickness and splenic fever. The animal food, poisoned in the disease-producing district, may show no signs of disease, unless subjected to a definite existing cause, such as being driven or frightened. In classifying trembles among the diseases of the lower animals we should undoubtedly place it among the effects of vegetable poisons, and study it as a very remarkable toxicological phenomenon. I should be disposed to deal with splenic fever in the same way. Southern cattle, accustomed to feed on certain pastures in Florida and Texas, thrive, and their systems become charged with principles which are thrown off in the excretions for many weeks, and probably two or three months after they leave their native soil. Herds of these animals necessarily deposit a large amount of whatever they excrete; and thus pastures are contaminated, the grasses of which prove deadly poisons to healthy and susceptible cattle. It is certain that the feeding of cattle on the land over which Texan animals have passed is the ordinary, and probably invariable, cause of splenic fever.

The circumstances under which the disease manifests itself tend to favor the view that it is allied to the numerous forms of anthrax fever which prevail very generally in hot countries, and usually in low lands. These diseases, it is true, are scattered throughout the temperate zone; but their development depends upon heat, wherever it appears on stiff, retentive soils, and in some sandy but fertile lands their ravages are especially witnessed during wet seasons. Heat favors and creates the manifestations of splenic fever. The malady springs in a warm country, and is propagated most readily with heat and drought. It is indigenous where vegetation is rank, and the soil is charged with an excess of organic life, which, for want of direction, tends to waste and mischief. During the hot summer months anthrax or carbuncular fevers force the stock-owners of Southern Europe to seek the hills with their flocks of sheep and goats; and to disregard this injunction involves, not only the death of their animals, but the destruction of other warm-blooded creatures, including man himself, by malignant pustule. To this category undoubtedly belonged the various pests of old; and, by traveling northward, the virulence of these diseases, the development of the anthrax poison, and the propagation, under any circumstances, by contagion, diminish by simple and imperceptible gradations, and ultimately cease. The black-water of Great Britain and of America is one of the forms of this deadly anthrax, which, even so far north as Aberdeen, in Scotland, has been communicated, by the flesh eaten, to a whole family of human beings, who succumbed from malignant pustule. The Siberian boil plague is one of the typical forms of anthrax, and its history in relation to splenic fever is interesting, inasmuch as it occurs in a vast country, where stock is driven in masses from the east westward; and an opportunity is thus afforded for contagious transmission which is not often witnessed elsewhere.

Many so-called blood diseases, all enzoötic in their nature, and capable of limited transmission, are classified by the ablest veterinary pathologists of France and Germany with the anthrax fevers. In Germany the most destructive forms are so often characterized by enlargement, softening, and even rupture of the spleen, that the forms of anthrax are included under a generic term, "*Milzbrand.*" The condition of the spleen in splenic fever would induce many a pathologist to classify it unhesitatingly among the forms of "*Milzbrand.*" But there is a line of demarcation which, in my opinion, can be fairly established.

Southern cattle capable of propagating this disease usually start from their homes in the winter or early in spring. They do not die, as is always the case where anthrax originates, in large numbers, so as to attract decided attention, on the lands which foster the development of that subtle poison they carry northward. Their systems are not charged with an inoculable virus, such as the anthrax poison always is, when there is a sufficient heat to develop it. The heat during the summer of 1868 was higher than is usually required for the production of the anthrax virus. The best and fattest animals in a herd are the first to die of anthrax, and death is sudden and unexpected; an animal in the apparent enjoyment of health at night is dead before morning, or seen well in the morning and found dead by noon. French authors speak of their dying "*d'une apoplexie fulminante.*" Had the cattle which have been slaughtered as human food during the past summer, in Chicago and elsewhere, been tainted with a true anthrax, as they have been with splenic fever, medical reports would have developed many instances of malignant pustule in man, which they have not done. With the thermometer at 108° or 110° such a result would have been inevitable.

There is one disease in Europe, which prevails in various parts of the United Kingdom, and is common on woodland pastures during the spring and summer months, which presents most of the characteristics of splenic fever. It is the black-water, enzoötic hæmaturia, or bloody urine, which on the banks of the Dee, in Aberdeenshire, is termed the "darn." The Germans call it "*Bluthamen,*" "*Rothharnen,*" "*Maiseuche,*" "*Weidebruch,*" and speak of it as an enzoötic occurring in spring and summer among "grazing" cattle. It is described as characterized by bloody urine and weakness of gait in hind quarters, associated in some cases with intense fever, and in others with the weakness of anæmia, or the bloodless state. There is sometimes discharge of a little blood with the fæces. There is occasionally diarrhœa, but more commonly the excrement is nearly of normal character. After death the bladder is found distended with bloody urine; the kidneys are dark colored, and their pelves distended with similar urine; the blood is dark, the liver usually light colored, but the spleen congested, and of a dark color, and there are blood extravasations on the mucous and the serous membrane. Indeed, Spinola speaks of the fourth stomach, and even the intestines, as being much inflamed. It is important and instructive to notice the circumstances under which enzoötic hæmaturia occurs in Great Britain, and other parts of Europe. Since the introduction of turnip husbandry, a malady has arisen among cows, after calving, which is usually known as "red water," due to the

16

condition of turnips grown on ill-drained lands. In 1856 I was engaged in investigating the diseases of Aberdeenshire and Kincardineshire, for the Highland and Agricultural Society of Scotland. I then distinctly ascertained that tracts of land of the same character, and adjoining one another, grew turnips capable or incapable of producing the disease, according to the state of drainage. Indeed, farmers whose lands were well cultivated were sometimes surrounded by poor people, growing turnips on small plats, or so-called "pendules," of the same lands, but without the advantages of good drainage. The farmers' cows were healthy; whereas those fed on the poor people's crops suffered from "red water," after calving. This is a distinct form of enzoötic hæmaturia, due apparently to some modifications in the character of a root, grown on damp and retentive soils. It is, therefore, proved that the conditions of soil may injuriously affect domestic animals, and produce a definite and distinct disease, through foods that are usually wholesome. But the enzoötic hæmaturia which does not depend on a root crop, and which attacks steers, heifers, pregnant and even calving cows, has usually been ascribed, like the milk-sickness of Illinois, to some definite poison; and the singular manifestations of the disease, as it travels from Texas, would give weight to such an opinion. The "darn" of Aberdeenshire was supposed at one time to be due to a harmless, wild anemone, and afterward to the "darnel grass," or *Lolium temulentum;* but the opinion which I formed on the spot was, that the cattle died from eating the young shoots of oaks, and other astringent plants.

Medical men have had their attention directed to this subject during the past summer; and, in some instances, they have referred to it as a malignant typhus or typhoid fever. It is widely different from both in its origin, development, and progress. The morbid lesions, so far as blood extravasations are concerned, might suggest an analogy to typhus; but this is not the only disease associated with blood changes and petechiæ. Who ever saw a spontaneous development of malignant typhus on the healthy, open prairies of this country, even in man? If it be typhus, how is it that it is not contagious, and certainly not infectious? If typhus, why do not the sick western steers communicate it as readily as the Texan cattle? It is assuredly neither typhus nor typhoid fever; and its origin, in the causes which we have reason to believe operate most in its production in the South, approaches ague more closely than any other disorder. Splenic fever is not an intermittent or remittent disease; but it probably manifests itself spontaneously in districts, such as are commonly invaded by malaria, and this is what we see constantly in relation to the enzoötic diseases of animals, and especially those in which the spleen has a tendency to congestion, hemorrhage, and enlargement.

There is really no analogue in man, so far as my observations extend; and, in stating that the circumstances of its development resemble the reputed results of malarious intoxication, it must not be thought that I believe in the commonly accepted, but very vague and unsatisfactory, notions as to the nature of malaria. The conclusions, therefore, which I am disposed to draw from all the facts and arguments adduced in relation to the causes and nature of splenic fever, are—

1. That southern cattle, especially from the Gulf coast, are affected with a latent or an apparent form of the disease.

2. That they become affected in consequence of the nature of the soil and vegetation on which they are fed, and the water which they drink.

3. That their systems are charged with poisonous principles which accumulate in the bodies of acclimatized animals that enjoy an immunity.

4. That southern cattle may be driven so as to improve in condition; and yet for some weeks, and probably not less than three months, continue to excrete the deleterious principles which poison the cattle of the States through which the herds are driven on their way north or west.

5. That all breeds of cattle in States north of those on the Gulf coast, without regard to age or sex, if they feed on grass contaminated by southern droves, are attacked by the splenic fever; that the disease may be, but is very rarely, propagated through the feeding of hay.

6. That the disease occurs mainly during the hot months of summer and autumn, and never after the wild grasses have been killed by frosts, until the mild weather in spring returns; that then the grasses are healthy, and continue healthy, unless fresh droves of Texan or of Florida cattle are driven over the land.

7. That heat and drought aggravate the disease in individual animals.

8. That there is not the slightest foundation for the view that the ticks disseminate the disease.

9. That the splenic fever does not belong to that vast and deadly group of purely contagious and infectious diseases of which the rinderpest, the lung plague, and eruptive fevers are typical.

10. That it is an enzoötic, due to local influences, capable of only a limited spread, and analogous to or identical with the "black water" of various parts of Europe.

11. That, however warm the weather may be, cattle affected with splenic fever have not developed in their systems any poison like the anthrax poison; and that the flesh, blood, and other tissues of animals are incapable of inducing any disease in man or animals.

12. That splenic fever is not malignant typhus or typhoid fever. That it has no analogue among human diseases, but is, however, developed under conditions which prevail where the so-called malaria injuriously affects the human health.

CURATIVE TREATMENT.

The great majority of epizoötic and enzoötic diseases never can, and never will, be arrested by the medical treatment of the sick. Even the benignant epizoötic aphthæ, which is rarely fatal, spreads rapidly through a country; and, in the long run, owing to the certainty and rapidity of its transmission, entails more loss than some of the most fatal diseases. Splenic fever may be classed among the incurable maladies, inasmuch as we know of no antidote to the mysterious poison inducing it; and, while we can alleviate some of the sufferings of the affected cattle, a very trifling measure of success attends the most assiduous nursing and medication. Bleeding has been, in some parts, a favorite remedy; and I have known one animal recover either in consequence or in spite of the remedy. Purgatives have been freely and fairly tried, with good result in very few instances, and with depressing and killing influences in many more.

The "red water" of cows in Scotland is often cured by opiates, which check the discharge of blood; and with alcoholic stimulants in moderation, with the free use of mucilaginous drinks. I have tried the same treatment in splenic fever, with little or no success.

Page after page might be filled with notes on the administration of nitrate and of chlorate of potash, iodide of potassium, quinine, salts of iron, sesquicarbonate of ammonia, Epsom or Glauber's salts, sulphur, ginger, calomel, soap, and oil; and even guano from the goose cote has been said "frequently to effect a cure, given in doses of one quart, until a thorough evacuation is produced." A reporter from Woodson County, Kansas, says this is "a sovereign and unfailing remedy for the dry murrain." None of these agents (and some have been extolled as specific) have affected the steady progress and fatality of the disease.

Shelter, protection from flies, linseed or flaxseed tea, friction of the limbs, and injections, are humane, and, to a trifling extent, useful expedients. I have seen cows return to nearly their full quantity of milk on such treatment, with the aid of half-ounce doses of sulphuric ether, in four ounces of the solution of the acetate of ammonia and a quart of water, given thrice daily. Relief has been afforded by giving an ounce of tincture of opium for the first day or two; but to enter further into the history of experiments on this point is to recount a history of failures such as the world is accustomed to, in speaking of the medical treatment of human cholera and small-pox, or rinderpest and the deadly forms of anthrax in cattle.

THE PREVENTION OF SPLENIC FEVER.

The main object of the investigation which has brought to light the facts noted in the foregoing pages, has been the discovery of means whereby the direct and the indirect losses sustained for several years past, but especially in 1868, may not again harass American farmers, and injure the traders in Texan cattle. Hitherto the only measures suggested, and very partially adopted, have consisted either in prohibiting the importation of southern cattle into certain States, or portions of States; and, in one instance, in preventing their introduction only during the summer months.

Stringent laws have failed to avert the most disastrous and wide-spread losses; and while on the one hand persons interested in the Texan trade have justified their inattention to legal restrictions by declaring them one and all unconstitutional, instances have not been wanting of mob law adopting its own expedients. Dealers and farmers who owned southern cattle have been threatened—they have been pounced on in the dead of night, that they might surely be found in their homes—and there and then they have been requested to attend meetings of indignant and impoverished neighbors. Lastly, the stampeding and shooting of Texan cattle, whenever and wherever they might be seen, have been the mild alternatives which seem to have satisfied a thirst for revenge; or, in some instances, human life would, in all probability, have been sacrificed. Indeed, threats have been numerous, and heavy bonds or the actual payment of cash for dead, dying, and infected stock, have alone saved the persons of traders, commission agents, and farmers, who happened to have any dealings in long-horned beeves. The prevention of splenic fever, therefore, implies, in many instances, the prevention of lawlessness and the preservation of the public peace.

We have seen that splenic fever is a malady indigenous to Texas. It is there an enzoötic, and whatever may be the plant or plants inducing the disorder, it is indisputable that the conditions exist there which are rife in all parts of the world where enzoötic blood diseases, fatal parasitic maladies, and periodic outbreaks of mysterious affections, which annihilate herds and even depopulate districts, occasionally prevail.

The extirpation of noxious plants, the purification of streams, the equalization of the balance between animal and plant life on a given extent of soil, are agricultural problems which cannot, in Texas, be solved for generations to come. Thorough drainage, breaking up pasture lands, fencing off low wood lands which are crammed with a disease-producing vegetation, are measures neglected even in Great Britain, and will tax the industry and capital of many of the sons and grandsons of the present race of farmers, north, east, and west, in the United States; how much longer, then, must the exuberant soil of Texas wait for the hands and the brains engaged in making two blades of grass grow where there was once but one? Fertile, and reeking with the decay of excess as it is, we cannot anticipate the time when it will be so densely peopled as to secure attention to definite sanitary laws which, if not impracticable under the circumstances, might be applied for the prevention of splenic fever in Texas, Florida, or wherever else it may be discovered to exist as an enzoötic.

The question next presents itself whether the trade in live cattle between the South and the North is to be permitted. Its annihilation would effectually prevent such outbreaks, as I have had occasion to study; but such an expedient, though it might commend itself to some short-sighted farmers in Illinois and Indiana, would not be tolerated. It is true that, notwithstanding all the difficulties experienced in the past, wherever attempts have been made in the South to slaughter, and consign their animal produce to northern and other markets, the time will arrive, in all probability, for some such outlet to be secured. But, with beef at twenty, twenty-five, or thirty cents per pound in Philadelphia, New York, and Boston, with the packing interests of Chicago, and the demands of Europe, especially in times of war, it is idle to contemplate the fencing in of steers, which may be purchased by thousands and tens of thousands at eight or ten dollars a head in Texas. The prairie lands of States favored by geographical position, and nearest the great centers of consumption for all animal produce, cannot be utilized for some time to come without the advantage of supplying food for stock bred at a little cost elsewhere.

To suit a northern trade the Texan will doubtless attend to crossing his cattle with short-horned blood; and this, while it will encourage the purchase of such animals by the farmers of Missouri, Illinois, and Indiana, will in no way tend to modify splenic fever. Fortunately for all, it is possible to establish rules which, if intelligently attended to, will effectually protect any susceptible animal from destruction by contact with members of its own race from the Gulf States. All these rules must aim at a complete isolation for a sufficient period of time.

With our present state of knowledge it is imperative that we should deal with all cattle from the Gulf States in the same way. But numerous observations warrant us in believing that a careful study of the geographical distributions of the splenic fever in the South would indicate that there are broad tracts of land in Texas where the stock is free from all contamination, and may, in all probability, be freely mixed with cattle in any part of the States. It would not be safe to indicate the regions supposed to be healthy, as they may be more or less intersected by plague-stricken spots; but it is safe to assert that the most decided and best ascertained manifestations of disease, and capability of communicating disease, have been observed among herds derived from and near the Gulf coast.

That the hardships and privations to which Gulf-coast cattle are subjected in being transported to New Orleans, and up the Mississippi in steamers, may act as existing causes to the full development of fatal symptoms is probable; but such and similar prejudicial influences do not, and cannot, engender the disease. They may facilitate intelligent observations; and a competent veterinarian, inspecting the dead and injured cattle taken into the port of New Orleans or landed at Cairo, might add very largely to our store of knowledge on this and allied subjects. Such inspection might be of value in securing the isolation of badly infected herds, inasmuch as ordinary observers have noticed, where opportunities were afforded for seeing many herds from the Gulf coast, that some were apparently sound, while others numbered many sick and dying animals. Wherever such cattle are landed there should be a sufficient amount of closely-fenced land, beyond which the cattle should not be permitted to pass on foot. They might be transported thence by rail, but only to definite points for immediate slaughter, or to certain stations on railroad lands, where they can be placed alone, and without coming in contact with other cattle.

There are serious impediments in the way which may prevent the adoption of the last suggestion; but, having stated the principles which should govern legislation in this matter, we must leave the practical working of any well-matured scheme to those whose interests are at stake. Thus, if the stock taken from the cars at Tolono (and which destroyed almost every cow owned there) had been unloaded by the inhabitants in inclosed yards at a distance from the town, and then driven through a fenced road on which no other cattle were permitted to pass, it would have caused no loss. It must be left to local authorities to state whence, when, and how such stock shall be driven to secure such isolation; and it will probably be found most practicable, under such circumstances, to limit the traveling of Texan cattle on foot to the winter season, when the grasses are withered and the local stock is tended at home. Indeed, if a definite tract of prairie ground is devoted anywhere to the Texan trade, the conditions required for the prevention of splenic fever consist in the people keeping their cattle on their own inclosed farms or in well-fenced yards and feeding sheds.

A visit to the far West will convince any impartial person that judgment and enterprise can be exercised with a certainty of success in enabling Texan drovers to drive to points on the Union Pacific Road, Eastern Division, where they can do no harm. Traveling north from Texas through the Indian Nation into Western Kansas can inflict no injury. With the completion of the Union Pacific Road to San Francisco, it is not improbable that drovers may find it to their advantage to drive further than they usually do now, and make for other stations; but, whatever course they adopt in this respect, they can safely relieve the overstocked State of Texas by utilizing the vast prairies of the West in their important trade.

The question to settle is whether they should travel earlier in the season or later. It is my opinion that, if they wish to hear no more of splenic fever, they should reach Western Kansas in the summer or in early autumn, keeping their stock fresh on the abundant grasses, and shipping it East when the packing season commences, about the middle of October. An experiment on a large scale has been made by Messrs. McCoy Brothers, at Abilene. This spot on the eastern division of the Union Pacific Road was selected as the most isolated, and it is situated within four hundred miles of the Texan frontier and one hundred and sixty-three miles west from the State line.

It is east of the sixth meridian, which is the line established by the laws of Kansas as the limit over which Texan cattle shall not pass; but, by common consent, the advantages offered by this spot have been hitherto secured to the Texan trade. The yards were completed by the 5th of September, 1867, and from that time to the close of the season one thousand car loads of cattle were shipped east from Abilene. The trade, therefore, began late, the season was wet, and the Texas fever gave no concern. This year, however, large herds were collected early in the spring in Texas, and the first car load of cattle left Abilene on the 10th of June.

The people of the new town and its neighborhood had accumulated more live stock than they had last year, and, without taking the precaution which could readily have been adopted, permitted their cattle to go over the ground traversed by Texan stock, and "black-water" appeared among them.

It is evident that, as the property of a very large and important town may be founded on this very traffic, precautionary measures should be adopted for the isolation of the local stock. There can be no difficulty in this; and, with the experience of 1867 before us, the system of driving late for the fall markets is calculated to preserve the most promising of all outlets for southern farmers and drovers. There are objections, perhaps, to this plan; but, since it is impossible for the trade to go on in a reckless and ill-regulated manner, it is for the interest of all that the least objectionable plan, and yet the one most certain to prevent the ravages by disease, should be adopted.

We are not in a position to recommend any system of quarantine; but all who intend to further the interests of this trade should remember that during the summer season they cannot, without damaging their business, intermingle southern with northwestern stock. The line of demarcation must be distinct; and whereas in some places the local stock must be fenced in, in others the Texan steers will have to submit to some crowding, and conditions which are not the most favorable for so large a trade.

GENERAL REMARKS ON THE PRECEDING REPORTS.

The diseases of cattle which form the subjects of the three reports herewith published are typical of three distinct classes of disorders which tend to the impoverishment of the farmer and the country at large.

The first and simplest in its origin and character is an enzoötic or indigenous affection, localized in corn-growing States and districts, where, under the influence of abundant moisture and inattention to conditions which prevent the propagation of parasitic plants on the farmer's crops, a fungus is formed which destroys the nutritive value of cornstalks and grain. These become indigestible, induce impaction of the third stomach and constipation, which speedily terminate in death. The malady is not propagated beyond the farm or stable where the diseased fodder is supplied to stock.

The third is the American cattle plague of 1868, which, from an ignorance of its origin and nature, created serious loss, and, what is probably as bad, a panic that cannot readily be forgotten, on both sides of the Atlantic. Its study has revealed characters hitherto unknown or undescribed in relation to any disease of man or animals. The facts rendered show that it is developed in the hotter parts of the United States bordering on the Gulf coast, where lands are rich, retentive, and undrained, and therefore constitute the hotbeds of malarious or periodic diseases in the human family. So far as present knowledge goes, it is capable of propagation in an intensified form among cattle which feed on pastures traversed, in any part of the country beyond the original centers of development, by southern herds. It is not improbable that comparative pathology may here shed light on the precise nature of remittent and intermittent fevers in man; and the fact that these have not been observed to extend by a form of contagion may be explained by the conditions essential to the propagation of the bovine periodic fever. Large masses of animals travel fresh from the breeding grounds of this indigenous disease, and discharge large quantities of excrement on the food which is the carrier of the morbid material into the systems of cattle that are contaminated and die. It is true that anthrax, Siberian boil plague, or carbuncular fevers generally, from a peculiar decomposition in the liquids and tissues of the affected animals, are capable of being transferred by its inoculation, under favorable circumstances, to healthy people, and indeed to all warm-blooded creatures; but there are indigenous maladies, somewhat allied to the splenic fever of cattle, developed under like conditions, and capable of moderate extension from the districts where they originate spontaneously. But the cattle in the South are affected with a malady that is not inoculable, that is not propagated by the bites of insects and by the transference of decomposed or poisoned blood and tissues into the structures of healthy men or animals, and manifests in its method of propagation more of the features of cholera than of other properly recorded malady. It does not belong to the group of epizoötics proper, or contagious diseases like pleuropneumonia, rinderpest, and the varied forms of variola. It is not an infectious disease; and the single observation reported by the New York commissioners cannot outweigh the hundreds we have observed and carefully traced, and which indicate that the cattle are not discharging, by their breath or skin, into the air around them, any principles capable of perpetuating the malady. The plagues proper spread regardless of soil, climate, food, geological formation, altitude, &c., wherever sick animals approach or touch healthy ones. Splenic fever is not communicated by a cow to its calf, and is absolutely stopped by a fence, unless some accident leads to the mingling together of the southern animals with others they are capable of injuring. The malady, engendered with peculiar virulence in western or eastern cattle, is not, unless exceptionally—and no properly attested exception has come to my knowledge—communicated by these to other animals that have not traversed the trails of Texan or other southern herds. It is a modification, a poisoning of the food and possibly of the water tainted by the manure of the southern cattle, whereby the malady is transmitted. It is thus with human cholera. I do not wish to be understood that splenic fever is at all allied to cholera beyond the peculiar and ordinary method of propagation from certain centers. We know nothing of the spontaneous development of cholera and the centers whence it springs. We can witness the independent and primary production of the Texas or Florida fever by transporting western or eastern cattle to the South, where, fed on the pastures apart from other animals, they contract the disease and die.

Annually the Texan steers suffer, so far as my observations on cattle of all ages go, from this same local influence, which, in their acclimatized systems, does not usually lead to death. There is doubtless something tangible and ponderable, which some future chemist may reveal, that renders the grasses, and perhaps the waters, of the South so deleterious.

The disease, therefore, to which the third of the annexed reports refers, is an indigenous or enzoötic malady, susceptible of moderate extension by the manner in which the grasses of healthy regions are modified by the manure scattered broadcast from the systems of southern herds. It is not a contagious plague, and will probably cease when the agriculture of the South is fairly and fully developed.

Not so with the destructive malady, the lung plague or epizoötic pleuropneumonia, which is silently but seriously ravaging the Eastern States. This affection constitutes the subject of my second report. Its method of propagation, by diffusion of a specific animal poison or virus through the air, offers an instructive contrast to the comparatively harmless disease of the South. The lung plague kills slowly and surely wherever it penetrates, without regard to latitude, breeds, soils, conditions of weather, or systems of cultivation. It can be stamped out; and its propagation in a mild form may be resorted to for the protection of cattle that have been suspected of entering an infected area. It attacks animals but once in their lifetime, and presents all the characters of specific eruptive fevers, of which the human or ovine small-pox may be regarded typical.

A few words may not be considered inappropriate as to the nature of our investigations. They have extended over a period of ten months, and in all parts of the United States except in the far west. The furthest point west which was reached is near the terminus of the Kansas Pacific Railroad, and southwest to Corpus Christi. The great object in view has been to determine and demonstrate with precision the causes and signs of the several diseases examined, with a view to the suggestion of means of prevention and cure. The history of special outbreaks, the methods of extension, the essential symptoms and pathological changes indicated by sick animals, and the institution of careful personal inquiries among those who have witnessed the maladies at different periods, have engaged special attention.

We were first in having opportunities for a careful study of the changes in temperature which occur in splenic fever, and, taken in conjunction with similar observations originally made by us in relation to the rinderpest or Russian murrain, and since in numerous outbreaks of pleuropneumonia, it will be found that very definite and highly practical results may be anticipated from persistence in this method of observation. Indeed, so important is the matter in connection with the entire subject of comparative pathology, that it may not be deemed inappropriate to give a résumé of our operations on this particular point.

Last July we first used the only available thermometers that could be obtained in Chicago, centigrade thermometers, of French manufacture. The Surgeon General, however, kindly acceded to a request made through the Department of Agriculture, and two carefully-compared self-registering thermometers, made by Mr. L. Casella, of London, were forwarded to the west for the purpose of our inquiries. With these we were enabled to correct and verify the earlier observations. The normal temperature of cattle varies from 100° to 102° Fahrenheit. The average temperature of Texan cattle is from one to two degrees higher than that of northern steers. There may be accidental deviations, of which the most noticeable is at the period of œstrum, when a cow may indicate a temperature as high as 106° Fahrenheit. It is, however, remarkable how difficult it is in healthy animals to cause any great deviation from a normal standard, even during the hottest days of a western summer. Comparative observations on a number of animals at the same time constitute a valuable and essential test. It was, however, striking and strange that in examining Texan cattle caught with the lasso, the temperatures obtained were the same as those among work cattle of the same herds, which could be handled readily near the wagons. Observations of this kind are referred to in the report on splenic fever.

The best part—and the only one which should be chosen—for the insertion of the thermometer, is the rectum. The instrument must be introduced as nearly as possible to the same extent in all cases, and retained in situ at least three minutes. Animals are apt to defecate soon after the thermometer is passed in, and the rectum then remains passive for a time. This necessitates the withdrawal and reintroduction of the instrument, and the time required for the observation must be taken from the second intromission.

By this means animals in apparent health, grazing and moving in perfect comfort, are often found sick; and in the case of a contagious disease like pleuropneumonia this timely warning is of the highest moment.

In relation, however, to the nature of a malady, much is taught us by the thermometer. The periodic fever of southern cattle begins, like the rinderpest, with an increased heat of the body. The local changes appear secondary to the general fever, though it is difficult to estimate the time that elapses from the first exaltations of temperature to the local manifestations. In pleuropneumonia it is probable, and indeed our observations are almost conclusive on the point, that there is first a local change and commencing deposit. A material grows and penetrates, charged with and dependent on the presence of a specific poison, and when it has sufficiently involved any important parts and become complicated with ordinary inflammatory changes, the general fever sets in. An elevated temperature is, however, observed in this disease long before a farmer or dairyman suspects that an animal is affected. This is the only way in which some latent cases of pleuropneumonia are recognized.

Scientific men have hitherto failed in tracing the distinctive characters of organic poisons which differ from each other, and are only recognized, by the very different effects produced on the animal economy. Some attack a single species of animal; others induce the same disease in a number of species. The lung-plague poison induces its characteristic effects on cattle; the poison of hydrophobia, most readily communicated among feline and carnivorous animals, is deadly to the omnivora and vegetable feeders. Of the peculiar principles which tend to the diffusion of those diseases which are known to us as indigenous in certain latitudes, and which we must distinguish at all times, in classifying diseases, from the contagious maladies of no known primary source, we have two equally remarkable instances in the splenic fever of the South and the charbon or anthrax of many parts of the world. The one passes from cattle to cattle; the other is deadly to men, horses, dogs, pigs, and other warm-blooded animals.

It is evident that principles which exert such a variety of definite influences must have fundamental characters to distinguish them—that the virus of smallpox may some day be capable of distinction in its virus form from the virus of rinderpest or the lung-plague.

As far back as 1849, Mr. L E. Plasse, a veterinary surgeon at Niort, Deux Sèvres, in France, published a work, illustrated by tables and a map, in which he announced the discovery of the causes of epizoötics and epidemics, with the distinguishing features of two forms of charbon or anthrax, the one gangrenous and the other virulent.* It is a common error, due mainly to the undetermined meaning of a much-used medical term, to regard epidemics and epizoötics as *typhoid* fevers. Thus confounding many maladies, M. Plasse, in vainglorious terms which characterize his whole volume of near 500 pages, says: "*J'ai reconnu que les fièvres typhoides, qui, chez les animaux, sont semblables à celles de l'homme, dépendent toujours d'une seule et même cause: des champignons microscopiques introduits dans l'économie animale par les aliments; et je démontrerai clairement que toutes les causes qui ont été indiquées ne sont qu'indirectes et déterminantes; qu'elles sont le résultat de l'erreur; et que la véritable cause est une et invariable.*" M. Plasse was by no means the first to point to the lower forms of vegetable life as causes of disease in men and animals; but it would be an unprofitable task to enlarge on the earlier hints in this great field of error and of mystery. Plasse has the credit of first publishing a comprehensive volume on the subject; and in his succinct *exposé* of the work before us—an *exposé* which he read before the Institute of France on the 9th of October, 1848—he says:

"I have had to substitute the general denomination of cryptogamy for the various expressions applied to the diseases called typhoid, and I have recognized four states of the cryptogamic maladies.

"First state, *cryptogamic incubation.* The toxic principle here may sojourn in the animal economy during a greater or less length of time without causing marked functional disturbance; the disease will nevertheless be recognized by certain general symptoms.

"Second state, *cryptogamic elimination.* This is the discharge of the poisonous principle from the animal economy, without apparent functional trouble, whether by the excretions, the embryo in abortion, or the sucking animal.

"Third state, *external cryptogamy.* The morbid principle is eliminated without apparent disturbance, and is fixed in a more or less apparent manner on the surface of the skin, or in certain cavities which have external openings. In this category are included glanders, farcy, scrofula, lupus, canker of horses' feet, (*crapaudine,*) elephantiasis, tinea, lepra, &c.

"Fourth state, *cryptogamic fever.* Here the toxic principle is precipitated in the incubative stage, either in the liquids or in the solids, in the interior, and in a manner whereby it determines a more or less intense and very various reaction, according to the kind of fungus and the system which is affected; thence the different forms of typhoid fevers, such as epizoötic aphthæ, grippe, the contagious typhus of cattle, *suette miliaire,* gangrenous pleuropneumonia, variola, scarlatina, &c."

M. Plasse heralded forth his great discoveries in terms of no doubtful meaning: "*C'est à la médicine vétérinaire qu'il était réservé d'arriver à ces grandes découvertes.*" It might be thought that he had arrived at this result after long and painful researches on cryptogamic botany, and in demonstrating the presence of the lower forms of plants in the tissues of such animals, or in the food which communicated disease. Suffice it to say that M. Plasse's observations referred rather to the character of seasons and localities remarkable for the development of cryptogamic vegetation, and supposed to induce epidemics and epizoötics. He has recorded some observations on intestinal disturbance, induced by grasses and grains attacked by fungi which he does not name; but, apart from these imperfect records, his entire work is based on the crudest hypotheses.

It is not my object here to give a history of the cryptogamic theories in relation to the origin of disease, nor to review the able work of Charles Robin on the parasitic plants living on man and animals, nor to analyze the observations of Swayne, Brittain, Budd, Baly, Sull, Griffith, Bennett, Robertson, Graves, Swain, Salisbury, Hallier, Richardson,

* Découverte des causes des Épizooties et des Épidémies; Causes et distinction de deux genres de Charbon, &c. Par L. E. Plasse. Poitiers, 1849.

Duvaine, De Bary, and many more. Apart from the views enunciated and slender facts recorded, it seems to me essential to the completion of the work undertaken to attempt some means whereby it may be shown whether the periodic, or Texas, fever and the lung-plague did owe their origin, as alleged by the New York commissioners for the first and Hallier and Weiss for the second, to a peculiar cryptogamic vegetation. When in the West last summer I had occasion to recommend an investigation of the causes of the prevailing cattle fever in the South; and, on its being resolved that I should visit Texas for the purposes of this inquiry, I obtained the assent of the Commissioner of Agriculture to the selection of Mr. H. W. Ravenel, of Aiken, South Carolina, so well known as an enthusiastic and reliable observer and collector in the field of cryptogamic botany, to accompany me.

At the same time Dr. J. S. Billings and Dr. E. Curtis, whose attention has been specially directed to the cryptogamic origin of disease, offered to coöperate with me, if I would supply material for satisfactory experiments regarding the two diseases named. By a favorable arrangement between the Agricultural and Army Medical Departments these reports are now enriched by observations of the most reliable and interesting description.

JOHN GAMGEE, *M. D.*

Hon. Horace Capron,
Commissioner of Agriculture.

APPENDIX.

WEIGHTS OF LIVER AND SPLEEN.

The following tables record the weight of the liver and the spleen, healthy and diseased, of cattle examined during the investigation referred to in the foregoing report:

August 26 *to August* 30.

CHEROKEE SPLEENS.

2½	2¼	2	2	2¼	2¼	2½	2¼	2¼	2½	2½	2½	2½	2½	2½	2½	2¼	2½
2	2	2¼	2	3¼	2¼	2¼	2¼	2½	2½	2¼	2¼	2¼	2¼	2¼	2½	2¼	2
2	2½	2¼	2½	2½	3	2½	2¼	2¼	2½	2½	2½	2	2½	2½	2½	2½	2½
2½	2¼	2	2	2	2¼	2½	2	3	2¼	2¼	2¼	2¼	2½	3	2½	2½	2½
2¼	2½	2½	2¼	2¼	2½	2	2¼	2½	2¼	2¼	2¼	2½	2½	2½	3¼	2½	2¼
2½	2¼	2¼	2½	2½	2½	2¼	2½	2½	2¼	2½	2½	2¼	2½	2¼	2½	2¼	2¼
2¼	2½	2¼	2½	2¼	2½	2½	2¼	2	2	2¼	2½	2¼	2½	2¼	2½	2¼	2¼
2½																	
Total.	......	......	......	......	......	......	......	......	......	......	......	......	......	......	......	.....	300½
Aver'e	......	......	......	......	......	......	......	......	......	......	......	......	......	......	......	.....	2.36

TEXAN SPLEENS.

3½	3	2½	3	3½	2¼	2¼	4	3½	3	2¼	3½	3	2½	3	2½	2	2½
2½	3¼	2½	2¼	2½	3½	3½	2¼	3	2	3	3½	2¼	2½	2½	2¼	3½	2¼
2½	3	3	2¼	2½	2	2½	3¼	2½	3	3¼	2½	4	3½	3	2¼	3½	3¼
3½	2¼	3¼	2½	2½	2½	2½	2¼	3½	2½	3	3¼	4	3	2½	2	2½	2½
3	3¼	3	2¼	2¼	3¼	3½	2½	3½	2½	3¼	2½	2¼	3½	2½	3	3	3¼
3	3½	3½	2½	2	2½	3½	3¼	3¼	2½	3	3¼	3	2½	3¼	2	3¼	3¼
2½	3½	3½	3¼	2½	2½	2½	3	3	3¼	3½	3½	2	2½	3¼	3½	3¼	3½
2½	3	3¼	3½	3½	2	2¼	2¼	3½	2½	2½	2¼	3	2½	2½	3¼	3¼	3
2½	2½	3½	3	2½	3	2	2½	2½	3¼	2½	3	3¼	2	2¼	3	2⅛	4
2½	2¼	2½	2½	3	2¼	2½	2¼	2½	3¼	2	3½	2½	3	2¼	2½	2	2½
3½	2½	2¼	2½	2½	3	2½											
Total.	......	......	......	......	......	......	......	......	......	......	......	......	......	......	......	.....	523
Aver'e	......	......	......	......	......	......	......	......	......	......	......	......	......	......	......	.....	2.79

NATIVE SPLEENS.

1½	1½	1½	1½	1½	1¼	1½	1¼	1¼	1¼	1¼	1½	1½	1½	1¼	1½	1¼	1½
1½	1¼	1½	1½	1¼	1½	1½	1¼	1½	1½	1¼	1¼	1¼	1¼	1½	1½	1½	1¼
1¼	1¼	1¼	1¼	1½	1½	1½	2	1½	1½	1¼	1½	1¼	1½	1¼	1¼	1¼	1½
1½	1¼	1½	1¼	1½	1½	1½	1½	1½	1¼	1½	1½	1	1½	1¼	1½	1½	1½
1½	1½	1¼	1¼	1¼	1¼	1¼	1½	1¼	1½	1½	1½	1¼	1¼	1¼	1½	1½	1¼
1¼	1½	1½	1½	1¼	1½	1½	1¼	1½	1½	1½	1½	1¼	1½	1¼	1¼	1¼	1½
1½	1½	1¼	1¼	1¼	1¼	1¼	1¼	1¼	1¼	1¼	1½	1½	1½	1½	1¼	1½	1½
1½	1¼	1½	1½	1½	1¼												
Total.	......	......	......	......	......	......	......	......	......	......	......	......	......	......	......	.....	183¾
Aver'e	......	......	......	......	......	......	......	......	......	......	......	......	......	......	......	.....	1.39

NOTE.—By the term "native," as here applied to cattle or their diseased organs, is meant cattle not raised in districts in which the infection originated.

Native cattle.

MALE.

Date.	Spleens.	Livers.	Date.	Spleens.	Livers.	Date.	Spleens.	Livers.	Date.	Spleens.	Livers.
Sept. 8	1	10	Sept. 10	1½	10	Sept. 11	1½	9	Sept. 13	1½	16
	1½	11		1½	11		1	11		1	8
	1	9		1½	9		1½	12		1	7
Sept. 9	1½	14		1½	16		1	10		1	6
	2	15		1½	10		1½	11		1½	11
	1½	15		1½	11		1½	11		1½	13
	1¾	13		1½	11		1½	11		1½	12
	1½	13		1½	11		1½	11		1½	10
	2	13		1½	12		1½	10		1½	13
	2	13		2	10		1½	9		1¼	7
	2	12		1½	9		1½	9		1½	9
	1½	10		1½	8		2	13		1½	12
	1½	12		1½	12		2	16		1½	16
	2	13		1½	11		1½	18		1	8
	1½	11		1½	11		1½	9		1	6
	1½	12		1½	12		1½	16		1½	9
	1¼	10		1½	13		1½	11		1½	12
	1	9		1½	11		2	14		1½	9
	1	8		1½	13		1	10		1	8
	1½	10		1½	11		1½	13		1½	10
	1	9		2	12		1½	12		1½	14
	1½	10		1½	12		1½	14		1½	10
	2	10		2	10		1½	16		1	5
	1	8		1	9		1½	9		1½	8
	1½	9		1½	15		1½	13		1	7
	1½	10		2	14		1½	12	Sept. 14	1½	10
	1¼	9		1	12		1½	12		1½	9
	¾	5		2	16		1½	13		1½	10
	1	8		1½	13		1½	14		1½	9
	1½	10		1½	12		1½	12		1½	9
	1	6		2	13		2	16		1½	8
	1½	10		1½	12		2	13		1½	8
	1	8		2	13		1½	14		1	6
	2	14		1½	12		1½	14		1½	11
	1	9		2	14		1½	13		1½	10
	1¼	9		1	9		1	10		1½	12
	2	8		1¼	9		1½	12		1½	16
	1	9		1½	10		1	9		1½	20
	1½	12		1	10		1½	14		1½	16
	1¼	9		1½	9		1½	12		1¼	13
	1½	12		1	10		1½	13		1½	9
	1½	10		1¼	11	Sept. 13	1½	11		1¼	6
	1½	13		1	10		2	12		1½	8
	1½	15		1¼	11		1½	13		1½	16
	1	12		1	9		2	15		1½	13
	1	13		1½	12		1	11		1½	12
	1½	10		2½	12		1½	12		1½	11
	2	17		1	8		2	12		1½	8
	1½	13		1	11		1½	12		1½	9
	1½	13		1	10		2	15		1½	10
Sept. 10	1½	9		1	11		1½	14		1½	10
	1	8	Sept. 11	1	10		2	13		1½	12
	1½	8		1	10		1½	10		1½	12

Native cattle—Continued.

MALE.

Date.	Spleens.	Livers.	Date.	Spleens.	Livers.	Date.	Spleens.	Livers.	Date.	Spleens.	Livers.
Sept. 14	1½	12	Sept. 15	1½	14	Sept. 15	1½	13	Sept. 15	1½	10
	1½	12		1½	13		1½	14		1½	11
		13		1½	12		1	9		1½	13
	2½	19		1	9		1	11		1½	9
	1½	12		1	10		1½	12		1	11
	2	11		1½	12		1½	13		1½	13
	1½	9		1½	14		1	10			
Sept. 15	1½	12		1½	14		2	16	Total........	373½	2,928
	1½	16		1	10		1½	13			
	1½	16		1½	15		1½	14	Average.....	1.46	11.39
	1½	14		1½	12		2	16			
	1½	15		1½	13		1½	11			
	1½	12		1½	14		1½	13			

FEMALE.

Date.	Spleens.	Livers.	Date.	Spleens.	Livers.	Date.	Spleens.	Livers.	Date.	Spleens.	Livers.
Sept. 8	2	16	Sept. 9	1½	11	Sept. 9	1¼	9	Sept. 10	1½	14
	1½	12		2	12		1¼	9		1	8
	1	15		1½	12		1½	11		1½	15
	2	11		1½	13		1½	13		1½	11
	2	14		1½	15		1½	13		1½	13
	1½	12		2	12		1¼	13		1½	10
	2	16		1¼	13		1½	14		1½	12
	1½	12		1½	14		1½	12		1½	14
	2	13		1½	13		1½	14		1½	12
	1	10		1¾	16		1½	10		1½	13
	1	9		1¼	12		1½	15		1½	15
	1½	14		2	20		1½	10		1	9
	1	11		1	13		1½	12		1¼	12
	1½	15		1	12		1½	10		1½	13
	1	9		1	16		1½	8		1¼	8
	1½	16		2	19		1½	12		1½	10
	1½	12		1	13		1	11		1½	12
	2½	10		1½	13		1	11		1	7
	1½	11		1	14		2½	9		2	10
	2	15		1½	16		1	10		1½	13
	2	16		1½	14		2	14		1½	7
	2	20		1¼	9		1½	11		1½	8
	1½	14		1½	12		1	8		1½	9
	2	13		1½	10		1½	11		1½	11
	1½	12		1½	10	Sept. 10	1½	13		1½	10
	2	15		1½	7		1	8		1½	13
	1½	16		1	7		1½	10		2	16
	2	13		1¼	9		3	11		1	8
	2½	12		1½	10		1½	9		1	8
	2½	15		1½	12		1	8		1½	11
	2	16		1½	10		1½	16		1½	16
Sept. 9	1¼	13		2	10		1½	12		1½	10
	1¼	11		1½	10		1½	12		1½	11
	1¼	14		2¼	14		1½	12		1½	10

Native cattle—Continued.

FEMALE.

Date.	Spleens.	Livers.	Date.	Spleens.	Livers.	Date.	Spleens.	Livers.	Date.	Spleens.	Livers.
Sept. 10	1½	9	Sept. 11.......	1	12	Sept. 11	1½	13	Sept. 13	1½	12
	1½	13		1½	13		1½	13		1	11
	1	8		1½	15		1	10		1	12
	1½	14		1½	13		1½	12		2	14
	1	8		1½	14		1½	13		1½	10
	1½	12		1¾	14		1½	14		1½	10
	1½	12		1½	15		1½	14		1	8
	1½	11		1½	13		1½	16		1¼	9
	1½	11		1	10		1½	12		1	8
	1½	11		1½	14		1½	10		1½	12
	1½	14		1½	12	Sept. 13	1	11		1	6
	2	10		1½	10		1½	13		1	6
	1½	16		1½	16		2	16		1½	15
	1½	7		1	7		1¾	12		1	8
	1	10		1	6		1½	14		1½	10
	2	16		1½	15		1¾	12		1½	9
	2	10		1½	16		2	15	Sept. 14	1½	9
	1	11		1½	14		1	16		1	6
	2	16		1½	13		1½	16		1	5
	1½	16		1½	14		1	12		1½	8
	3	13		1½	12		1½	15		1½	9
	1	11		1	9		1	12		1	6
	1	8		1½	15		1	15		1½	11
	1½	16		1	8		1	10		1½	10
	2	16		1½	16		1	12		1½	8
	2¼	16		1½	16		1	10		1½	9
	1½	16		1½	14		1½	12		1½	10
	2	14		1½	10		2	15		1	4¾
	1½	14		1½	15		1¾	16		1	6
	1½	15		1½	12		2	13		1½	10
	1	12		1½	15		1½	13		2	16
	1	14		1½	12		1	11		2	21
	1	12		1½	14		1½	12		1½	18
	1½	13		1	9		1	12		1½	22
	1½	14		1	11		1½	12		1½	10
Sept. 11	1	9		1½	12		1	12		1½	9
	1¼	11		1½	14		1	12		1½	9
	1½	12		2	16		1	12		1½	8
	1¼	13		1½	14		1	10		1½	9
	1½	12		1½	13		¾	12		1½	10
	1½	15		1	10		1	10		1½	9
	1¾	16		2	11		1	12		1½	10
	1½	12		1½	13		1	9		1¾	17
	1	13		1½	14		1	12		1½	16
	1½	12		2	16		1½	12		1½	12
	1½	13		1½	12		1¾	13		1½	8
	1¼	15		1½	13		1	13		1¼	10
	1¼	15		1½	10		1½	10		1½	12
	1½	14		1½	11		1½	12		1½	10
	1	17		1½	13		1½	11		1½	12
	1½	14		1½	9		1¼	10		1	6
	1¼	15		1½	11		1	11		1	5
	1	11		1½	11		2	11		1½	9

Native cattle—Continued.

FEMALE.

Date.	Spleens.	Livers.	Date.	Spleens.	Livers.	Date.	Spleens.	Livers.	Date.	Spleens.	Livers.
Sept. 14	1½	12	Sept. 14	1¼	9	Sept. 15	1½	14	Sept. 15	2	13
	1¾	18		1¼	8		1½	14		2½	13
	1½	14		1½	9		1½	12		1	9
	1½	16		1½	10		1	16		1½	11
	1½	14		1½	11		1½	14		2	12
	1½	10		1½	13		1½	14		1	11
	1½	12		1¼	14		2	16		1	11
	1½	10		1½	15		1½	14		1½	13
	1¼	8		1½	16		1½	13		1½	11
	1½	10		1¾	17		1½	14		1½	12
	1½	10	Sept. 15	1½	14		1½	12		1½	12
	1½	10		1½	12		1½	10		1¾	13
	1½	10		1½	12		1½	10		1	11
	1¾	15		1½	12		1	10		1¼	11
	1½	14		1½	12		1	10		1	13
	1	5		1¼	11		1½	11		1½	12
	¾	4		1½	14		1½	13		1	10
	1½	13		1	12		1½	13		1¼	12
	1¾	15		1	9		2	14		1	8
	1½	10		1½	11		1	13		1	10
	1½	8		1½	12		1½	13		1	11
	1½	9		1½	8		1½	13		1	9
	1½	10		1¼	14		1½	12		1	11
	1¼	9		1¾	10		1½	13		1	10
	1½	8		1	12		1	12		1½	11
	1½	10		2	15		1½	13		1½	15
	2	19		1	12		1½	13		1½	13
	1¾	17		1	12		1½	12		1½	14
	1½	18		1	12		1	10		2	15
	1½	11		1½	12		1	11		1½	15
	1½	12		1	12		1	10		1	11
	1½	14		1½	12		1½	10		1½	12
	1½	6		1¼	11		1½	11		1½	16
	1½	9		1	12		1½	11		2	16
	1¾	10		1	12		1	12		1½	11
	1½	16		1	11		1½	9		2	12
	1½	9		1	11		1½	14		1½	11
	1½	8		1½	12		2	15		2	12
	1½	12		1	9		1½	11		2¼	13
	1½	10		2	11		1	12		2	12
	1½	9		1½	13		1	12		1½	14
	1¼	8		1	12		1½	15		2	12
	1	5		1½	10		1	11		2½	13
	1	6		1½	12		1¼	11		1½	11
	1¼	9		1	10		1½	12		2	12
	1½	12		1½	12		1½	12		2	11
	1½	14		1	13		2¼	13		1½	12
	1	5		2	15		1	11		1	10
	1	6		2	12		1½	10		1½	12
	1¼	12		1½	13		1½	12		2	10
	1½	20		1½	12		1½	11		1½	11
	1¾	21		1½	13		1½	10		1½	11
	1½	10		1¼	14		1½	11		2	10

Native cattle—Continued.

FEMALE.

Date.	Spleens.	Livers.	Date.	Spleens.	Livers.	Date.	Spleens.	Livers.	Date.	Spleens.	Livers.
Sept. 15	1½	11	Sept. 16	1½	12	Sept. 18	1	12	Sept. 18	1	11
	2	10		1½	13		1	10		1	11
	1¼	8		1½	14		1½	9		1½	12
	1	14		1	13		1¼	12		1	13
	1½	10		1	15		1½	10		1	14
	1¼	8		1½	13		1½	14		1½	13
	2	12		1½	13		1	15		1	12
	1½	13		1	10		1¼	14		1	13
	1	10		1	13		1½	15		1	12
	1½	9		1½	14		2	17		1½	11
	2	11		1	13		1	16		2	15
	2	12		1½	12		1½	14		1	16
	1½	13		1½	13		1½	13		1½	14
	1¾	15		1½	14		1	12		1	13
	2	13		1	13		1	11		1	12
	1¼	15		1½	12		1½	13		1	15
	2	10		1	12		1	15		1	17
	2	10		1	13		1	10		1	16
	2½	12		1½	14		1	11		1½	13
	1	10		1	11		1½	13		1½	14
	1½	12		1	10		1½	12		1	12
	2	10		¾	14		1	14		1½	14
	1	12		2	15		1	14		1	15
	1½	11		2	13		1½	13		1½	14
Sept. 16	1½	14		1½	12		1	12		1½	15
	2	16		1½	14		1	13		2	16
	1½	17		1	15		1	12		2	17
	1½	16	Sept. 18	1½	13		1	13		1½	13
	1½	15		1¼	16		2	15		2	11
	1½	15		1¼	14		1	17		1	15
	1½	17		1½	11		1½	15		1	10
	1½	17		2	17		1	14		1	9
	1½	12		1¼	16		1	12		1½	13
	1½	13		2	12		1½	13		1	11
	1½	13		2	13		1	14		1	11
	1	14		1½	15		1	15		1½	12
	1½	14		2	12		1½	14		1	13
	1	13		1	10		1	15		1	14
	1½	14		1½	12		1½	14		1½	13
	1½	13		1½	13		1½	15		1	12
	1½	14		2	14		2	17		2	17
	1½	14		2	11		1	16		2	14
	1¼	15		1¼	13		1½	14		1½	14
	1¼	15		1½	15		1½	13		1½	14
	1½	17		2	10		1	12		1	12
	1	14		1½	11		1	11		1	13
	1	14		1¼	10		1½	13		1½	11
	1	13		1½	11		1¼	14		2	15
	1½	13		1¼	12		1	15		1	16
	2	15		1½	13		1	10		1½	14
	1½	12		1¼	9		1½	11		1	13
	1	13		1½	10		1½	13		1	12
	1½	15		1½	10		1	14		1½	14

Native cattle—Continued.

FEMALE.

Date.	Spleens.	Livers.	Date.	Spleens.	Livers.	Date.	Spleens.	Livers.	Date.	Spleens.	Livers.
Sept 18........	2	17	Sept. 18 and 20	1½	13	Sept. 18 and 20	1	14	Sept. 24	1	13
	1½	15		2	10		1½	16		1½	15
	1½	17		2¼	12		1	12		1	16
	1½	14		1¼	9		1½	10		1½	15
	1½	13		1	11		1¼	11		1½	15
	2	17		1	8		1	13		1	14
	1½	14		1½	11		1½	8		1½	12
	1	15		2	12		1½	10		1½	14
	2	13		1¼	11		1½	12		1	15
	1½	11		2	9		1¼	14		1½	15
	1½	14		1¼	10		1½	16		1¼	12
	1½	15		1½	12		1¼	10		1½	10
	1	11		1¼	13		1½	13		1	9
Sept. 18 and 20.	2	13		1¼	12		1½	12		1¼	8
	1½	15		1	11		1	13		1½	12
	1½	9		1½	10		1½	15		1	14
	1¼	8		2	9		1½	14		1	16
	1½	8		1¼	12		1½	10		1¾	14
	1	9		1	14		1½	12		1	9
	1¾	10		1¾	11		1	8		1½	10
	1	9		1	10		1¼	12		1¾	12
	2	13		1½	8		1½	10		1	10
	1½	12		2	9		1¾	12		1¼	12
	1½	14		1½	10		1½	12		1½	10
	1½	13		1¼	13		1¼	10		1¼	13
	1½	12		1½	12		1¼	9		1¾	13
	1	10		1¼	10		1½	13		1	12
	1½	12		1¼	12		1½	12		1½	12
	1½	10		2	14		1¼	14		1½	13
	1¾	12		1½	10		1½	16		1	10
	1½	11		1¾	16		1¾	15		1¼	12
	2	9		1¼	11		1½	13		1¾	13
	1½	11		1½	12		1	10		1¾	9
	2	12		1	10		1½	12		1½	10
	1½	13		1½	11		1½	9		1	9
	1	12		1	9		1¾	13		1½	14
	1¾	13		2	12		1	10		1¼	12
	1½	12		1½	13		1¼	11		1½	13
	2	10		1	8		1	10		1½	14
	1¾	11		1½	10		1¾	8		1	14
	1½	13		1¼	12		1	9		1¼	10
	1	12		2	14		1½	10		1½	10
	1¼	10		1½	13		1¾	13		1¼	14
	1	10		1½	10		1¼	15		1¾	9
	1¾	12		1½	12		1½	16		1	8
	2	9		1¼	14		9	21		1¾	11
	1½	10		1½	10	Sept. 24	1½	16		2	12
	1	12		1	11		1	15		1½	13
	1¼	13		1¼	12		1½	16		1½	10
	1½	11		2	13		1½	17		1¼	12
	1¾	12		1½	16		1	16		1½	14
	1	10		1½	15		1½	15		1½	10

Native cattle—Continued.

FEMALE.

Date.	Spleens.	Livers.	Date.	Spleens.	Livers.	Date.	Spleens.	Livers.	Date.	Spleens.	Livers.
Sept. 24	1½	12	Sept. 24	1½	15	Sept. 24	1¼	14	Sept. 24	1½	12
	1	11		1½	15		1½	16		1	13
	1¼	16		1¼	11		1½	15		1½	14
	1½	10		1	14		1	14		1½	14
	1½	15		1½	16		1½	15		1	15
	1¼	10		1	11		2	16		1½	16
	1	12		1½	15		1½	14		10	12
	1½	14		1	10		1	14	Total	1,461½	12,402¾
	1¼	10		1½	12		1½	15	Average.....	1.441	12.231

MALE AND FEMALE.

Date.	Spleens.	Livers.	Date.	Spleens.	Livers.	Date.	Spleens.	Livers.	Date.	Spleens.	Livers.
August 20	1	12	August 20	1	9	August 20	1	9	Sept. 2	2	20
	1½	14		1½	12		1½	11		1½	14
	2	9½		1	14		1	8½		1	13
	1½	13		2	15		1	14		1½	12
	1	15		2	17		1	12		1¼	14
	1¼	16		1	14		1½	14		1½	13
	2	9½		1	13		1½	12		1	14
	2	14		1½	14		1½	9		2	20
	2½	13		1	15		1½	12		1½	14
	1¾	12		1	16		1	14		2	20
	1	12		1¼	16		1	12		1½	14
	1	13		1	14		1½	9		1	13
	1¼	13		1½	15		1	12		1½	12
	1	12		1	12		1½	13		1¼	14
	1½	14		1	13		2	14		1½	13
	2	12		1	14½		2	16		1	13
	2	13		1½	9		2	18		1¼	14
	2	15		1¾	12		1¼	9½		1½	12
	1¾	18		2	14		1	14		1	16
	1½	16		2	15		1½	15		1¼	13
	1	12		1¼	16		1	12		1½	14
	1	9½		2	17		1¾	16		1	14
	1¼	14		1¼	16		1	12		1¼	14
	1	12		1½	12		1½	15		1	13
	1	8½		1¾	10		1	14		1¼	15
	1½	12		1¾	12		1	15		1½	18
	1	12		1	16		1	12		1¼	14
	1½	14		2	18		1	9		1½	17
	1	15		1½	16		1½	8		1¼	13
	1	16		1¾	12		¾	12		1½	18
	1	12		1	12		¾	8½		1½	16
	2	9		2	10		¾	8		1½	14
	2	10		1	12		1	9		1¼	14
	1½	14		1½	13		1½	9½		2	19
	1	15		1	14		1	12		1½	18
	1½	13		1	15		1	12		1	13
	1	14		1¾	16	Sept. 2	1	16		1½	14
	1	12		1	12		1½	18		1½	14
	2	13		1¼	14		1¼	14		1¼	14

Native cattle—Continued.

MALE AND FEMALE.

Date.	Spleens.	Livers.	Date.	Spleens.	Livers.	Date.	Spleens.	Livers.	Date.	Spleens.	Livers.
Sept. 2	1½	12	Sept. 2	1¼	10	Sept. 3	2½	12	Sept. 6	1	15
	1¼	14		1	9½		1¾	10		1½	18
	1½	14		1	9		1½	8		1½	16
	2	16		1	8½		1½	8		1¼	15
	1½	15		1½	9		1½	7		1¼	14
	1¼	14		1½	8½		1	10		1¼	17
	1½	14		1	8		1½	9		1¼	14
	1¼	15		1	8½		1½	9		1½	15
	1¼	14		1½	9		1½	12		1¼	14
	1½	15		1¼	8¼		2	10		1¼	15
	1½	13		1¼	8		2½	9		1½	18
	1½	15		¾	8		1½	9		1¼	17
	1¼	16		1½	9½		1½	10½		1¼	17
	1	11½		1	10		2	11		2	11½
	2	9½		1½	10		2	12		1¼	10¾
	1½	11½		1	11		2½	12		2	13
	1½	11		1	11		1½	12		1¼	14
	1¼	12		1¼	11		1¾	12		1½	10
	1½	12		1	10		1	11		2½	9½
	1½	11		1½	12		2	12		1½	10
	1½	12		2	9½		2½	10		1½	11½
	1¼	10		2	12		2¾	9		1½	11½
	1½	11		1½	10		2	8		1	13¼
	2	12		1	10½		2	10		2½	11½
	2	13		1½	11		2½	11		2	13½
	2	10		2	11		1½	12		1½	13
	1½	9		2	12½		2	9		1	10
	1½	9½		2	9		2	10		1½	11
	1	9		2	10		2½	9		2	9
	1	9½		1½	11		2	10		2	9½
	2	12		1¼	11		2	11		1½	11½
	2	10		1½	12		2	12		1½	11
	2	11		1½	12		2	11		1½	13
	2½	12	Sept. 3	2	10	Sept. 4	1½	14		1¼	9½
	1	9		4	9		1½	12		2	10½
	1½	12		2½	13		1½	14		2	9½
	1	10		2½	16		1½	14		1½	13
	1	13		2¾	10		1½	12		1½	13½
	¾	9½		2	10		1¼	10		1¼	10
	1	11		2	11		1½	14		1	12½
	1	12		2½	13		1½	14		1	9½
	1½	10		2½	15		1½	16		1¼	11
	1½	11		2½	15		1¼	14		1¼	10
	2	10½		2	10		1½	14		1¾	12½
	2	11		1½	11		1½	12		1¾	11½
	2	12		1¾	13		2	14		1¼	11
	1	11		2	12		1½	13		2	15¾
	1	12		2	12		3	18		1½	11
	1½	10		2¼	13		1½	14		2	13
	1	11½		2½	14		1½	12		1½	13
	1½	12		3	14		1¼	14		1¾	11½
	1½	13		3	13	Sept. 6	1	16		1¼	11
	1	11		2½	14		1¼	14		2	11½

Native cattle—Continued.

MALE AND FEMALE.

Date.	Spleens.	Livers.	Date.	Spleens.	Livers.	Date.	Spleens.	Livers.	Date.	Spleens.	Livers.
Sept. 6........	2	12	Sept. 7.......	1½	11	Sept. 7.......	1	12	Sept. 10......	1¾	14
	1½	9½		2	13		1¼	16		1	11½
	1½	9¼		2¼	13		1¼	14		1½	11
	1¼	9½		2	11		1½	15		1¼	10½
	1½	9		1½	12		1½	18		1½	9
	1½	9½		1	11		1	13		1½	14
	1	9		1½	12		1¼	14		1	10
	2	10		1	11		1½	15		1½	12
	1¼	12		1½	10		1½	18		1	10
Sept. 7........	1	11		1	10		1¼	14		2	12
	1¼	10		1	12		1¼	14		2½	11
	1	12		1½	13		1½	17		2	12
	1	13		1	10		1½	15		1½	14
	1¼	10		1½	12		1¼	14		1	10
	1½	10½		1	9½		2	18		1½	15
	1¼	11½		1¼	12		1½	17		1¾	15
	2	8		1½	13		1¼	15		1	11
	2¼	8½		1½	11		1¼	17		2	9
	1¾	12½		2	10		1	16		1½	13
	1¼	12		1½	11		1¼	14		1¾	11½
	1½	10		2¾	12		1½	18		1¾	12
	1¼	9		1½	15		1¼	15		1½	15
	1¾	11½		3	13		¾	14		1½	15
	1½	11		2	10		1¼	10¾		1¼	14¼
	1¼	11½		3	15	Sept. 9.......	1	11		1	12
	1¼	12		1½	13		2	12		1	10
	1	12		2½	14		1½	13		1½	9½
	1½	11½		1½	16		1½	15		1½	13
	1¼	11		1½	13		1	14½		1¼	13
	1½	12		2	10		2	12½		1	13
	1½	13		2½	10		1	13		1	9
	1¼	10		2¾	11		1½	9½		2	9½
	2	11		2½	12		1¼	15		1½	15½
	2	10		1½	11		1½	11		1½	11
	1½	12		2	13		1¼	13		1¼	12
	1½	10		2	15		1½	14		1¼	13
	1	11		3	10		1¼	10¾		1½	9½
	1¼	12		1½	10		1¾	15		1	15
	1½	11½		1¾	13		1½	12		1	8
	1	12		1½	16		1½	15		1½	13
	1½	13		1½	13		2	14½		1½	12
	1¼	9½		1½	12		2	15		1¾	12
	1½	12		1½	13		1¼	10½		2	15
	1¼	10½		2	10		1	12		2	16½
	2	9½		2	11		1½	13		1¼	11½
	1½	10¼		2	13		1	15½		1½	12
	1½	11		3	15		1½	10		1	14
	1	12		2½	8		1¼	12		1½	13
	1½	10		1	16		1¼	11½		2	12½
	1	9½		1¼	15		1½	14½		1	12
	1½	10		2	20		1¼	16		1	13
	1	12½		1½	18	Sept. 10......	1¼	12		1½	14
	1¼	13		1¼	14		1¾	13		2	10

Native cattle—Continued.

MALE AND FEMALE.

Date.	Spleens.	Livers.	Date.	Spleens.	Livers.	Date.	Spleens.	Livers.	Date.	Spleens.	Livers.
Sept. 10	2	15	Sept. 11	1½	13	Sept. 14	1½	13	Sept. 14	1	12
	1½	10		1¼	16		2	9½		1¾	15
	1¼	14		1	9		2	16		1½	12
	1½	13		¾	10		1	15		1	14
	1¼	10½		1¼	13		1½	12		2	9½
	1¾	11		2	9½		1¼	10		2	14
	1½	12		2	12		1¼	8½		2½	15
	2	13		2	11		1¼	16		1	12
	2½	13½		1½	13		1½	14		1½	13
	1¾	15		1¼	14		1½	8		2	15
	1½	9		2¾	15		1	9		2½	16
	2	8½		1½	13		1	8		1	9½
	1¼	11		1½	14		¾	8½		1¼	9½
	1½	12		1	15		2	19		1¼	9
	1½	13		1½	11		1	12		1½	12
	1¼	11		1¾	10		1	13		1½	15
	2	14		1	16½		1	15		1¼	16
	1½	15		2	12		1½	10		2	15
	1½	14		1	13		1¼	9½		1	14
	1¼	10½		1	14		1½	14		1½	15
	2	15		1½	12		2	16		1	16
	1½	13		1¼	14		2	15		1¼	14
	1½	11½		1½	11½		2½	15		2	9½
	1¾	13		2	13		1½	12		2	10
	1½	12		1¼	14		1½	14		1½	15
	1¼	13		1½	15		1½	9½		2	13
Sept. 11	1	10		1½	12		1½	9		2½	14
	1½	13		2	10		2	16		1½	16
	¾	8		1	11		1	12		1	14
	1	14		1½	12		1½	13		1½	13
	1	9		1¾	13		2	14		2	14
	1½	13		1	11		2½	13		2,	14
	1½	12		1½	11		2	14		1	12
	1	13		1¾	12		1½	15		1½	13
	2	9		1½	12		1¼	15		2	14
	1	11		1¼	11		1¼	14		1¼	15
	1½	13		1½	11		1¼	12		1¼	16
	1	14		1¾	13		1	10		1½	12
	1	14		1	8½		1¼	14		..	9½
	1½	15		1	13		1	12		1¼	14
	1½	10		2	14		1	13		1½	12
	2	16		1	12		1½	9½		1½	14
	1	14		1	14		1½	10½		1¼	10
	1	15		1	16½		2	12		1	15
	1½	13		2	12		2½	13		1½	16
	1¼	16		1	16		2	12		1	14
	1	9		1½	13		1½	15		1½	13
	¾	10		1¼	14		1½	16		1¼	14
	1¼	13		1	12		1	17		2	12
	1¼	14	Sept. 14	1	12		1	14		2½	13
	1	12		1½	14		1	9		2¼	16
	1	14		1	15		1¼	14		1½	10
	1	15		1¼	16		1	16		1½	11

Native cattle—Continued.

MALE AND FEMALE.

Date.	Spleens.	Livers.	Date.	Spleens.	Livers.	Date.	Spleens.	Livers.	Date.	Spleens.	Livers.
Sept. 14	1¼	10	Sept. 14	¾	8	Sept. 15	2	12	Sept. 15	¾	8½
	2	12		1	12		1	14		2	14
	2	14		1½	14		1	15		1½	16
	1½	15		1	15		2	10		1	13
	1	12		3	9		2	11½		1½	12
	2	10		3	9½		1½	14		1	10
	1	14		4	10		1½	15		1	9½
	1½	12		3	11		1	13		2	11
	1¾	10		3½	10		1	15		2½	12
	1	9		1	12		1½	16		1	14
	¾	8		1½	14		2	12		1½	12
	¾	8		2	10		1	11		1	11
	1	12		2½	14		1	9½		1½	14
	1½	15		1½	15		1	14		1	12
	2	9½		1½	14		1	13		2	11
	1	14		1	14		1½	14		1½	9
	1½	15		1½	15		1¼	16		¾	8
	1	12		1½	13		¾	9		¾	8
	1½	11½		1	9½		3	10		2	9
	¾	8		2	12		1	14		2½	12
	1	11		1½	14		1	12		1	11½
	1½	10		1¼	15		1½	14		1½	9
	1½	14		1	16		1	17		2	9½
	2	9		¾	8½		1	11		1½	15
	2¼	9½		1	12		1½	10	Sept. 16	1	8
	1	11		1	14		1¼	9		1	7
	1½	12		1	12		2	11		1½	8
	1¼	14		1	14		1¼	9		1½	8½
	1½	15		2	12		2½	13		¾	8
	2	9½		1½	14		1	12		1	9½
	2	16		1½	9½		1	9		1	7
	1½	12		1	12		2½	13		1½	7½
	1¼	15		1½	12		2	14		1	14
	1½	14		2	9½		1	15		1½	15
	1¼	14½		1	11½		1	12		1¾	14½
	1½	11½		2	12		1½	10		1½	11
	2	10		2	14		1	11½		1¼	8½
	1½	9½		1	14		1	14		1¼	9
	1	12		1½	14		1	17		1½	11
	1	14		1	15		1¾	16		1	13
	1½	15		1½	13		¾	8¼		1½	16
	1¼	16		2	14		¾	12		2	14
	1	12		1	14		¾	10		1	11
	1½	16		1	15		1¾	14		2	11
	1½	12		2	13		1½	14		1½	11
	1	11		2	14		1	15		1	13
	1½	9	Sept. 15	1	14		2	14		2	12
	1½	10		1½	15		1	11		1	13
	1½	9		1¼	16		1	12		1	17
	2	12		1	17		1	13		1½	16
	1¼	14		1	9½		1¼	14		2	14
	1	13		1¼	14		1	11		1½	17
	1	12		2	9½		1	8		1	9½

Native cattle—Continued.

MALE AND FEMALE.

Date.	Spleens.	Livers.	Date.	Spleens.	Livers.	Date.	Spleens.	Livers.	Date.	Spleens.	Livers.
Sept. 16	1¼	9	Sept. 17	1	9	Sept. 17	1	10	Sept. 18	2	14
	1½	16		1	8½		2	12		2½	16
	2	16½		1	8		1½	14		1¾	13½
	1	18		1½	9		1	12		2	14
	1¾	14		1½	10	Sept. 18	1	14		1	14
	1½	13		1	7		1½	15		1½	10
	1¾	16		1½	8½		1	8½		1	15
	1	13		1	8		1½	13		1½	16
	2	16		1½	9		1½	11½		1	13
	1	14		1½	8		2	9		1¾	12
	1½	15		1½	12		1	12		1	16
	1	12½		1½	12		2	13		1½	14
	1¾	15		2	14		2	15		1 1/10	7½
	1	10		1½	13		1	12	Sept. 23	1	14
	1	12		1	9		1	9		1½	15
	1	13		1	12		1½	14		1	12
	1	14		1	15		1½	12		2	16
	1	9		1½	14		1½	12		1½	15
	1½	8		2	13		1½	14		1	12
	1	7½		1½	13½		2	13		1½	15
	2	15		1	12		1½	13½		2	13
	1¼	13		1½	13		1	9		1¾	15
	1½	11		1½	15		1	11		1	14
	1	12		1	16		2	14		1½	16
	1	13		1½	12		1½	15		1	10
	1½	11		2	14		1¾	16		1½	9
	1	13		1½	16		1	13		1	13
	2	14		1	12		2	11		1½	12
	1½	9		2	12		1½	11		1¼	14
Sept. 17	2	15		1	8½		1	13		1	13
	2¾	14		1½	13		1	15		1½	15
	1	14		1½	14		1¾	13½		2	12
	2	14		2	12		1½	16		2	9½
	2	16		1½	11½		1	9½		1¾	15
	2	15		1	12		1¼	9		1	14
	2	14		2	13½		2	12		1½	13
	1½	12		1½	13		2	12		1	15
	2	15		1½	11		2	15		1½	14
	2	16		1	8½		2½	14		2	13
	1½	14		2	12		1¾	14		1	15
	1	15		1½	13		2	14½		1½	16
	2	13		1½	14		2	16		1	13
	2	14½		2	12		1¾	15		2	14
	2	15		1½	11		1½	13		1¼	12
	1½	14		1	12		1	12		1	16
	1	8½		2	15		1	10		1	15
	1	9½		2	13		1¼	14		2	9½
	1½	9		1	9		2	13		¾	8
	1½	10		1½	12		2	15	Sept. 24	1½	12
	1	8		1	14		1¾	14		1½	14
	¾	9½		1½	13		1½	16		1¼	16
	1	7		2	14		1	12		1	12
	¾	7½		2½	15		1¾	13		1½	13

Native cattle—Continued.

MALE AND FEMALE.

Date.	Spleens.	Livers.	Date.	Spleens.	Livers.	Date.	Spleens.	Livers.	Date.	Spleens.	Livers.
Sept. 24	1	15	Sept. 24	1	16	Sept. 25	1	12	Sept. 25	1	11
	1¾	14		1½	15		2	15		1	12½
	1	12		1	16		1¼	14		1	11
	1¼	15		1½	15		1	12		1	11½
	1	12		1	14		1	11		1¼	10
	1	13		1	15		1½	10		1¼	13
	1¼	15		1¾	10		1	9		1½	12
	1	10		1¼	14		1½	12		1	11
	1	9½		1	13		1	8		1	8
	1	9½		1½	12		1½	8		1	8
	1	8½		1¼	15		1½	9		1	10½
	1¼	14		1	16		1½	11		1½	11
	1¾	15		1	12		1	13		2	9
	1	9½		1½	9½		1	9½		2	11
	1	12		1½	12		1½	11		1½	11
	1¾	14		1	14		1	11		1½	12
	1½	15		1	15		1½	12		1	9
	1	9½		1¼	12		1½	10		1	12
	¾	14		1	9½		1¼	8		1½	13
	1½	9½		¾	11		1½	12		1	12
	1¼	15	Sept. 25	3½	13½		1½	9		1½	14
	1½	13		1½	12		1	10		1	12
	1	14		1¼	12		1½	11		1½	13
	2	12		1¼	10		1	12		1	14
	2	15		1	12		2	11		1	12
	2	16		1½	12		1¼	14		1	14
	1½	15		1	13		1	15		2	15
	1¼	15		1½	12		1	10		13	38
	1¾	16		2	13		1½	12			
	1½	14		2	11		1½	13	Total	1,980½	16785¼
	2	16		2½	13		1½	14			
	1½	15		1	10		1	14	Average	1.459	12.362

Cherokee cattle.

MALE.

Date.	Spleens.	Livers.	Date.	Spleens.	Livers.	Date.	Spleens.	Livers.	Date.	Spleens.	Livers.
Sept. 8	2	10	Sept. 10	1½	9	Sept. 10	2½	14	Sept. 13	1½	8
	1	10		2	12		1½	14		1½	12
	2	10		1½	13		1½	10		1½	10
	1½	12		1½	7	Sept. 13	1½	12		2½	12
	2	9		1½	9		1½	13		2	12
	1	7		1½	13		1½	14		2¼	10
	2	10		1½	8		2	13		2¼	14
	1½	8		1	8		2½	10		1½	11
Sept. 9	2	10		1½	10		2	12		1½	9
	1½	9		1½	11		2	12		1½	12
	2	10		1½	10		2	13		2	15
	2	13		1½	11		1½	12		1½	10
	1	8		2	10		1½	8		2	14
	1½	8		1½	10		1½	10		1½	12
Sept. 10	1½	7		1½	10		1½	10		1½	10

Cherokee cattle—Continued.

MALE.

Date.	Spleens.	Livers.	Date.	Spleens.	Livers.	Date.	Spleens.	Livers.	Date.	Spleens.	Livers.
Sept. 13	1½	10	Sept. 15	2½	12	Sept. 15	2	13	Sept. 18	2	12
	2	12		2	13		1½	13		1	7
	2¼	15		2	12		1½	11		1	9
	2	10		1½	11		1½	9		1½	11
	1½	12		2	12		1½	11		1	12
	1½	13		2	12		1½	10		2	12
	2	13		1½	11		1½	11		1½	12
	1½	12		1½	10		2	13		1	12
	2½	16		1½	11		2	12		1	7
	2	12		1½	10		1½	11		1	9
	1½	9		1½	11		1½	9		1½	13
	2	12		2	12		1½	9		2	14
	1¼	14		2	12		1½	11		1	11
Sept. 14	2½	14		2	12		2	13		1	7
	2	12		1½	11		1½	11		1½	8
	1½	9		1½	9		2	13		1½	8
	1½	13		1¼	8		2	12		1	9
	1½	10		2	11		2	13		1½	9
	1½	13		1½	11		1½	11		1	8
	1½	12		1½	12		2½	14		1	9
	1½	10		2	12		2	13		1½	11
	1½	10		1½	11		1¾	14		1	8
	1½	10		2½	13		2	13		1	7
	2	14		2	12		2	13		1	9
	1½	10		1½	11		2	12		1½	10
	1½	12		1½	11		1½	10		1	10
	2½	15		2	13		1½	11		1½	13
	1½	11		1½	9		1½	12		1	11
	2¼	10		1½	9		1½	9		1	11
	2	11		1½	8		1½	10		1	11
	2½	12		1½	11		2	11		1½	10
	3¼	11		1½	12	Sept. 18	1½	7		1	11
	3	14		2	12		1	7		2	13
	1½	10		1½	11		1½	8		2	12
	2	9		1½	12		1	7		1	11
	3	10		2	13		1	5		2	12
	2½	9		1½	9		1	7		1½	13
	3	12		1½	10		1	8		2	9
	2	11		2	11		1¼	8		1	7
	2	10		1½	12		1	11		1½	8
	2	10		1½	10		1½	7		1	9
	3	10		2½	14		2	9		1½	9
Sept. 15	1½	8		1½	10		1½	8		1½	9
	1½	7		1½	11		1	7		1	8
	1½	8		1½	11		1	6		1	7
	2	12		1½	11		1½	9		1	8
	1½	13		1½	10		2	10		1	8
	1½	9		1½	11		1½	9		1½	9
	2	13		1½	12		1	7		2	10
	1½	9		1½	10		1¼	10		1½	11
	2	10		1½	9		1	8		2	13
	2	10		1½	13		1½	7		1	7
	2	10		1½	12		2	10		1½	8

Cherokee cattle—Continued.

MALE.

Date.	Spleens.	Livers.	Date.	Spleens.	Livers.	Date.	Spleens.	Livers.	Date.	Spleens.	Livers.
Sept. 18.......	1½	11	Sept. 18......	2	12	Sept. 18......	1	8	Sept. 18......	1½	7
	1	13		2	12		1	9		1½	9
	2	12		2	13		1½	7		1	8
	2½	13		2	13		1½	5		1½	7
	2	13		1½	11		1½	7		1½	7
	2½	11		1	11		1	6		1	8
	2	12		1½	13		1	5		1½	9
	1½	10		1½	10		1	7		1½	8
	1½	10		1	9		1½	8		1½	7
	1½	10		1	8		1	9		1½	9
	1½	11		1	11		1	7		1	8
	2	11		1½	13		1½	8	Sept. 25	1½	9
	2½	12		1	9		1½	9		1½	11
	2½	14		1	10		1	9		2	12
	2½	14		1½	10		1½	10		1½	9
	1½	10		1½	11		1½	10		1	8
	2	12		1½	11		1	8		1½	9
	2	12		1½	8		1	7		2	11
	1½	11		1	7		1	6		1½	10
	1½	10		1½	8		1	5		2	12
	1½	13		1½	9		1½	7			
	2	11		1	8		1	8	Total	577¾	3,756
	2½	13		1	9		1	6	Average.....	1.60	10.404

FEMALE.

Date.	Spleens.	Livers.	Date.	Spleens.	Livers.	Date.	Spleens.	Livers.	Date.	Spleens.	Livers.
Sept. 8	1½	11	Sept. 10......	1½	12	Sept. 13......	1½	8	Sept. 14......	2	12
	1½	10		1	6		2	11		2¾	11
	2	10		1½	8		2	12		2	11
	2	9		1½	9	Sept. 14	2½	13		2½	9
	1	7		1	7		1½	13		1½	8
	1	10		1½	13		1½	15		2	10
	2	10		1½	10		1½	14		2	10
	2	9		1½	12		1½	12		1½	10
	2	8		1½	10		1½	13		2½	9
Sept. 9	1	5		1½	11		1½	10		1½	8
	1½	9		1	7		1¼	10		2½	9
	1	6		1½	9		1½	11		1½	8
	1½	12		1½	9		1½	16		2¼	14
	1½	12	Sept. 13	1½	10		1¾	14		1½	9
	2	10		2	15		1½	10		1¾	11
	2	12		2½	12		1½	10		1¾	8
	1½	9		1½	8		1½	10		2¼	9
	1½	9		2	12		2	13		2	10
	1¼	12		2½	14		1½	12	Sept. 15	1½	11
	1	8		2	10		1½	12		1½	11
	1	5		1⅛	12		1½	10		1½	10
	2	10		1½	13		1½	12		1	9
	1½	10		2	14		1½	13		1	9
	1½	8		2½	18		1¼	9		1½	11
Sept. 10	1½	14		2	15		1½	8		1½	11
	1	10		1½	10		1½	10		1½	12

Cherokee cattle—Continued.

FEMALE.

Date.	Spleens.	Livers.	Date.	Spleens.	Livers.	Date.	Spleens.	Livers.	Date.	Spleens.	Livers.
Sept. 15.......	2	12	Sept. 15......	1½	10	Sept. 15......	1½	11	Sept. 18......	1½	11
	2	13		1½	11		1½	10		1½	9
	2	12		1	9		1½	10		1	7
	2½	14		1½	11		1½	11		1½	8
	1½	11		1½	12		1½	12		1½	9
	1½	11		1½	12	Sept. 18......	1½	11		1½	7
	1½	11		1½	11		1	9		1	9
	1½	12		1½	11		1½	13		1	8
	1½	12		1½	10		1½	13		1½	9
	1½	12		1½	11		1½	11			
	1½	13		1½	11		1½	12	Total........	244¼	1,611
	1	9		1½	11		1½	13			
	1½	10		1½	12		1	12	Average.....	1.606	10.6

MALE AND FEMALE.

Date.	Spleens.	Livers.	Date.	Spleens.	Livers.	Date.	Spleens.	Livers.	Date.	Spleens.	Livers.
Aug. 20........	3	9	Sept. 3.......	2½	14	Sept. 3.......	2½	13	Sept. 3.......	2½	10
	3½	8		2½	13		2	10		2¼	9
	3	12		2½	12		2½	12		2½	10
	2¾	10		2¼	14		2¼	13		2¼	9
	2	11		2½	13		2	10		2½	8
	2¾	9		2	13		1½	9		2¼	8
	2¾	12		2¼	14		1¼	10		2½	9
	3	8½		2½	13		2	11		2¼	9
	3	11		2½	13		1¾	11		2½	10
	3	9½		2½	14		2¼	12		2¼	9
Sept. 2	3	9½		2½	13		2½	11		2½	9
	3	11		2¼	13		2¼	10		2¼	9
	3	11		2¼	13		2¼	12		2	8
	2½	10		2	10		2	11		2¼	9
	3	9½		2¼	11		1½	10		3	10
	2½	9		2	11		1½	12		2½	10
	3	9		2½	12		2¼	12		2	9
	3	10		2¼	11		1¼	10		2½	9
	3	10½		2	10		2¼	11		2½	16
	3	9		2½	13		2¼	12		2½	12
	3¼	9		2½	11		2½	10		2¾	15
Sept. 3	2¼	10		2¼	12		2¼	8		4	13
	2½	13		1½	9		2½	8		2	10
	2¼	10		2	10		2½	9		2	11
	2	11		2¼	11		2½	10		2	10
	2½	14		2¼	10		2½	9		3	11
	1½	10		2	11		2½	10		3	12
	1¼	11		2¼	10		2¼	8		2	9
	2½	12		2½	13		2½	10		2	15
	2¼	11		2¼	10		2½	10		2½	12
	2¼	13		2¼	12		2¼	9		2	13
	2½	14		2	10		2¼	8		2¾	12
	2¼	12		1½	8		2½	10		2½	12
	2	13		2¼	12		2¼	8		2	11
	2½	13		2½	13		2	8		3	11
	2½	14		2¼	10		2¼	8		1½	12

Cherokee cattle—Continued.

MALE AND FEMALE.

Date.	Spleens.	Livers.	Date.	Spleens.	Livers.	Date.	Spleens.	Livers.	Date.	Spleens.	Livers.
Sept. 4	2¼	12	Sept. 4.......	2	9	Sept. 6	2¼	10	Sept. 10......	3	11
	2	10		2	10		2¼	11		3½	9
	2¼	11		1½	9		2	9		3	9½
	2½	13		2¼	11		2	8		4	9½
	2	9		2½	10		1½	13		3	10½
	1¾	8		2¼	10		1¼	8		2¾	9
	1½	9		2½	12		2¼	11		2¾	10
	1¼	8		2¼	11		2½	13		2½	9
	1½	10		2½	13		1¼	8		2¾	14
	2	11		2¼	11		2¼	12		3	11
	2¼	12		2	10		2¼	13		3½	9½
	2¼	12		2	12		1¼	8		4	9
	2¼	11		1½	9		1¼	9		4¼	9½
	2	9		1½	11		1½	11		3	10
	2½	12		1¼	10		2¼	12		3½	9
	2¼	10		2½	13		2	10		3¼	8½
	2	9	Sept .6.......	2	13	Sept. 7	1½	10		2¾	9½
	1¼	8		2¼	13		1½	12		2½	11
	2½	12		2	12		1¼	12		3	9½
	1¼	9		2¼	13		2¼	14		3¾	9
	2	12		2	11		2¼	12		3½	9½
	1½	10		2	10		2½	13		2½	8½
	2½	12		1½	10		2	12		3	9¾
	2¼	11		1¾	8		2¼	14		4	9½
	2¼	11		1½	9		2¼	14	Sept. 11	2¾	8
	2½	12		1½	11		2	10		3	9½
	2½	12		2¼	13		1½	9		3	10
	2	9		2¼	13		1½	10		3½	9½
	1½	9		2½	12		2¼	12	Sept. 14	2	15
	2	8		2	10		2¼	13		1½	10
	1½	9		2	9		2¼	13		1½	10
	1½	11		2¼	12		2¼	13		1½	12
	2½	12		2½	11		2½	14		1¾	13
	2½	12		2¼	13		2½	13		1¾	14
	2¼	11		1½	9		2¼	14		1½	10
	2¼	12		2	10		2½	15		1½	16
	1½	9		1½	12		2½	14		1½	13
	1¼	9		2	11		2	10		1½	10
	2	10		2¼	12		2	11		1½	12
	2¼	12		2¼	11		2¼	13		1½	12
	1½	11		2½	10		2¼	14		1½	10
	1½	11		2¼	9		2¼	13		1½	9
	2¼	12		2	10		2¼	14		1¾	14
	2¼	12		2	9		2	10		1½	12
	2½	12		2½	13		2¼	14		1½	18
	2¼	11		2½	12		2½	13		1½	10
	1½	9		2½	12		2¼	12		1½	12
	1½	9		2½	12		2½	13		1½	10
	2	11		2½	13	Sept. 10	2¼	9½		1½	9
	2½	10		2	10		2½	10		1½	12
	2¼	11		2	9		3½	10		1½	12
	2½	11		2½	13		2½	11		1½	12
	2¼	12		2¼	14		2½	9¾		2	13

Cherokee cattle—Continued.

MALE AND FEMALE.

Date.	Spleens.	Livers.	Date.	Spleens.	Livers.	Date.	Spleens.	Livers.	Date.	Spleens.	Livers.
Sept. 14	1½	10	Sept. 14	3	9½	Sept. 17	2½	10	Sept. 23	3½	12
	1½	10		4	8		2½	10		2	9
	1½	10	Sept. 16	2½	8	Sept. 18	2	9½		2½	8½
	1½	8		2½	9		3	8½	Sept. 24	3	10
	1½	14		3	11		3	9		3	9½
	1¾	16		3½	10		2½	11		3	9
	1½	14		3	9½		2¾	10		2¾	10
	1½	13		2½	8½		3	9		3½	10
	1½	12		3	9½		3½	8½		3½	9½
	1½	14		3½	8		2	12		3	10
	1½	13	Sept. 17	2½	9		2½	11		3½	11
	1½	15		2½	8½		2¾	12		3¾	11½
	3	9		3	9		3	9		4	10
	3	8		3	9½		3½	9½		4	10
	4	10		2¾	11	Sept. 23	3	10		3½	12
	4½	12		3	12		3½	9		3	9½
	3	9		2½	11½		2½	9½		2¾	9
	3	11		3	9½		3	12		2½	9
	3½	12		3	10		3	11		2½	10
	3¾	9		3½	11		2½	10	Total	1,034½	4,767½
	3	10		2	11		2¾	14			
	3½	8½		2½	14		3	10	Average	2.345	10.81

Texan cattle.

MALE.

Date.	Spleens.	Livers.	Date.	Spleens.	Livers.	Date.	Spleens.	Livers.	Date.	Spleens.	Livers.
Sept. 8	3½	12	Sept. 10	2½	13	Sept. 11	3	13	Sept. 11	2½	12
	3½	10		2½	12		3	14		2½	10
	3½	10		3	12		2½	14		2½	11
	3	9		3	14		2½	13		2½	10
	3½	12		2½	13		3½	10		3	13
	3	10		3	17		3	10		3	14
	3½	12		3	14		3	12		3	12
	3	11		2	13		2½	13		3½	13
	3½	12		2½	11		3	14		2½	14
	3½	14		2½	14		3	14		2	13
	3	10		2	13		3	14		2½	14
Sept. 9	1½	13		2½	14		3	12		2	13
	2½	11		2½	12		3	12		2½	13
	2	13		2½	13		3	12		2½	12
	2	14		2	12		3	12		2	9
	2½	14		1½	10		3	14	Sept. 13	3	14
	2½	16		2	10		2½	13		2½	13
	2	12		2½	12		2½	12		2	13
	2	11		2	10		3	14		3	14
	2½	11		2	9		3½	13		2½	11
	2½	11		2½	12		2½	12		3½	16
	3	11		2½	14		2¾	11		3	21
	2½	12		1¾	8		3½	14		2	10
Sept. 10	3	16		1	9		2½	10		3	12
	2½	14		2	11		2½	14		3	13

Texan cattle—Continued.

MALE.

Date.	Spleens.	Livers.	Date.	Spleens.	Livers.	Date.	Spleens.	Livers.	Date.	Spleens.	Livers.
Sept. 13.......	2½	12	Sept. 15	2½	13	Sept. 16	2½	13	Sept. 16	1½	12
	3½	13		2	12		2	12		1	11
	3	13		3½	10		2	12		1	12
	2½	16		2	11		2	13		2	13
	2	12		3	13		2	13		3	14
	2½	14		2½	12		2½	13		2½	13
	3	13		2	12		2	13		2½	13
	2½	12		3	13		2	12		2	13
	3	13		2	15		2	13		2	13
	2½	10		1½	12		2	13		2	13
	2	12		2	11		2	14		2	13
	3	14		3¼	10		1½	11		1½	12
	3	14		3	12		1½	12		2	13
	3	13		2½	13		2	12		2	13
	3½	15		3	10		2	13		2	13
Sept. 14	2½	10		2½	9		2½	15		1½	11
	3	12		2½	12		2½	15		1½	11
	3	14		3	13		2½	13		1½	11
	3½	13		2½	15		3	14		1½	12
	2½	10		2	10		2	15		2	11
	2½	11		3	12		2½	13		1½	13
	3	12		2½	15		2½	13		2	11
	2¾	10		3	10		2½	12		1½	13
Sept. 15	2½	24		2¼	13		2	12		2	13
	2½	12	Sept. 16	2½	14		2½	12		1½	13
	2½	10		2	15		2	11	Sept. 18	3	10
	2½	11		3	15		2	12		3½	13
	2	13		2½	12		2½	13		2¼	15
	3	13		2	13		2½	12		2½	12
	3¼	14		2	12		2	13		3	13
	2¼	10		2	13		2	14		2	16
	1¼	10		2	12		2½	13		1½	15
	2	8		2½	13		2½	12		3	13
	3	13		1½	11		2	14		2	10
	2½	15		2	12		2	13		3	15
	2½	13		2	13		2	12		3	11
	2	10		2	13		2	13		2½	12
	2½	12		2½	13		2	12		1½	11
	3	16		2	12		1½	11		2	12
	2½	15		2	13		1½	11		3	13
	2	12		2½	14		1½	10		2½	11
	2½	13		2	13		2	12		3	12
	1½	10		2	14		2	15		2½	10
	2	11		2	14		2½	14		3	11
	3	13		2	14		2½	13		2	10
	3	12		2	13		2	13		2½	12
	2	9		2½	14		2	12		2	11
	3	12		2½	14		1½	11		2½	13
	1¾	9		2	13		1½	10		3	10
	2	10		2½	13		1½	10		2	15
	2½	13		2½	14		1½	11		2½	9
	1½	12		2	13		1½	12		2	14
	2	12		2½	14		1½	11		3	13

Texan cattle—Continued.

MALE.

Date.	Spleens.	Livers.	Date.	Spleens.	Livers.	Date.	Spleens.	Livers.	Date.	Spleens.	Livers.
Sept. 18	1¾	8	Sept. 18	2	13	Sept. 18......	2	11	Sept. 25	2	11
	2	10		3	14		2½	13		2	13
	3	15		3	13		1½	11		2	15
	3	13		3	13		1½	11		2	10
	3	15		2½	13		2	12		2½	13
	3	10		2	12		2	12		2	13
	3	12		2½	12		1½	12		1¾	11
	2½	15		1	11		1	11		2	12
	2	12		1½	12		1½	12		2	13
	3	13		2½	13		2	13		2½	13
	2	12		2	13		1½	11		2	12
	3	11		1½	14		1½	11		1½	11
	2½	12		1½	13		2	13		1	10
	2¼	10		2	14		2	10		2½	13
	3	11		2½	13		2	11		2	12
	2½	13		2	14		2	11		2½	13
	2	10		1½	13		2½	12		2	14
	3	13		1½	14		2	13		2½	12
	2½	11		2	13		2½	11		2	13
	3	10		2	14		2½	13		2	12
	2½	12		2½	15		1½	9		1½	13
	3	13		2	13		1	10		1	9
	2	10		1½	14	Sept. 24	1½	11		1½	10
	2½	11		1	12		1½	9		1½	12
	3	13		1½	13		1½	12		1	9
	2	13		2	11		2½	14		1½	12
	1½	11		2½	13		2	13		2	13
	1	11		2	13		2	14		2	12
	1½	13		2	11		2	15		2½	14
	1½	10		1½	12		2	13		2	13
	1	9		2	14		2½	14		2½	14
	1	8		1½	13		2	13		2	13
	1	11		2	14		2½	14		1½	10
	1½	13		2	13		2½	14		1½	11
	2	13		2½	12		2	13		2	12
	2½	12		2	13		2	12		1½	11
	2	13		1½	11		2½	14		1½	10
	1½	11		1½	10		2½	13		2½	13
	2	13		2	13		2	14		2	12
	2	13		2½	14		2½	14		1½	12
	2½	12		2	13		2	13		2	13
	1½	11		2½	13		3	15			
	1	10		2	12		2½	14	Total	1,109¼	6,070
	1½	12		2	11		3	15			
	2	14		2	11	Sept. 25	2	10	Average	2.259	12.36
	1½	13		2	12		1¾	12			

FEMALE.

Date.	Spleens.	Livers.	Date.	Spleens.	Livers.	Date.	Spleens.	Livers.	Date.	Spleens.	Livers.
Sept. 8	2½	11	Sept. 8.......	2¾	12	Sept. 8.......	2	10	Sept. 8........	2½	15
	2¼	10		2½	12		2½	11		3	12
	2	10		2½	10		3	13		2½	16

Texan cattle—Continued.

FEMALE.

Date.	Spleens.	Livers.	Date.	Spleens.	Livers.	Date.	Spleens.	Livers.	Date.	Spleens.	Livers.
Sept. 8........	2¼	14	Sept. 8	2½	16	Sept. 10......	1½	9	Sept. 13.......	3	13
	2	15		3	15		2	10		2½	12
	2½	13		2½	13		2	10	Total	69¼	360
	3	16		2¾	16		1¼	10			
	2½	15	Sept. 10	2	11		2	10	Average.....	2.387	12.413

MALE AND FEMALE.

Date.	Spleens.	Livers.	Date.	Spleens.	Livers.	Date.	Spleens.	Livers.	Date.	Spleens.	Livers.
Sept. 2	3	12	Sept. 4.......	1½	10	Sept. 4.......	2½	14	Sept. 4.......	2¼	12
	3	10¾		2½	11		2½	12		2¼	13
	3	9½		2	12		2¼	14		2½	15
	4	12		2½	16		2½	13		2½	14
	3	11		2	14		2¼	12		2¼	13
	3	10		2½	10		2¼	13		2¼	14
	2½	12		2	12		2	11		2¼	14
	3	12		2½	12		2¼	14		2	10
	3	11		1¾	13		2¼	13		2¼	12
	3	11½		2	15		2½	13		2½	13
	2½	10		2	12		2¼	13		2½	12
	2¾	10		2	13		2¼	14	Sept. 6	2½	14
	2½	11		2½	15		2½	14		2¼	14
	2½	11		3	12		2¼	13		2¼	13
	3	11		3	11		2¼	14		2¼	13
	3	12		3	12		2½	14		2½	14
	3½	10		3	10		2	11		2¼	13
	3	12		3	10		2½	14		2¼	13
Sept. 3	2¾	9½		3	12		2½	14		2½	14
	3	10¼		2½	9		2½	13		2	12
	2½	11		2½	12		2¼	12		2¼	14
	2¾	13		2	13		2¼	10		2¼	14
	3	12		3	10		2¼	11		2	12
	2¾	11		3	12		2½	14		2½	14
	2½	9		2	12		2½	14		2¼	13
	3½	11		2½	12		2½	12		2½	14
	4	13		2	10		2¼	10		2½	15
	3½	10		2	10		2½	12		2¼	13
	3¾	11		2½	12		3¼	13		2¼	14
	3½	9		2½	12		2½	13		2¼	13
	3¼	10		2	12		2½	14		2½	14
	3	10½		2¼	14		2¼	13		2¼	13
	3¾	11		2½	13		2¼	13		2¼	14
	3	10		3	14		2¼	12		2¼	13
	3	10		2½	13		2¼	13		2½	14
	3½	11		2¼	12		2¼	10		2½	15
	3½	9		2¼	11		2¼	10		2	12
	3¾	11½		2	10		2½	14		2¼	12
	2½	9		2½	13		2½	13		2¼	13
Sept. 4	2	10		2¼	12		2¼	12		2½	12
	2	11		2¼	13		2½	13		2¼	13
	3	12		2	10		2¼	14		2	10
	2½	10		2¼	18		2½	13		2¼	12

Texan cattle—Continued.

MALE AND FEMALE.

Date.	Spleens.	Livers.	Date.	Spleens.	Livers.	Date.	Spleens.	Livers.	Date.	Spleens.	Livers.
Sept. 6........	2½	10	Sept. 7........	2¾	11	Sept. 7........	2½	14	Sept. 9........	3½	9
	3	10½		2¾	9½		3	15		3¾	10
	3½	11½		2	8½		3¼	14		4	9½
	2½	11½		3½	9½		2½	13		4½	11
	4	10		2½	14		2¼	14		3½	11
	2	9½		2¼	14		2	11	Sept. 11.......	3	9
	2½	10		2	12		3			2¾	8½
	3½	11¾		2½	14		2½	13		1	14
	2¾	11½		2¼	12		2¾	16		3½	10
	3	11		2½	14		1½	12		4	11
	3¾	12		2½	12		2½	10		3½	9½
	2½	12		2½	13		3	12		3½	12
	8	13		2	9		2½	13		3½	9
	3½	10		2¼	10		2	13		3½	11
	3	10		2½	13		2¾	10		3	10
	3½	9½		2½	15		2½	12		3¾	12
	4	10		2½	14		2½	11⅛		3	8
	3½	11		3	13		1¾	24		3	9
Sept. 7........	3	9½		4	15		2	13			
	3½	10		2½	14	Sept. 8........	3	12	Total..........	699	3.126
	3	10½		2½	14		3½	11¼			
	4	9½		2½	15		4	9½	Average......	2.667	11.931
	4½	9¾		2½	14		3	9¾			
	3	10		2½	14	Sept. 9........	2½	10			

REPORT OF RESULTS OF EXAMINATIONS OF FLUIDS OF DISEASED CATTLE WITH REFERENCE TO PRESENCE OF CRYPTOGAMIC GROWTHS.

SIR: In accordance with your request, and with instructions received from the Surgeon General United States Army, to investigate the question of the possible cryptogamic origin of cattle diseases, we have carefully examined many samples of blood and secretions from diseased cattle, furnished us from time to time by Professor Gamgee, and have experimented with them in various ways. The results of our investigations we have to report as follows.

The questions which we have endeavored to answer are these:

1st. Are any forms of cryptogamic growth present during life in the blood or secretions of the diseased animals?

2d. If so, of what character are they, and what is their probable source?

Supposing the foregoing queries answered, there would still remain the problem of the nature of the connection between the cryptogam and the disease, a problem which we have not attempted to discuss.

As the fungi are the only cryptogams which it is necessary to consider, reference will be made to these only.

The fungi which are supposed to cause disease in animals are, when in their perfect state, or at least in such a state that they can be identified, composed of mycelium and spores. But according to the advocates of the cryptogamic origin of disease, neither the mycelium nor the spores of the fungus that produces the malady are necessarily or even usually to be found in the fluids or tissues of the affected animal, their theory being that the disease is produced by the presence in the economy of minute particles of protoplasm, (micrococcus of Hallier,) resulting from development and breaking up of the spores or mycelium of a fungus; from which granules, they assert, can be developed perfect forms of fungi, of recognizable genera and species, by proper "cultivation" outside of the body of the animal fluids containing them.

Thus, when the blood of a pleuropneumonic cow, fresh from the vein, is examined with a magnifying power of 1,200 diameters linear, nothing distinctive or unusual may appear; the red and white blood corpuscles may be perfectly normal, and nothing like spores or mycelium will be seen. But there will probably be, either single or in masses, some minute granules or molecules appearing as glistening points scattered over the field. If such are not present at first, by keeping the blood exposed to the air for a few hours they may be found in abundance.

Now, it is these little molecules which are asserted to cause disease by their presence in the animal economy, and which are claimed to be vegetable in their nature, as being developed from and capable of reproducing certain common fungi, popularly known as rusts, smuts, or molds.

To prove the truth of the latter statement, experiments have been made by various investigators on the principle of placing the fluids containing the micrococcus in the proper conditions as regards warmth and moisture for the development of fungi; supplying the germs with suitable pabulum for their nourishment, and adopting such precautions as are possible against the fortuitous introduction of spores of fungi from the atmosphere. And if, under such circumstances, a mold or mildew appears upon the suspected matter, the argument is that such mold necessarily sprung from the micrococcus granules as its parent germs, and therefore represents the perfect fungus of which such micrococcus is a special form.

Now, since the spores of the common molds are almost omnipresent, the conclusiveness of all such experiments must depend upon the possibility of showing that all extraneous bodies have been perfectly excluded from the fluids cultivated.

In detailing our own experiments in this direction, therefore, we give a somewhat minute description of the apparatus and processes employed, partly that the value of the results obtained may be judged by it, and in part because it may be of use to others attempting a similar line of research.

The first thing to be done is to obtain the suspected fluids in a state of purity, without risk of contamination by spores floating in the atmosphere, and in such a manner that they can be preserved for some time without risk of material change.

To effect this we take a glass tube about three-sixteenths of an inch in diameter, seal one end by the flame of a lamp, and, at a point about three inches from the sealed end, draw it out to a slender tube, (*a*.)

The tube is then held nearly upright in the flame of a Bunsen burner until the whole of the sealed end up to the narrow neck is red-hot. The part in the flame is held with pincers, the other end in the fingers, and when the requisite heat is obtained the slender neck is rapidly drawn to a point and sealed. We now have a pointed, hermetically-sealed tube, (*b*,) in which there is a partial vacuum, and in which by the red heat all organic matters have been destroyed.

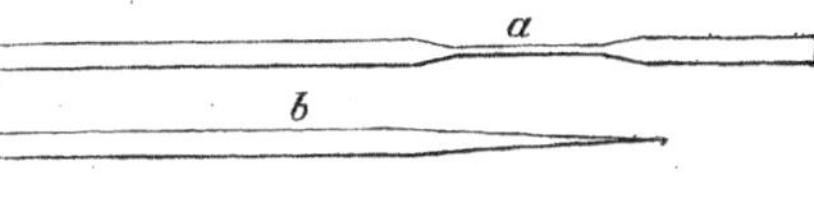

This we call a "vacuum tube."

Suppose, now, that we want some blood for experiment. As soon as possible after the death of the animal, lay bare the jugular vein, prick it with a lancet, introduce the pointed end of the tube and break it off within the vein, pressure being at the same time made upon the vessel from above and below toward the opening by the fingers of an assistant. The blood will rush into the tube, and if it has been properly made, will fill it for three-fourths of its length. Then, holding a lighted spirit lamp or candle close to the vein, withdraw the point of the tube directly from the vessel into the flame, and hold it there until sealed.

If the operation has been properly performed, and the blood be healthy, it will coagulate and then remain unchanged for an indefinite period.

Exudates in the pleural or peritoneal cavities, bile, urine, &c., are obtained and preserved in the same way.

The next step is to place the material thus obtained in favorable conditions for the growth and development of any fungus germs which it may contain. The requisites for this purpose are warmth, moisture, a supply of nutritive material, and exclusion of foreign spores.

With regard to this last point, we reasoned as follows:

By no amount of precautions or of complexity of apparatus is it possible to secure such absolute isolation of a fragment of tissue or a quantity of blood from possible contact with foreign spores, that the results obtained from its cultivation can be considered as positively conclusive. By no means known to us can a piece of lung be transferred from the body of an animal to the interior of a glass flask without contact with the atmosphere and with instruments, nor even with the more manageable blood can we be absolutely certain, when we see its surface covered with mold, that the possibly single spore from which that forest sprang must infallibly have been in the vein of the animal whence the blood was drawn. It was felt, therefore, that to adopt at the outset extraordinary precautions against the introduction of foreign spores would be more apt to lead to error than even taking none at all. The method of comparison was therefore resorted to.

Let us first see, we argued, whether, without taking special pains to prevent the entrance of extraneous matters, the tissues and fluids of a diseased animal will produce fungi which healthy tissues and fluids placed side by side with them will not. The apparatus employed consists of the following:

1st. The so-called "isolation apparatus."

This consists of a thin flat-bottomed flask, of four to eight ounces capacity, closed by a cork dipped in paraffine. Through the cork passes a glass tube bent twice at right angles, reaching about two inches into the flask, and having the external end loosely closed by a pledget of dry cotton or jewelers' wool.

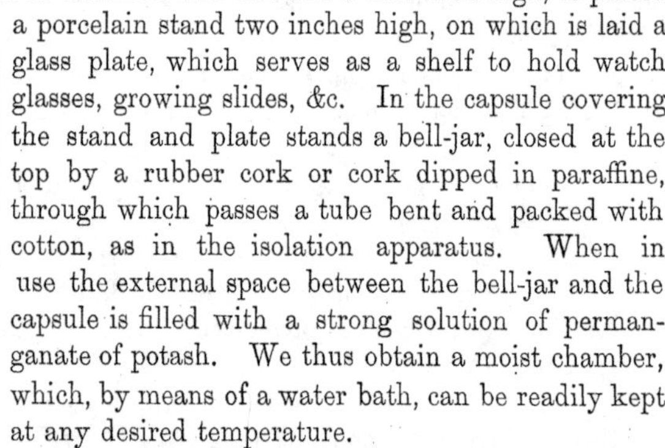

This is used in operating upon considerable quantities or masses of material which are to remain undisturbed for several days, weeks, or months.

To follow out the changes which occur from day to day, and especially to trace under the microscope the commencement and progress of any fungous growth, growing slides of various patterns, and the so-called culture apparatus, were employed. This last was made as follows:

In a flat glass capsule, six inches in diameter and one and a half inch high, is placed a porcelain stand two inches high, on which is laid a glass plate, which serves as a shelf to hold watch glasses, growing slides, &c. In the capsule covering the stand and plate stands a bell-jar, closed at the top by a rubber cork or cork dipped in paraffine, through which passes a tube bent and packed with cotton, as in the isolation apparatus. When in use the external space between the bell-jar and the capsule is filled with a strong solution of permanganate of potash. We thus obtain a moist chamber, which, by means of a water bath, can be readily kept at any desired temperature.

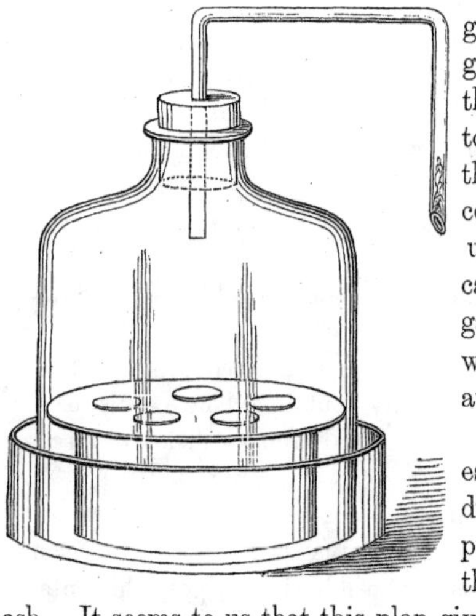

The above-described forms of apparatus are essentially those used by Hallier, but he provides for drawing into the flask or bell-jar fresh air, which he purifies from foreign matters by causing it to pass through alcohol or a solution of permanganate of potash. It seems to us that this plan gives more complexity and trouble without additional security; for we have repeatedly caused spores of various species of fungi to germinate after they had been one or two minutes in alcohol; and spores being not easily wet by water, they would readily pass without injury in a bubble of air drawn through any aqueous solution. The risk of spores passing through an inch of dry cotton loosely packed in a tube, unless by the aid of a strong and long-continued current of air, is probably very small.

Of course the most satisfactory proof of the presence of fungous germs in the blood would be to see them actually develop under the microscope, and produce the forms by which they could be identified. To this end we have made use of the various forms of growing slides known to microscopists, but with results not very satisfactory. For the general purposes of a growing slide, that which has given the most satisfaction is made by laying on an ordinary glass slide, three inches by one, a piece of thin, fine, white blotting paper of the same size, with an opening in the center three-fourths of an inch in diameter, or a little less than that of the thin glass cover used. The edges of the paper may be cemented to the glass with a little Canada balsam, although this is not necessary.

To use it, put in strong alcohol for ten minutes, then in distilled water for the same length of time; free the central opening from water; place in it a drop of the fluid to be cultivated, and cover it with a very thin glass cover Care must be taken to keep it perfectly flat. Place the slide in a culture apparatus, in which water alone is used as the isolating fluid; let one end of a piece of sewing thread rest on the end of the slide and the other dip into the water.

If the slide is to be used without being placed in a moist chamber, the paper should be covered with a piece of thin sheet-rubber or oiled silk, of the same shape and size, and with a corresponding opening. If it be desired to use high powers, or to trace the germinations of a spore found in examining a slide, the glass cover may rest on the slide, and the blotting paper be placed on instead of under it.

If it is desired to develop the fruit, the drop of alimentary fluid should be small, and a groove should be cut in the paper to the edge of the slide to allow the admission of air. The amount of moisture can be regulated at will by varying the size and number of the threads used to keep the paper wet. This slide is simple, cheap, and susceptible of being so modified that it is available for almost every purpose for which a growing slide is required.

De Bary's growing slides were also used several times, and were very satisfactory.

Another form of development apparatus, which was used toward the close of our experiments, consisted of a six-ounce glass beaker, having a little water at the bottom, and hermetically closed by a piece of thin sheet-rubber tightly stretched over the top. From the center of this cover there was suspended by a thread a strip of thin blotting paper which had been previously soaked in alcohol and distilled water, and on which the material to be cultivated had been placed. The thread was attached to the cover and the paper by Canada balsam. This is a sort of isolation apparatus, and is more satisfactory than the one used by Professor Hallier.

The material or substratum upon which the cultures are made, and which is intended to furnish nutriment to the fungi, is of various kinds. We used extract of beef, healthy blood, condensed milk, solutions of cane and grape sugar, pulp of lemon, orange, potato, &c.

The solutions of sugar used were made with crystallized sugar, and a little tartrate of ammonia and ashes of yeast were added to furnish the nitrogen and salts required for the growth of fungi.

All the apparatus was thoroughly cleansed previous to use, by washing with alcohol and freshly-boiled distilled water, and the solutions of sugar, milk, beef juice, &c., were thoroughly boiled; and, if filtered, reboiled before they were used.

SERIES I.—EXAMINATIONS OF BLOOD AND SECRETIONS FROM CATTLE AFFECTED WITH CONTAGIOUS PLEUROPNEUMONIA.

A cow, four years old, died with the usual symptoms of pleuropneumonia, near Washington, on the 10th day of February, 1869. Examination was made twenty minutes after death. The lungs were stuffed with exudation, and the pleural cavity contained a quantity of turbid, very fetid liquid, which, under the microscope, appeared full of actively moving monads and bacteria. No communication was found between the lung and the pleural cavity, but it is not positive that such did not exist. The blood, under a magnifying power of 1,200 diameters, presented no abnormal appearance. Vacuum tubes were filled with the blood, and specimens of the pleural fluid and of the bile were also preserved. The latter presented no unusual appearance under the microscope.

Experiment 1, February 10, 1869.—Three six-ounce isolation-flasks were prepared; an ounce of Tourtelot's extract of beef placed in each, boiled five minutes, and allowed to cool to 90° Fahrenheit. To the first were added the contents of one of the vacuum tubes from the cow above referred to; to the second that of a tube of blood from a healthy cow; to the third, nothing. The flasks were then placed in a water bath, and kept at a temperature of 85° Fahrenheit. On the 14th of February the flasks were opened. N . 1 contained large numbers of motionless bacteria, single and in pairs; No. 2 contained a very few of the same; No. 3 contained none. The flasks were kept one week longer, at the end of which time there was no change from the appearances above mentioned.

Experiment 2, February 10, 1869.—Six watch-glasses were arranged as follows: No. 1 contained pulp of fresh lemon and pleuropneumonic blood; No. 2 contained pulp of fresh potato and pleuropneumonic blood; No. 3 contained pulp of fresh lemon and healthy blood; No. 4 contained pulp of fresh potato and healthy blood; No. 5 contained pulp of fresh lemon alone; No. 6 contained pulp of fresh potato alone. All the watch-glasses were placed in a culture apparatus, which was kept at 80° Fahrenheit in a water bath. February 14th a beautiful growth of *Aspergillus glaucus* (Lk.) and *Penicillium glaucum* (Fr.) appeared on watch-glasses Nos. 1, 2, 3, 5, and 6—most profusely on Nos. 1 and 3. Watch-glass No. 4 contained nothing.

Experiment 3, February 10, 1869.—Six watch-glasses were arranged, three with pulp of lemon, and three with potato. To four of them a few drops of the pleural liquid were added. They were placed in the culture apparatus, and in four days aspergillus and penicillium were in fruit in all.

Experiment 4, February 10, 1869.—This was a duplicate of experiment 1, with the exception that bile was used instead of blood. At the end of ten days' careful examination failed to discover any organic forms in either of the flasks.

Experiment 5, February 25, 1869.—One of the vacuum tubes of blood from the above-mentioned cow, and a tube of healthy blood which had been put up at the same time, were opened and carefully examined. The blood in each was coagulated, free from offensive odor, and under the microscope presented no unusual appearance. The contents of each tube were placed in a one-ounce vial with a slip of purified blotting paper, the vials sealed and kept at a temperature of 70° Fahrenheit. Ten days later bacteria and vibriones were present in each, but no trace of mycelium or of fungus fructification.

On the 26th of February, 1869, a cow in the last stages of pleuropneumonia was killed near Washington, and vacuum tubes were filled from the jugular vein. Tubes were also filled with the serum contained in bullæ formed by the false membrane lining the bronchial tubes.

About four inches of each jugular vein were removed, ligatures having been first applied. Eighteen hours afterward the blood in the veins from which the tubes had been filled was carefully examined with a power of 750 diameters. It was coagulated, and the serum contained some molecules, single or in chains of two or three, which were motionless, (see plate, fig. 1.) Blood from one of the vacuum tubes contained no such bodies. The lung serum contained molecules like those in the vein.

Experiment 6, February 26, 1869.—In a culture apparatus were placed three watch-glasses and two growing slides, arranged as follows: The growing slides and watch-glass No. 1 contained boiled potato and diseased blood; watch-glass No. 2 contained boiled potato and healthy blood; watch-glass No. 3 contained boiled potato and lung fluid. Twenty-four hours later, in the growing slides the red corpuscles had nearly disappeared; bacteria and monads, single or in short chains, were seen; a few moving, but the greater part at rest. Seven days later there was no change; motionless bacteria and monads were present in all the glasses, but no trace of mycelium or spores.

Experiment 7, February 26, 1869.—Seven watch-glasses and five growing slides were arranged as follows: Watch-glass No. 1 contained potato boiled in distilled water; watch-glass No. 2 contained lemon boiled in distilled water; watch-glass No. 3 contained lemon boiled with diseased blood; watch-glass No. 4 contained diseased blood alone; watch-glass No. 5 contained healthy blood alone; watch-glass No. 6 contained boiled potato with diseased blood; watch-glass No. 7 contained boiled potato with healthy blood; growing slide A contained boiled lemon with diseased blood; growing slide B contained boiled lemon with healthy blood; growing slide C contained boiled potato with diseased blood; growing slide D contained boiled potato with healthy blood; growing slide E contained boiled potato alone. These were placed in four sets of culture apparatus, and kept at a temperature of 78° Fahrenheit. In twenty-four hours a few small cells were seen in slide B, which rapidly developed into ordinary yeast, continuing to bud and increase for four days. The fluids in watch-glasses 4 and 5 rapidly putrefied, and were filled with bacteria and monads. In watch-glasses 1 and 2 and growing slide E no change had occurred in eight days. In the others a few motionless bacteria appeared on the second day, after which there was no change. The precautions taken in this experiment to exclude extraneous bodies were great, embracing every point which could be thought of as liable to lead to error. In April one of the tubes containing lung serum from this cow was given to Mr. Reid, residing near Washington, and with its contents he successfully inoculated several cattle, producing in each case the same effects, and, judging by the after results, conferring

21

the same immunity against the disease as if perfectly fresh virus had been used. The jugular vein from this cow, which had not been opened, was suspended in a glass jar, closed with a cork dipped in paraffine. This was kept at the ordinary temperature of the room and in diffuse daylight.

June 3, 1869, the jar was opened and the contents examined. The serum had drained from the vein and collected in the bottom of the jar, was of an offensive odor, and contained bacteria, moving and at rest. No trace of mold on the outside of the vein. The contents of the vein showed no bacteria or molecular forms.

The contents of the vein and the serum which had drained from it were cultivated upon various substrata and in the several forms of apparatus, with the usual results, viz: luxuriant development of cryptococcus and penicillium.

On the 3d of June, 1869, three months after it had been put up, one of the vacuum tubes of blood from this animal was opened, and the contents carefully examined. They could not be distinguished from freshly coagulated blood; the corpuscles were perfectly normal, and there was no trace of bacteria or micrococcus.

This blood was cultivated on growing slides and in the beaker isolation apparatus—in one case with negative results, in others with the productions of the usual penicillium forms. Healthy blood kept for the same time and treated in the same way gave the same results.

Other experiments were made with the pleuropneumonic fluids by cultivating them with solutions of cane and grape sugar, which will be referred to subsequently.

The general conclusion from all the observations and experiments we have made is, that in the contagious pleuropneumonia of cattle there is no peculiar fungus germ present in the blood or secretions, and that the theory of its cryptogamic origin is untenable.

The significance of the appearance of bacteria, monads, penicillium, &c., in the experiments above given will be hereafter referred to.

SERIES II.—EXAMINATIONS OF BLOOD AND SECRETIONS FROM CATTLE AFFECTED WITH THE TEXAS OR SPLENIC FEVER.

On the 30th of April, 1869, two four-year old steers were killed at Corpus Christi, Texas, and vacuum tubes were filled by Professor Gamgee with the blood, urine, and bile. Professor Gamgee's notes state that the spleen of these animals weighed respectively three and a half and three and three-quarters pounds; the livers were fatty; the true stomachs presented erosions, and there were punctiform ecchymoses in the pelvis of the kidneys and in the bladder.

The blood and secretions were examined microscopically by Professor Gamgee, immediately after the death of the animal, with a power of five hundred and fifty diameters, but nothing unusual was discovered.

On the 25th of May one of the blood tubes was opened, and the contents examined with a power of eight hundred diameters.

The blood was dark, firmly coagulated, and without offensive odor. No white corpuscles were seen; the red corpuscles were mostly normal, a few being crenated or triangular. Patches of granular matter, a few motionless bacteria, and molecules, single or in chains of two or three, having a vibrating, swarming motion, were observed.

In short, all the appearances were those usually presented by blood when the white corpuscles have disintegrated and it is in the incipient stage of putrefaction. But besides these there were present yellow globular bodies, smaller than the red blood corpuscles, mostly united by twos and threes, though in some cases four or six were strung together, and presented the general characteristics of minute spores. Ether, liquor potassæ, and sulphuric acid had no particular effect on them. (See plate, fig. 11.)

In two of the tubes from the same cattle, opened one month later, the contents were putrefying, and micrococcus and bacteria were abundant.

On the 29th of May vacuum tubes of blood and secretions from two yearling steers, killed at Houston, Texas, May 18, 1869, were received and examined. These animals presented the usual lesions—enlarged spleens, erosions of the stomach, &c.

The blood from these tubes was in an advanced stage of putrefaction, and filled with bacteria and micrococcus.

The bile from the four-year-old steers was normal in appearance; that from the one-year-old animals was very dark and tenacious. Micrococcus was found in each, but not abundant. In each there were found moving rods, (bacteria?) which were somewhat peculiar, one end being bent, forming a little knob or hook. (See plate, fig. 12.) They were of an orange color, probably owing to imbibition of biliary coloring matter.

The urine in each set of tubes was found to contain micrococcus, bacteria, and cryptococcus.

Experiment 1.—Blood from the first series of tubes was placed in a De Bary's growing slide, on blotting-paper, in a beaker isolation apparatus, and in a watch-glass under a culture apparatus, with a few drops of freshly-boiled solution of sugar. In the growing slide cryptococcus forms were observed in thirty-six hours; in twelve hours more, delicate mycelium filaments appeared, and on the fourth day the usual fructification of *Penicillium crustaceum* was seen in the air space in the slide. The isolation apparatus was opened on the fifth day, and penicillium found on the blotting-paper. In the watch-glass cryptococcus was developed on the second day; two days later this was very abundant, and of various sizes and forms, including *C. guttulatus* of Ch. Robin.

Four days later mycelial filaments, with dilatations of various forms and sizes, (*Schizosporangia* of Hallier,) covered the surface of the blood. (See plate, fig. 13.) One month later careful examination showed nothing but penicillium.

Experiment 2.—The precautions taken in this case were very great, and were as follows: The beakers, culture apparatus, watch-glasses, slides, blotting-paper, and thread were treated with dilute nitric acid, then with liquor potassæ, and finally rinsed with hot, freshly-distilled water. The knife, glass rod, and file used were cleansed in hot alcohol just before being used. The vacuum tubes were cleansed with liquor potassæ and alcohol just before being opened. The sheet-rubber was thoroughly washed with the same fluids.

To prepare the beaker isolation apparatus, after the articles used had been treated as above, the cover with blotting-paper was placed on the beaker, strong alcohol having been first poured in, and then it was thoroughly shaken. The alcohol was then removed by similar treatment with fresh distilled water. The apparatus was then taken to a room in which no experiments had been made, and the fluids added to the blotting-paper. During this operation the interior of the apparatus was exposed for about one minute.

Blood from four-year-old steer (first set of vacuum tubes) was placed in a De Bary's growing slide, in a watch-glass with pulp of lemon, same with pulp of orange; also in beaker isolation apparatus on lemon and orange.

Blood from one-year-old steer (second set of vacuum tubes) was arranged in the same manner.

And, lastly, a similar series of apparatus was arranged with lemon and orange without blood.

The growing slides and watch-glasses were examined daily, with powers ranging from 200 to 1,000 diameters.

At the end of five days the isolation beakers were opened. The phenomena in all, with one exception, were the same. *Penicillium crustaceum* (Fr.) was developed in all, more slowly and less luxuriantly where no blood had been added. The exception referred to above was in the watch-glass to which the putrescent blood from the one-year-old steer was added; in this there was a luxuriant growth of *Mucor racemosus*, (Fres.,) and also coremium, a luxuriant and fasciculated form of penicillium.

It is considered needless to give the details of all the culture experiments undertaken with this blood; suffice it to say that it was placed on various substrata and compared with healthy blood, and the results were in all cases the same, that is, production of penicillium, coremium, and mucor.

In cultures undertaken with the urine, either no result was obtained or the usual penicillium made its appearance.

Culture of the bile upon lemon gave the same results, but the penicillium growth was much less than when the blood was used. Disk-like masses of mycelium, (the *Sclerotia* of Hallier,) usually bright yellow in color, were produced alike with diseased and healthy blood.

To judge, therefore, from the specimens that we have had the opportunity of examining, it would appear that in the blood, bile, and urine of cattle slaughtered in Texas, apparently healthy while alive, but presenting after death the appearances considered characteristic of the splenic fever, there are present minute bodies corresponding to the micrococcus of Hallier, which exhibit the same behavior with reagents as the spores of fungi.

In the bile and urine bacteria and cryptococcus cells also occur. The micrococcus granules, however, have no specific characteristics, and cannot be distinguished from similar bodies which are to be seen in any blood in an incipient stage of putrefaction. Thus, on the 4th of June, vacuum tubes were filled with blood from a healthy sheep slaughtered near Washington, and this blood, examined sixty hours afterward, contained in equal abundance these same bodies (micrococcus) that were found in the blood of the Texas cattle. The attempt to give these micrococcus molecules a special and important character by the "cultivation" in various ways of the blood containing them, also failed. In all cases the fungous growth that appeared upon the cultivated material was composed of the commonest molds, and, instead of being unique as to species or even genus, comprised various forms and sizes of cryptococcus, torula, penicillium, coremium, mucor, and the so-called schizosporangia of Hallier, of all forms and sizes; these various fungi being either simultaneously or successively developed. Moreover, all these varieties of fungi can be also developed by a similar cultivation of healthy blood, though not so rapidly nor in so great luxuriance.

The fact that in our cultivations we never obtained any growths of ustilago, coniothecium, or tilletia, which were so frequently produced in Hallier's experiments, is probably due to the circumstance that no specimens of those fungi were ever brought into the room where our experiments were conducted.

In cases of splenic fever of cattle our experiments, therefore, fail to establish the presence of any peculiar or special cryptogamic germs in the blood; and, instead of supporting the notion that the micrococcus granules which are present in any way cause the disease, tend rather to show that their occurrence should be considered as an effect of the malady, whether constant and inherent, or altogether fortuitous; for since these granules, if fungous in their nature, must be, as indicated by the cultivations, forms of the very commonest moulds, it is certainly a much more probable hypothesis that the disease so destroys the vitality of a part of the blood as to render it capable of supporting and nourishing a low form of these ubiquitous fungi, which perish when introduced into a healthy subject, than it is to imagine a deadly disease, occurring only under certain rigidly prescribed conditions, as caused by the presence, in the economy of the germs, of fungi notoriously harmless and of universal occurrence.

It is, of course, possible that these fungi, developed in the fluids of a diseased animal, may become the carriers of contagium. This can be determined only by a series of inoculations upon healthy cattle.

While the experiments reported above were still in progress, we were fortunate enough to obtain a copy of the Transactions of the New York State Agricultural Society for 1867, containing the "Report of the New York State Cattle Commissioners," in connection with the "Special report of the Metropolitan Board of Health on the cattle disease." This report we read with interest.

The conclusions of Professor Hallier we do not accept, for three reasons: First, because the fluids sent to him were not put up with the proper precautions for exclusion of extraneous spores; second, because the culture apparatus used by him does not give reliable results, as we have found by experiment; and lastly, because his reasoning is based on a peculiar theory of his own, that penicillium, mucor, &c., are merely unripe forms of certain ustilagineous fungi, a theory which cannot be discussed here, but of which it is sufficient to say that it has been accepted by no other prominent mycologist.

The statement of Dr. Stiles, that "the fungous origin of zymotic diseases is now conceded by the highest authorities in mycological research," will no doubt surprise the said authorities; for Berkeley, Curtis, and De Bary, the highest authorities in England, America, and Germany, most assuredly concede nothing of the kind.

With a culture apparatus, a lemon, and a little albuminous fluid, such as blood, serum, white of egg, &c., it is very easy to obtain almost any kind of mold; but the laws of development of such organisms are not yet sufficiently known to enable one to draw decisive inferences from the results.

With regard to the magnifying power necessary for the examination of minute cryptogamic forms, it has usually been overrated. A good one-fifth objective is all that is necessary, and in making observations on growing slides is the highest power that can be conveniently used. We have, it is true, used much higher powers, but do not consider them necessary, or even desirable, in microscopic investigations of this character.

REMARKS.

In a general way it may be stated that all abnormal appearances observed in the fluids examined were such as might be attributed to putrefaction. Although much remains to be learned as to the causes and nature of this process, the tendency of modern science is to class it as a species of fermentation, which may be defined as a particular mode of decomposition of organized bodies, accompanied by the growth of cells of a fungoid character, supposed to be the active agents in the process.

In fluids undergoing the alcoholic, the acetic, lactic, or butyric acid fermentations, in wine affected with the bitter fermentation, or in a solution of tannic acid changing to gallic acid, we find minute cells, in German called "*Hefe*," in French "*mycoderms*," in English "*yeast*." Although the cells of ordinary yeast and those of the *Mycoderma vini, aceti*, or *lactis*, differ in shape and size, it is supposed that these variations are due to the character of the fluids by which they are nourished, and that they are all really derived from the same source, namely, the ordinary molds. Common brewers' yeast (*Cryptococcus cerevisii*) is now thought to be not a distinct species of plant, but merely a stage of development of several different genera of fungi, such as penicillium, aspergillus, mucor, and perhaps several others. And the same is probably true of the other mycoderms.

When organic substances rich in nitrogen decompose, the action is termed putrefaction; and in all such, when examined with a sufficiently high magnifying power, there will be found little molecules, either single or in chains of from two to six, and minute colorless rods, single or in chains of two or three, straight or spirally twisted, rigid or flexible. All of these may be at rest or in motion; if the latter, it may be a vibrating, trembling motion, without change of place, or a direct propulsion through the fluid. These minute organisms have been successively considered as animals, as algæ or water plants, and as fungi. The globular molecules are termed monads, and more recently micrococcus. The rods have received many names, but are usually known as bacteria. The tendency of investigators of this subject is to consider these monads and bacteria as the mycoderms of the putrefactive fermentation, and to suppose that they also are but one form of development of penicillium and other common molds. Mrs. J. Luders asserts that she has seen the bacteria emerge from spores of penicillium placed in meat juice, and the production of yeast by adding putrefying fluids to saccharine solutions has been repeatedly accomplished.

We have performed some experiments on this subject which may perhaps be of interest.

Our aim was to develop in a saccharine solution an unmistakable yeast cell, with its attendant special form of fermentation, from a vibrio or bacterium contained in a putrefying fluid; and the practical problem was to devise some means whereby the putrid fluid might be added to the sugar solution, without at the same time any yeast cells, which it might accidentally contain, also passing into the solution and so vitiating the result. To accomplish this end we availed ourselves of the different behavior of yeast cells on the one hand and the various cryptogamic organisms of putrid fluids on the other, in respect to their ability to pass through certain tissues. Now, bacteria, vibriones, and molecules, either single or in chains, (*Monas*, *Microzymas*, *Micrococcus*, *Leptothrix*, *Zooglea*, and *Schizomycetes*, of various authors,) will readily pass through thoroughly moistened filtering paper; while, as originally shown by Mitzscherlich, (Pogg. Annal., 1855, p. 224,) and again proved by the following experiments, yeast cells will not. Furthermore, none of the above-mentioned bodies will pass through vegetable parchment, although fluids will. If, then, upon adding a putrefying fluid to a saccharine solution, through the intervention of filtering paper, we produce yeast and fermentation in that solution, while upon making the addition through vegetable parchment we produce none, the method of the experiment leaves no doubt that the yeast must have been developed from cryptogamic germs other than yeast contained in the putrid matter. To carry out this plan of experiment, the following apparatus was used:

In a four or six-ounce glass beaker (not lipped) was placed a tube, made by cutting off the bottom of a common test tube, three-fourths inch in diameter, and as high as the beaker. This tube was open at the top, but closed at the bottom by two layers of fine, strong filtering paper tied tightly over the flaring end with waxed string, and rested on a fragment of glass rod placed in the beaker; all these articles having been carefully washed, were put together as described, and about two ounces of hot strong alcohol were poured into both the tube and beaker. A piece of thin sheet-rubber was next tied over the top, hermetically closing both beaker and tube, and the whole apparatus, having been thoroughly shaken, so that the hot liquid should come fully in contact with every part, was then set aside to cool until wanted.

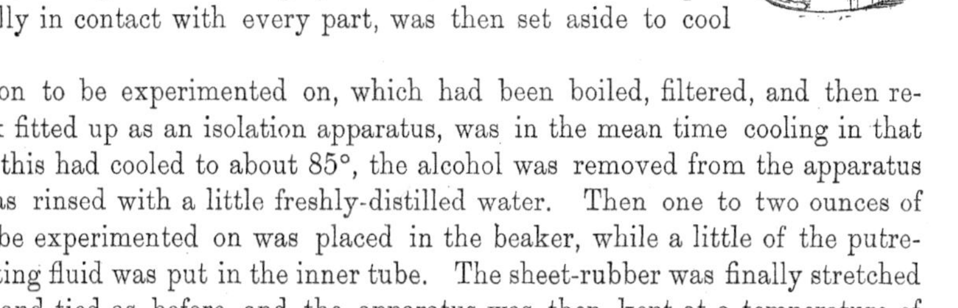

The solution to be experimented on, which had been boiled, filtered, and then reboiled in a flask fitted up as an isolation apparatus, was in the mean time cooling in that vessel. When this had cooled to about 85°, the alcohol was removed from the apparatus and the tube was rinsed with a little freshly-distilled water. Then one to two ounces of the solution to be experimented on was placed in the beaker, while a little of the putrefying or fermenting fluid was put in the inner tube. The sheet-rubber was finally stretched tightly over all and tied as before, and the apparatus was then kept at a temperature of 75° Fahrenheit to 85° Fahrenheit in diffused daylight, (see plate, fig. 4.)

The solutions used were of cane or grape sugar, mixed with extract of beef, or with tartrate of ammonia and ashes of yeast.

The following formulæ gave the best results:

A.

Cane sugar	10 parts.
Tourtelot's extract of beef	10 parts.
Water	100 parts.

B.

Cane sugar	10 parts.
Tartrate of ammonia	5 parts.
Ashes of yeast	5 parts.
Water	80 parts.

Experiment 1.—On the 24th of March, 1869, solution A was placed in five beakers, the tubes of which were closed with paper. In the tube of No. 1 was put a teaspoonful of fresh yeast; in those of Nos. 2 and 3 some putrefying fluid from lung of a pleuropneumonic cow; in No. 4 was placed a fluid containing large and lively bacteria taken from a can of preserved roast meat which had spoiled; to No. 5 nothing was added. Two ounces of the solution were also retained in the flask which had remained uncorked for fifteen minutes.

In twenty-four hours the rubber cover of No. 1 was distended, presenting a well-marked convexity. Bubbles of gas were rising in the tube, but none in the beaker. The covers of Nos. 2, 3, and 4 were slightly distended, and a few bubbles appeared on the outside of the tubes. No. 5 was unchanged.

In forty-eight hours the covers of the first four beakers were strongly distended, showing that the closure was perfect, (an important point.)

In No. 1 the bubbles were still confined to the inside of the tube, while in Nos. 2, 3, and 4 they were chiefly on the outside of the tubes. No. 2 was now opened. The fluid in the beaker was turbid, filled with molecules, chains of granules, and bacteria. It also contained well-marked yeast cells, separate, and just beginning to bud.

The next day, March 27, beakers 1, 3, and 4 were opened. In No. 1 the yeast was confined to the tube, in which it was in full growth. Not one yeast cell could be found in the outer fluid.

In Nos. 3 and 4 there was abundant growth of yeast in the beakers; greatest in No. 4. In No. 5 there was no change, nor has any occurred at this date.

At the same time that the beakers were arranged a series of growing slides was prepared and charged with the same fluids. The changes in these corresponded precisely with those in the beakers, except that they were more slow.

Experiment 2.—Two beakers were arranged with solution A. The tube of No. 1 was closed with vegetable parchment, that of No. 2 with filtering paper. Putrefying fluid from the lung of a pleuropneumonic cow was placed in the tubes, care being taken in No. 1 that this fluid should stand at the same height as the solution of sugar in the beaker.

In twenty-four hours decided osmose from the tube to the beaker had occurred in No. 1, and the rubber cover was concave. In forty-eight hours the cover was still concave, and the fluid in the tube was three-fourths of an inch lower than in the beaker. In beaker No. 2 the cover was distended, and yeast was evidently in active development.

Four days later the beakers were opened. The cover of No. 1 was now very slightly convex; yeast cells were found in the tube, but none in the beaker, although the latter contained molecules or micrococcus. In No. 2 the cover was now concave, owing to fructification of penicillium within the tube. Yeast cells were found abundant in the beaker.

Experiment 3.—Eight beakers were arranged with solution B, the tubes being adjusted as follows:

Nos. 1 and 2, closed with filtering paper; contents, putrefying roast beef. Nos. 3 and 4 closed with filtering paper; contents, blood of pleuropneumonic cow. No. 5, closed with filtering paper; contents, fresh yeast. No. 6, closed with vegetable parchment; contents, fluid as in Nos. 1 and 2. No. 7, closed with vegetable parchment; contents, fluid as in Nos. 3 and 4. No. 8, closed with vegetable parchment; contents, nothing added.

To each beaker, except 6 and 7, two growing slides were prepared with the same fluids. April 14 the beakers were opened. Nos. 1, 2, 3, and 4 contained abundance of yeast, and the covers were strongly convex. Nos. 5, 6, and 7 contained yeast cells in the tube, but none in the beaker; the yeast in No. 6 was very scanty. No. 8 remained unchanged. The growing slides were watched from day to day. Yeast cells appeared in those corresponding to beakers 1 and 2 in forty-eight hours; in those corresponding to 3 and 4, one day later. They appeared in those corresponding to beaker No. 8 on the sixth day, but none had appeared in the beaker on the tenth day.

A number of other experiments were made on this subject, the results of the majority of which were in accordance with those above given. Several times the conclusions were vitiated from the fact that yeast developed in the sugar solution when nothing was added.

It seems probable, in view of the results of the preceding experiments, that some of the bacteria and micrococcus germs are really fungoid in character and capable of development into higher forms.

It is unlikely that all the minute organisms above referred to are of the same character, but any attempt at classification of them is of very doubtful utility. If it is ever successfully done it will probably be by the application of chemical tests. We may mention that a solution of sulphate of quinine stops the motion of bacteria very quickly, while strychnine has no particular effect; and, again, in a solution of pure carbolic acid, two grains to the ounce, we have seen them quite lively twenty-four hours after they had been placed in it.

We do not suppose the above will hold good for all bacteria; indeed, we have seen some that were rendered motionless almost instantaneously by solution of carbolic acid.

If the foregoing view of the nature of those bodies be accepted as probable, the results of the culture experiments with the fluids of diseased and healthy animals can be readily understood. In many animals, whether healthy or diseased, there are no fungous germs in the blood. We have kept vacuum tubes of blood for four months, and at the end of that time the contents were perfectly normal. In other animals there are probably germs in the blood during life, as shown by the fact that in vacuum tubes filled from them the blood putrefied and the usual mycoderms developed; but that these germs can develop and multiply without dead organic material as a pabulum is very doubtful.

The fungi which are developed from blood containing these germs are, as might be expected, the common molds, the spores of which are almost ubiquitous—most frequently penicillium, next mucor, next aspergillus.

Other forms may appear, and those above mentioned may vary greatly in size, color, and rapidity of development.

As was stated in the beginning, our object was to determine the presence, and, as far as possible, the nature of these germs. The query as to the connection between them and disease, whether they should be considered as specific causes of the disease, or as carriers of contagium, or as the signs of destruction of vitality of a part of the fluids or tissues in which they are found, the destruction being due to some other cause, is one of great interest, but for the answering of which the "lancet and injection tube" will probably be far more efficacious than the microscope and "culture apparatus."

J. S. BILLINGS,
Bvt. Lt. Col. and Asst. Surg. U. S. Army.
EDWARD CURTIS,
Bvt. Maj. and Asst. Surg. U. S. Army.

Hon. HORACE CAPRON,
Commissioner of Agriculture.

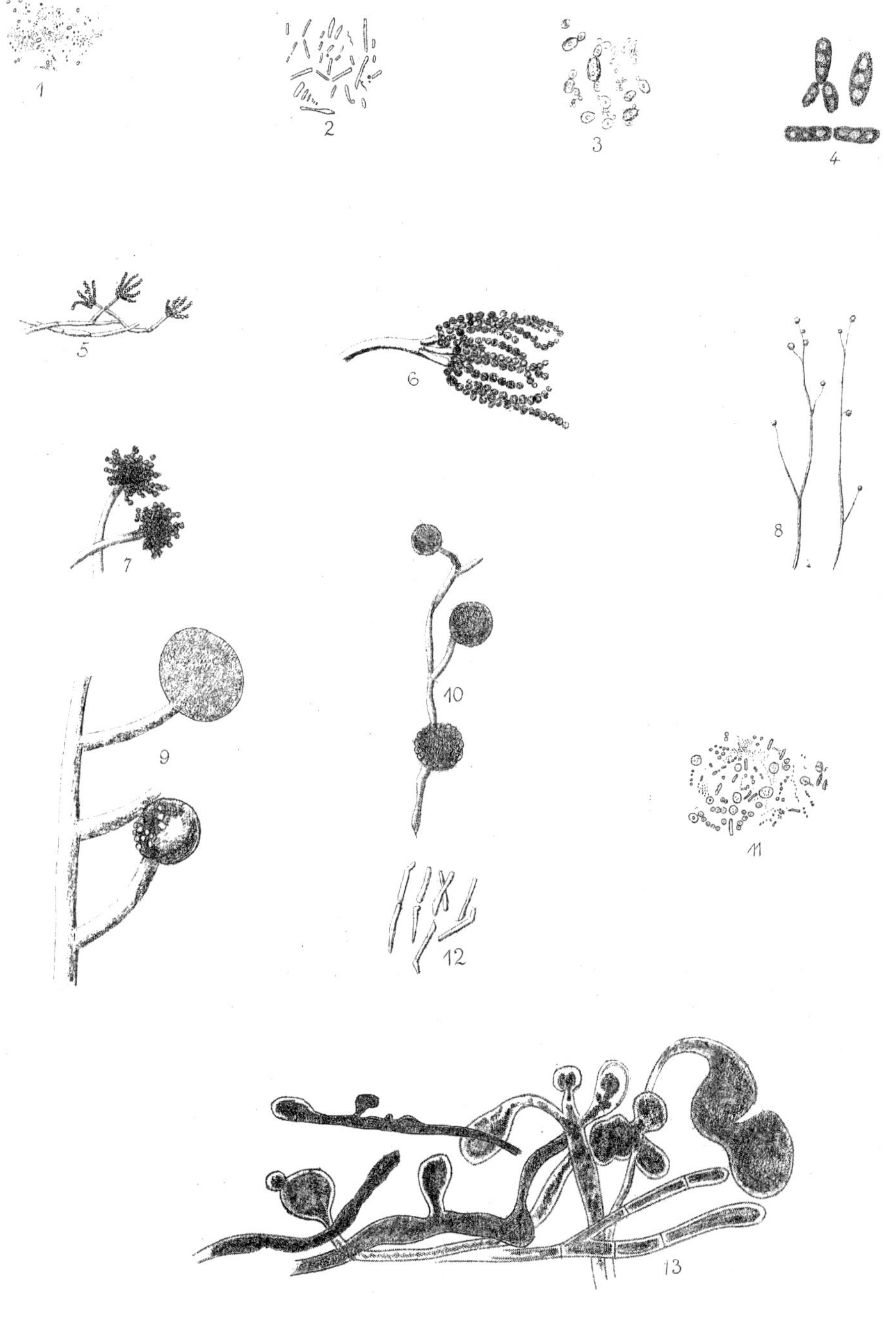
1
2
3
4
5
6
7
8
9
10
11
12
13

REPORT ON THE FUNGI OF TEXAS.

SIR: In accordance with an invitation to accompany Professor Gamgee to Texas, and to make an examination of the botany of the country where he investigated the cattle disease, and especially to direct attention to the lower cryptogamic flora, the fungi, and algæ, and also to examine the grasses and other plants furnishing food for cattle, I reached Galveston on the morning of the 28th of March, and proceeded at once to Houston to join Professor Gamgee.

After making a cursory examination into the pastures of the neighborhood of Houston, I accepted an invitation from Colonel Ashbel Smith to visit his farm at Galveston Bay, Harris County, and reached that place on the 30th. Here I had an opportunity of seeing a variety of soils, prairie as well as heavily-timbered land, the latter rather rare in this part of Texas. Colonel Smith offered me ample facilities for investigation, and, from his long residence in the country and extensive information, I was enabled to derive much benefit. I spent five days at this place, and made large collections of fungi and some few grasses. I made an examination also of hay which had been cut last summer and stacked in the fields. It was perfectly sound, and of bright and healthy color, without any indication of moldiness or parasitic growth. The hay was cut from a body of prairie land, inclosed by a fence, a portion of which had been burnt off for the purpose. The remaining portion, in the old dried grasses of the last season, presented no difference in appearance from dried grasses in similar situations; nothing to indicate any increased growth of parasitic fungi, or of having suffered from that cause. Colonel Smith was good enough to furnish me with notes of his place, which I append, to give an idea of the quality and situation of his lands:

The Evergreen estate is situated in 29° 42′ north latitude, at the head of Galveston Bay, within the debouchure of the united waters of Buffalo Bayou and the San Jacinto River, over Clopper's Bar, and on the east side of the river. It is washed in its rear by the Cedar Bayou, which empties into Galveston Bay some two miles lower down. This bayou is from twenty-five to thirty feet deep. There is scarcely any swamp or bottom, properly so called. The geological formation is alluvial. The soil on the San Jacinto or bay side is chiefly a sandy loam; that at the Cedar Bayou is a very black, stiff soil, and commonly known in this State as "hog wallow," from numerous depressions of the surface as if made by the wallowing of hogs. The estate comprises about four thousand acres, pretty equally divided in quantity into prairie and heavily-timbered land. Oak and cedar are the prevailing timber. There are also pines, hackberry, pecan, elm, ash, plum, persimmon, &c. There are four species of grapes at least. The mustang and muscadine abound in immense quantities. Both these vines, which are heavy bearers, make an excellent wine. The grasses are numerous; those growing spontaneously on the black lands, when protected from the feeding of animals by inclosure, make an excellent hay. The adjacent waters modify the temperature of the air most sensibly, both in summer and winter. The winter cold is about five degrees milder than that of Houston, as shown by a comparison of thermometers. The fields, when cultivated in corn, cotton, and sugar-cane, as before the war, yield abundantly.

After my return to Houston I went into the country, about three miles from the town, to a farm-house on the Buffalo Bayou, where I employed about two weeks in examining the pastures and grasses and making collections of *Fungi* and other *Cryptogams*. The wooded growth along the banks of the bayou—consisting of *Magnolia*, *Laurus*, *Ilex*, *Ungnadia* or Spanish buckeye, *Pecan*, *Tilia*, &c., affords a fine field for the *Fungi*, and at this place I collected about two hundred distinct species. The pastures were quite green, but the grass was still young and scarcely sufficiently grown to be identified. I collected here all that were in flower and could be distinguished. My attention was directed to their examination especially to ascertain the presence of the lower entophytal forms of *Fungi* or *Algæ*. I found them remarkably free of such parasites, as I expected from the early period of the year, (the *Uredos*, *Ustilagos*, *Puccinias*, *Tilletias*, and other entophytes most generally appearing later in the season,) with the exception of a few species, and they not in any abundance; and a *Helminthosporium* which infests the same grass (*Sporobolus indicus*) here in the Southern Atlantic States. I found no fungus on the grasses or other cattle food to attract my notice. This place, (Dr. Perl's beef packery,) on the Buffalo Bayou, and Colonel Smith's farm, are both in Harris County. With very few exceptions, my entire collection of *Fungi*, amounting to nearly three hundred species, was made at these two places; and it was also here that Professor Gamgee had the opportunity of examining some twenty-five or thirty cattle, collected from the neighboring pastures and slaughtered at the packery.

On the 23d of April we left Houston by steamer, and reached Galveston the next morning, and on the 26th took the steamer for Indianola, where we arrived on the morning of the 27th. Finding a sail packet ready to start for Corpus Christi, we took passage and reached the latter place on the 29th. The next day we rode out into the country some six or eight miles from the town, passing through the "*Chaparral*," or pastures densely set with cactus and various thorny shrubs. For several miles above Corpus Christi we passed through the mixed growth of prairie and *Chaparral*. On the Nueces Bay, at the mouth of the river, the face of the country was beautiful, with a gentle rolling surface some fifteen or twenty feet above the waters of the bay, thickly covered with grasses and flowering plants; and, interspersed with clumps of the graceful mesquite tree, (*Algarobia glandulosa*,) it presented the appearance of a well-kept lawn. On these prairies the grasses were much further advanced in growth than further north, and I added to my collection many I had not previously seen, and especially one or two species of mesquite grass.

On our return to Indianola, about one hundred and ten miles north of Corpus Christi, we went out some twelve or fifteen miles into the country—all prairie; and here I was also enabled to add largely to my collection of grasses and other *Phenogamous* plants. I saw but few *Cryptogams* either at Corpus Christi or Indianola, a few lichens and two or three species of *Fungi* comprising all from those localities. These prairie grasses were as free of cryptogamic growth as those about Houston, and, although my attention was specially directed to them, I could see nothing to excite suspicion as to their being differently affected from grasses in other places. There were certainly no entophytal fungi infesting them at that time in sufficient quantity to attract my notice.

The lands which I saw in Texas were all fertile, some of them extremely so. Most of the surface was of a fine clayey loam, in some places rather tenacious. From this cause during a wet spring, as the last one was, it was difficult to prepare for cultivation. I was informed along the coast that the best pastures and the most nutritious grasses were found higher up, from fifty to sixty miles above, and there are the best grazing lands.

About Houston the grasses are killed for a few months during winter, but at Corpus Christi and along the southern coast they remain green and furnish good pasture all the year round. I here present an analysis of my collection of fungi according to their natural orders, and a comparison with those of Rev. Dr. Curtis's North Carolina collection, the only full catalogue published in the United States:

Orders.	Texan.	Fungi.	North Carolina.	Fungi.
	No. of species.	*Percentage.*	*No. of species.*	*Percentage.*
Hymenomycetes	64	22	935	39
Ascomycetes	151	52	715	34
Gasteromycetes	13	4	150	6
Hyphomycetes	26	9	188	8
Coniomycetes	28	9	341	14

My whole collection amounts to three hundred and fifteen numbers; but deducting thirty, for species too old to be determined, and some represented under other numbers, the whole number may be estimated at about two hundred and eighty-five good species.

It will be seen by the preceding comparison that the Texan falls below the North Carolina collection in relation to numbers of Hymenomycetes, an order which contains the *Agarics*, *Boleti*, and other large and fleshy species very difficult to preserve except in dry weather. The number, however, which I saw were few, and I was impressed at the time with the very few representatives of the order in Texas. Perhaps later in the season that inequality would not have been observed. I was also surprised to find so few, comparatively, of the entophytal coniomycetes which infest living plants, the rusts, smuts, bunts, &c. This difference would also probably be less at a later period of the season, as it is mostly toward autumn, when the seeds of grasses are maturing and the leaves declining, that they are in the greatest profusion.

Attention has been drawn in the last few years to the "Texan cattle disease," and much interest has been elicited as to the nature and cause of this disease. In the voluminous and very able "Report of the New York State Commissioners in connection with the Metropolitan Board of Health of New York City," this subject has been very thoroughly investigated, and one of the results which seem to be definitely reached is the constant and universal presence in the blood and bile of the diseased animals of certain cryptogamic forms of vegetation, (*Micrococci* and *Cryptococci*, so called,) primordial spores or cells, and which, under the skillful manipulation of Professor Hallier, of Jena, have developed themselves into a distinct fungus plant, which he names *Coniothecium stilesianum*, after the distinguished microscopist on the New York board, who first discovered them. Professor Hallier, in his letter of December 18, 1868, to Dr. Harris of the Metropolitan Board, says in regard to the plant: "Perhaps you may succeed in finding out the places where this Coniothecium grows in nature. At all events, it is a parasitical fungus growing on plants, and to be looked for in the food of the wild bullocks."

Whether my examination of a limited portion of the flora of Texas, and comprised in so short a time, will throw any light upon these interesting questions, I cannot tell. My observations were made with as much diligence and care as I could command, and present, as faithfully as I am able to give them, the true condition of the pastures and the cryptogamic vegetation of the region of country visited. As far as I was able to examine, I found no species of Coniothecium on pasture grasses or on the dried hay. This, I know, is only negative evidence. The spores of these minute fungi, when they exist, are generally in great abundance, and may be wafted about by winds and carried by rains into rivers and pools of surface water which the animals drink. The *modus operandi* of these subtle agents of mischief, (*semina morborum*,) and the manner in which they gain access to the animal system, have long baffled the scrutiny of scientific men. To establish the fact of direct agency in any of these forms of vegetation, and to trace satisfactorily the connection between cause and effect, will require cumulative proof of very strong and unquestionable character. The phases through which they pass, and the different forms they assume at various periods of their growth, suggesting an analogy with the *partheno-genesis* (or alternation of generations) in the animal kingdom, are another element of difficulty in the solution of this question. Such investigations, however, as those undertaken by the New York commissioners, conducted, as they have been, in a truly scientific and philosophical spirit, must necessarily result in throwing light upon the subject, and be ultimately crowned with success.

My collection of phenogamous plants comprises about one hundred and seventy species. Of these about two-thirds consist of *Gramineæ* and *Cyperaceæ*, comprising the grasses proper and the rushes, sedges, and reeds, and water grasses. I am now engaged in their examination, and will furnish to the Department of Agriculture a full series. Besides these, I collected such lichens and mosses as I could readily obtain, specimens of which will also be prepared for the Department.

Recapitulation of collection made in Texas.

	Species.
Grasses and other phenogamous plants, about	170
Fungi, about	285
Algæ, about	25
Musci and Hepaticæ, about	35
Lichens, about	85
Total, about	600

Respectfully submitted.

H. W. RAVENEL.

Hon. HORACE CAPRON,
Commissioner of Agriculture.

REPORT

OF

STATISTICAL AND HISTORICAL INVESTIGATIONS

OF THE

PROGRESS AND RESULTS OF THE TEXAS CATTLE DISEASE.

DEPARTMENT OF AGRICULTURE,
Statistical Division, June 10, 1870.

SIR: Two years prior to the initiation of the series of investigations chronicled in the preceding pages, and long before the public mind of the Atlantic States was aroused to the dangers of the summer transportation of cattle fresh from the plains of the Gulf States, there was undertaken, under my direction, a systematic investigation of the facts, stated and reiterated by reliable farmers in the track of Texas cattle migration, stoutly denied by Texans, referred by drovers to every cause but their own cattle, and faintly believed or mildly doubted by the people, and even by the papers, of the East. Some affected to regard the reports from Kentucky, from Missouri, and from Kansas, as wild exaggerations of the truth, or fabrications in extenuation of controversies and violence begotten of encroachments upon the ranges of cattle-growers of the border. But the reports were too general, the statements too direct, and fortified by substantiations too strong, to be wholly ignored. Besides, they had been repeated year after year since the introduction of the southern cattle, not only in those States, but in the more eastern States of similar latitudes or climatic conditions. The drovers of Florida and Georgia, in the past generation, had witnessed similar results from the movement of coast cattle; and indeed the disease characterized in the preceding report as splenic fever can be distinctly traced back into the eighteenth century, as I propose to show.

It has been in existence ever since cattle were first driven from the country bordering on the coast of the Mexican Gulf to the upland regions to the northward, wherever cattle were present on the line of march to receive the infection. If the Indians, prior to the settlement of the States, ever brought with them, in their northern migrations, Spanish or Mexican cattle which were native to or had been acclimated in the lowlands, it is more than probable that this disease was communicated to the cattle of the higher latitudes.

The existence of this disease, proven by adequate testimony from many places and through a long period of time, was still either positively unknown or practically ignored by agriculturists at a distance from the places of its prevalence; so that, on the introduction of Texas and Cherokee cattle, through the swift intervention of steam, by river and by rail, into the heart of the Ohio valley, the results hitherto invariably occurring among Kansas or Missouri stock now visited, with equal severity, the cattle of Illinois and Indiana; and forthwith the doubt and indifference with which a distant calamity was regarded were exchanged for apprehension and alarm, which spread rapidly eastward, awakening the anxiety of stock owners, arousing to action city boards of health, and causing panic among purchasers of meats. Even agricultural editors, ignorant of the real character of the disease, wrote of the probabilities of its dissemination from farm to farm like the virus of rinderpest—a result of which no fears could reasonably have been entertained, native stock, having the disease, not communicating it to others.* Yet this alarm, notwithstanding the extravagance of its manifestation, accomplished good results, calling public attention to abuses in cattle transportation, exciting inquiry which resulted in more intelligent views of the subject, and promoting legislative action protective of the stock-growing interests.

The first notice of this disease which I have been able to find is contained in a lecture delivered before the Philadelphia Society for Promoting Agriculture, by Dr. James Mease, November 3, 1814, upon the diseases of domestic animals, in which it is stated that cattle of a certain district in South Carolina "so certainly disease all others with which they mix in their progress to the North that they are prohibited by the people of Virginia from passing through the State." It was mentioned as a singular fact that the South Carolina cattle had the power of infecting others with which they associated, while they themselves were in perfect health; and also that cattle from Europe or the interior, brought to the vicinity of the sea, were attacked with a disease that generally proved fatal. Dr. Mease corroborates these views from personal observation in Pennsylvania in 1796. September 20, 1825, he read before the same society an "account of a contagious disease propagated by a drove of southern cattle in perfect health." The following extract is given:

"In the month of August of the year 1796, I was on a tour for the recovery of my health, and having called at Anderson's ferry, [now Marietta, above Columbia, in Lancaster County,] on the Susquehanna, I found the people of the house in great distress on account of the death of some of the cattle and sickness of others, which had occurred in a few days after a drove from the south had left the place. Upon inquiry, I was informed that the drover merely requested and obtained permission to confine his cattle for one night in a plowed field, and I was assured that the stock of Mr. Anderson had no intercourse with the drove, which, after staying all night, pursued their journey in the morning to Lancaster. There several head were disposed of to different persons, and in every instance, as I was informed, they communicated disease to the stock with which they mixed. The admission of a single head was enough to give rise to it. As the drove of cattle exhibited no mark of illness, the mystery of the cause was inexplicable, and is so to this day. They stopped a day or two near Downingtown, thirty-two miles from Philadelphia, on the western turnpike, and soon after, the field they occupied received another drove which had been purchased by the late Mr. Stricker, of Columbia, on the Susquehanna. It consisted of two hundred and sixty head, and, as I was afterward informed by Mr. S., had been purchased by him in Maryland in the vicinity of Hagerstown, and between that and the Cove Mountain. Sixty of this drove were sold by Mr. S. near the Billet, in Montgomery County, the greater part of which died. Several others were sold at the Middle Ferry on the Schuylkill, eight of them were bought by the late Isaac Coates, above Dowingtown, and all died. Some taken to Germantown shared the same fate. Part of the South Carolina drove was sold at Blue Bell Tavern, a well-known sale place for drove cattle, and

* No fact in connection with the Texas cattle disease is more firmly established than this. Among all the records of its ravages, in all the years of its history, no instance of a secondary generation of the virus, no statement of its communication from a sick northern animal to a well one, is noted, with a single exception, (referred to hereafter,) which, if really an exception at all, only serves to establish the rule.

of these forty-six head were purchased by Messrs. Weed & Holstein, who then rented the meadows on State Island, (where I then resided as lazaretto physician,) and were mixed with near two hundred and seventy others, a part of which had been purchased, half fat, in the month of June, preceding. In about four days after the southern cattle had been turned out on the meadows they were brought up to the yard round the barn to be branded, and after remaining there a few hours they were returned to pasture. The disease first appeared, after a few days, among the cows in a field near the barn, and which were regularly milked in the yard used to confine the southern cattle until branded, and in a pair of fine working oxen, which were regularly and daily fed and yoked in the same yard. Several other cattle were successively attacked, to the number of at least twenty; all of them, except one, died. All those purchased half fat in June died. My advice being asked, I went to the field where several of the cattle lay ill, and was told that the first symptoms were loss of appetite and weakness of limbs, amounting to inability to stand; when they fell they would tremble and groan violently. I saw several in this condition. Some discharged bloody urine, others bled at the nose. The bowels are generally very costive. Upon being opened, the kidneys were found inflamed and sometimes in a state of suppuration, and intestines filled with hard balls. I prescribed strong purgatives. To one I gave two ounces of calomel, in sweet oil on the second day of the disease; but without producing any evacuation. Bleeding was tried without success. The blood was in a state of decomposition, and did not coagulate. As a preventive, I recommended smearing the nose, horns, forehead, hoofs and tail with tar, to counteract the contagion of the disease by creating an artificial atmosphere around the animal, and also the obvious expedient of an entire separation of the old stock from the strangers. *None of the southern cattle died.* The circumstance of the cattle from a certain district in South Carolina infecting others with the disease above alluded to, has long been known, but the precise locality, or its extent, I have not as yet been able to ascertain, notwithstanding my inquiries on the subject. The country of the long-leaf pine has been said to be the native place of the infection, but with what certainty I am unable to say. The cattle alluded to are said also to emit a peculiar smell which is easily perceived on a warm day, and to be well known in South Carolina."

Old residents of the piedmont region, between the tide-water areas and the Blue Ridge, are familiar with this form of disease; and the cattle drovers who have brought stock from the country of the long-leaf pine to greater elevations and higher latitudes, testify with remarkable unity to the constancy of its appearance and the uniformity of its prominent characteristics. The following statement obtained by the Statistical Division of the Department of Agriculture, in April, 1867, from Mr. J. Wilkinson, of Athens, Georgia, a reliable cattle dealer of good judgment and great experience, embodies the essential points of this oft repeated testimony:

"I have been a cattle dealer for twenty-five or thirty years, and in that time have had many deaths among my stock by this disease, and have in consequence taken some notice, meanwhile endeavoring to learn its causes and how it was brought about. I notice that cattle scarcely ever take the fever if let remain where they were raised, and I am fully convinced it is generally brought on by a change of climate. For instance, you take cattle from the mountain country to the low country and they will take the fever in a short time and die, but their disease will not affect the cattle raised there; but, on the other hand, take cattle raised in what we call the distempered part of our country, that is, the low country, from warm latitudes up into a colder one, they will themselves improve all the time; but, without being sick themselves, they will spread the fever and kill the cattle in the section of country into which they are taken, till they travel on, or have staid long enough for the fever to leave the system. I have been in the habit of driving cattle from Florida to Virginia, and have found my cattle to improve and do well; but after I passed the line of 34 degrees they began to spread the fever all along the line of travel among the stock raised in that section of the country, till I struck the line of Virginia, which is a distance of about two hundred and fifty miles; then it ceased, and all went on well. I suppose the reason for its stopping was that my cattle had been out of the low country long enough to become acclimated. Hence, I think the disease is originated from a change of climate, either from a colder to a warmer climate, or taking them from a warm climate to a cooler and more healthy one. How it is that they carry the disease with them and give it to others, without injury to themselves, is a mystery I am not able to solve, and will leave that to be discussed by the bureau of investigation."

THE INVESTIGATION OF 1867.

A knowledge of the peculiar features of this disease, first described without a name, afterward as an "unknown disease," or sometimes "murrain," (an unmeaning term appliëd to various diseases in the South,) in later times as "Spanish fever," and in the investigation of 1868 as "splenic fever," has been mainly confined, until recently, to localities in which its effects have been felt. A few paragraphs relating to it found their way into agricultural papers, but nearly all that was generally known of its real character and the extent of its prevalence, up to the time of its outbreak in Illinois in the summer of 1868, was obtained by the Statistical Division and published in the Monthly Report of Agriculture.

In 1866 inquiries were made at several points, and the existence of the disease was ascertained in Southern Kentucky, Southwestern Missouri, and Southern Kansas. In 1867, the statements hitherto received being more suggestive than complete or satisfactory, a circular was issued inquiring as to the places and dates of its appearance, the amount of loss sustained and the remedial treatment adopted.

The replies demonstrated the truth of previous information and the traditions of the early cattle trade in the South, showing that the disease had hitherto been developed among natives, on the arrival of the Texans in Southern Kansas and Missouri, in the more elevated sections of Arkansas, in parts of Tennessee, in Southern Kentucky, in North Carolina, and on the hill lands of Georgia and South Carolina. It was not reported further north than Southern Illinois, and its very existence appeared to be unknown in Ohio, Pennsylvania and Maryland. A fact suggestive of its climatic origin showed its existence in the mountain lands of Georgia, where it was generated by the presence of lowland cattle that had scarcely been removed a distance of fifty miles. It appeared that cattle driven from Texas to New Orleans did not communicate the disease to the cattle of Louisiana. Nor was there any evidence that the cattle of any one lowland section, when driven to another, caused an outbreak of the disease. A marked instance was reported from Arkansas, eight hundred Texas cattle having been driven directly from Texas into Mississippi County, in

1866, where they remained and mingled safely with the native stock This county lies in a latitude sufficiently high to awaken expectation of a fatal result of such migration; but it is on the Mississippi, in a miasmatic region.

The Texas correspondents were indignant in their comments on the "Texas cattle fever." Many claimed that their cattle were not subject to any prevailing diseases. One, in Collins County, admitted that cattle brought there from the North are liable to a disease similar in its symptoms. This corresponds with the statement made seventy-five years ago concerning the introduction of European and upland cattle into the coast districts of South Carolina, and with thousands of similar cases since, which are by no means incompatible with the climatic theory which all the facts seem to sustain, but furnish strong corroboration of it.

There is no doubt that the cattle of Texas are thrifty and comparatively free from diseases, while post-mortem examinations, in Texas and in the abattoirs of the northern cities, show enlargement of the spleen and traces of former derangements of the digestive organs. It is also a fact that the annual reports of condition of farm stock, made to the Department of Agriculture, contain accounts of fatal "murrains," and diseases of various names, from the miasmatic sections of the country, more frequently than from elevated locations and higher latitudes. In 1867, in Baker County, Florida, (according to the report of a correspondent,) two thousand cattle were destroyed by an unknown disease. "Murrain" was reported, in the returns of the spring of 1867, from many portions of the South, often without a detail of symptoms or circumstances, but in many cases with descriptions highly suggestive of "splenic fever," as in Towns County, Georgia, the return noting the prevalence of "murrain," and stating that cattle "pastured with cattle from the South take the murrain and invariably die, though those brought from the South do well." In Barton County, Georgia, twenty cases of "Spanish fever" were reported, and a few in Newton County. The investigation of 1867 showed that the Texas cattle migration northward, which had been closed during the period of the war, its interruption resulting in total exemption from the Texas cattle disease for precisely the same period, had been vigorously prosecuted anew on the return of peace, bringing with it the old disease, which raged just in proportion to the extent of the movement of southern droves. Its ravages, in 1866, were mainly confined to Kansas and Missouri, with a few instances of its prevalence in Kentucky and Southern Illinois. A few extracts from these returns will illustrate the peculiar features of this disease.

Kansas.—In Linn County it had "been prevalent in summer and fall, but is seldom, if ever, known in winter." "A disease made its appearance in Burlingame (in Osage) about the 1st of August, called by some, Spanish fever; by some, dry murrain. Afterward it prevailed in other parts of the county. It was principally confined to the Santa Fé road, which runs east and west through the county. Not one in twenty recovered. The damage could not be less than $5,000. Blooded stock were more frequently attacked and rarely recovered. The usual remedies for murrain were tried, but were of no avail. After that medicines were given as an experiment, but the cures were so few, if any there were, that nothing was established. The first symptoms were a moping and an apparent weakness about the loins. A high fever set in, and the animal kept on foot, eating and drinking as usual, until it laid down to die. Some were packed in wet cloths; some were drenched with salts; to some sulphur, saltpeter, sweet spirits of niter, lard, copperas, garlic, poke-root, and other medicines, in indefinite quantities, were administered. Let alone was the best remedy. The animal died in about a week after being attacked. There seemed no difficulty in getting physic to operate; the bowels were generally active and open. After death there seemed to have been a high fever in some localities; sometimes in the stomach, sometimes in the kidneys, sometimes in the lungs. As a general rule the stomach was dried up; the bladder full of red water, but not bloody. The eyes looked as usual and the fore-quarters seemed strong. I account for the different appearance in different animals by the fact that injurious medicines of different kinds had been given to different animals which I examined. All this stock had pure water and good grass. The first case that occurred was that of an ox, which belonged to a logging team of seven yoke. This ox, on account of his breachy propensities, was kept at night in a stable, and watered from a well of pure water. When not at work in the day-time he was staked out to grass with a long rope About two weeks before he was attacked with this disease a herd of Texas cattle came along and were stopped and fed around him for an hour or more. Soon after the rest of this team were attacked, and all died but one, which escaped the disease. Along the trail of this Texas herd, which left the Sante Fé road at Burlingame, and traveled north, almost every farmer lost stock. Cattle that belonged to Burlingame, and ranged north over this trail, nearly all died, while those which ranged south all escaped, though they were herded at night in the same yards. Another herd of Texas cattle passed through the county eight miles east of Burlingame, in another direction, and they left their trail, whole herds dying where they passed along. People here are unanimously of the opinion that the disease came from Texas. Cattle from the Cherokee country do not bring that disease. Neither do these cattle after they have been wintered here." "Spanish fever was brought in by Texas cattle, (in Leavenworth,) but was confined to certain limits, on uninhabited Indian reserves, as the people would not allow any to be pastured around farms in the settlements. It appeared from three to four weeks after the Texas cattle came in or passed by, among cattle that grazed on the same ground where the Texans had grazed over night, or staid for a greater length of time. It appeared in the latter part of July. The Texans arrived in June. At four different times in seven years this has been the case, always three or four weeks subsequent to the Texan arrivals. Loss, ninety-five per cent. of those attacked. Bleeding, cathartics, stimulants, hydropathy, &c., have been tried by multitudes. I have personally exhausted the whole range of cattle medicines, and lost very largely in 1857, 1858, and 1859, but found no remedy in any direction; in a word there is none known. All were attacked that were exposed to the cause." "The Spanish fever broke out in December, (in Woodson,) and raged until the 1st of January, when the cold weather set in and checked it. In the immediate localities where the Texas cattle crossed the country the losses were heavy. Some farmers lost all they had, and no less than thirty per cent. of the cattle have died. The methods of treatment have been various. I have treated the disease in its incipient stages, and have seen everything tried that ingenuity could devise. Calomel did no good; salts and alkalies all failed." "The Spanish fever, or something similar, (in Douglas,) made its appearance about the 1st of February among a few cattle that were driven from the South. I think the severity of the winter caused the greatest loss; about one-third of all the cattle brought from the South have died. The only treatment was to give the weaker ones a little more care, and separate them from the stronger ones." "The Spanish fever appeared during the first part of last May, (in Fort Scott,) about the time Texas cattle commenced driving, and continued all summer. Texas cattle did not appear to suffer any ill effect from the disease, but fully one-half of the native cattle in the county died with it. No remedy has been found for this disease." "Within the last ten years we have had the Spanish fever in this county three times, (in Franklin,) and it is indisputable that in every case cattle from the South had been driven through our county. Yet I have frequently heard those who have resided in Texas say that the disease known here as Spanish fever is unknown in the section they came from. I think it is generally admitted that it is only when cattle are driven in droves in hot weather that the disease manifests itself."

Missouri.—"There were a few cases of Spanish fever among cattle in this county, (Howard,) immediately on the public roads on which Texas cattle had been driven. No other disease. August was the month in which the above fever occurred. No treatment was instituted, and all died." "The Spanish fever appeared in July and August, (in Cass,) after the passage of droves of stock from Texas and Arkansas. Some sections of the county did not suffer; others, through which the travel mainly passed, lost fully five per cent. of their stock. The loss throughout the county is fully two per cent. of the whole number of cattle. Various remedies were tried to save the sick cattle, but nothing found effectual." "We lost some cattle last summer with the Spanish fever, (in Callaway,) immediately on the trail of a drove of Texas cattle that passed through our county. Almost every one living on the road where they passed lost more or less, if their cattle ran outside or grazed on the same pasture or prairie; but it did not spread from those farms on the road. Almost all that were attacked died. We know of no cure for it." "Spanish fever was introduced into the western part of this county (Christian) by droves of Texas cattle passing in October. Was very fatal, but spread over only a small portion of the county. No remedy applied." "The Spanish fever appeared about the 1st of July, (in Newton,) and continued until the 1st of October. Various remedies have been tried, but none proved effectual. The fever appeared to be caused by Texas cattle passing through the county. Many droves were stopped last summer by the citizens, and not allowed to pass until October. There was no sign of disease among the Texas cattle." "The Spanish fever is the only disease that has prevailed (in Bates) among the cattle in this section of the country. The disease is never seen until from ten days to two weeks after the passing through the county of Spanish cattle, which generally commences about the 1st of June and continues through the season. The loss in our county for the year 1866 will not fall short of sixteen hundred head. In some cases it killed entire herds. There is no effectual remedy known to the inhabitants of this county." "The Texas or Spanish fever prevailed to some extent in our county, (Chariton,) on the road traveled by a drove of Texas cattle through the county, but the disease was not in other parts of the county. The number lost was about sixty. No remedy was discovered that tended to alleviate the disease. Nearly all the cattle attacked died in a short time." "Spanish fever has prevailed wherever Texas cattle have passed, (in Cedar,) and attacks our native cattle directly, or soon after feeding on the same ground, in the spring, summer, or fall. It is thought that our cattle would not take the disease in the winter season, but this may only be conjecture, as no large droves have yet been driven here from the South in the winter. The loss is great, say eight-tenths. No remedy or treatment has yet been successful."

Kentucky.—"The Spanish fever was introduced into this county (Oldham) in June last by cattle brought from Texas by parties to sell to grazers. I have not seen any of the diseased cattle this season. The number that died did not exceed fifty head, as the Texas cattle only passed through one corner of the county. The 24th day of June, 1860, there were driven on my farm, to stay over night, about fifty head of Texas cattle. Some forty days after they left, about the 18th of August, the disease broke out among my milch cows and heifers and work cattle. I lost fourteen head, worth seven to eight hundred dollars. At the same time I was grazing a lot of large fat cattle for one of my neighbors—about sixty head; out of the number eleven head died, valued about the same as my own. This was the first appearance of the disease in this State. I tried all the remedies I could think of. Some of the diseased ones recovered, though I will not say what remedy reached the disease. Work oxen that crossed the road traveled by these cattle took the disease and died. In the last stages of the disease greenish and yellow matter exudes from the nose. The animal will live, in some cases, ten or twelve days after being attacked. This county has not been entirely free from the disease in the last ten years. Almost every farmer has a remedy of his own. I have had the disease in my herd twice; the first time I lost one hundred and fifty—nearly all I had." "Last summer my son bought at auction, in Lexington, (Fayette,) twenty-four Kentucky raised cattle. Shortly after the purchase five of the cattle were taken sick, four of which died. It was ascertained that these five cattle had been driven along the road over which some Texas cattle had traveled. The former had been given green corn, and the one that eat freely of it recovered. They were all taken sick the same day, and the four died the second and third days after. None of the other cattle were affected, though all were in the same pasture. It is a well-known fact that Kentucky cattle pastured with, or shortly after Texas cattle, or driven along the road after them, will take this fever. It is believed, however, that it is never taken from the native stock. The Texas fever had been very destructive in the neighborhood from which these five cattle were driven from Lexington."

Illinois.—"In the southern part of this county (Perry) Spanish fever appeared in July last, among cattle that were pastured on ground that had been previously occupied by a drove of Texas cattle. The loss was about seventy head. Various remedies were tried, but none of them were effectual. I understood that all the cattle were attacked with the disease that followed the Texas cattle in the pasture, and that all that were attacked died. It appears also that the Texas cattle, while feeding in the pasture, had no appearance of disease."

The losses had now become so heavy in Missouri and Kansas, notwithstanding repressive State enactments and organized violent opposition to the cattle movement which had proved an effective bar to the malady in certain instances of vigorous enforcement, that Congress was formally called upon for aid in a scientific investigation. The Commissioner of Agriculture, in calling the attention of Congress to the following resolution of the Legislature of Kansas, reported progress in his efforts to obtain the actual facts relative to this singular and fatal disease, which he feared might "result in great loss to the people of Kentucky, Missouri, Kansas, and possibly to those of other States, if Texas cattle should be allowed unrestricted range through them:"

"Whereas there annually prevails a contagious disease among the cattle of this and adjoining States, commonly known as 'Spanish fever,' destroying large numbers, thereby seriously affecting the interests of productive industry; and whereas such disease is propagated by the introduction of cattle from the State of Texas and the Indian Territory, south of Kansas; and whereas the want of a scientific investigation of the said disease has rendered void any effort to arrest its ravages: Therefore,

"*Resolved by the House of Representatives of the State of Kansas, (the Senate concurring,)* That our Senators and Representatives in the Congress of the United States are instucted to urge and support an appropriation by said Congress to enable the Department of Agriculture to make the said scientific investigation, and that a copy of this resolution be forwarded to each of our Senators and Representatives in Congress, and also to the Commissioner of Agriculture."

It was stated, in connection with this resolution, that the people of Southern Kansas, conscious of their danger, and distrustful of the efficacy of governmental action for their defense, were then taking the matter into their own hands, and organizing vigilance committees to arrest and force back the Texas cattle movement. A meeting, representing the farmers living in the vicinity of McDowell, Humboldt, Clark, and Lyon Creek, had just organized a large committee of resolute farmers, fully able to put in force an illegal but salutary restriction.

THE OUTBREAK IN 1868.

Early in June of 1868, the "Spanish," "splenic," or "Texas cattle" fever, appeared at Cairo, Illinois, the most southern point in the State, and the place of transhipment of Texas cattle from steamboat to railroad cars. It was a new and speedy mode of obtaining Texas cattle, by which they were introduced into the prairies of Illinois in less time than was previously occupied in reaching Kansas on foot. As might have been expected, the cattle in the vicinity of Cairo were soon dying in large numbers; and as repeated shipments were dispatched into the interior, the stations at which they were yarded and fed, preparatory to distribution by different railroad lines, became centers of infection, spreading disease among native stock coming upon the same herding grounds or drinking from the same streams or ponds.

At Tolono, the junction of the Illinois Central and Toledo and Wabash railroads, where the disease appeared about the 20th of July, it swept away nearly all the cattle of the neighborhood, two hundred and thirty-five cows dying prior to the 1st of August.

It spread rapidly through Illinois and Indiana, appearing only where Texas cattle had been dropped at cattle yards, or on routes over which they had been driven to feeding grounds; and in a few instances in Ohio, New York, New Jersey, and in New England, it was communicated by the southern long-horns to native cattle.

The alarm became general, and repressive measures were everywhere adopted by boards of health, city governments and State authorities. The Commissioner of Agriculture, in continuance of efforts now beginning to be appreciated, authorized an investigation by a veterinarian then in the country, who had been prominent in similar labors in Europe, Prof. John Gamgee, of London. Upon this tour of observation and examination he was accompanied by H. D. Emery, editor of the Prairie Farmer, as a volunteer assistant. The results of that and other practical inquiries into the nature, causes and operations of this mysterious disease are recorded in this volume.

Up to this point the statistical investigations conducted during the two preceding years had resulted in the accumulation, from a wide range of territory, of a mass of facts, which were singularly explicit and uniform, pointing to certain marked peculiarities of the disease. About the middle of August, at the outset of the medical investigation, I made public a summary of results, obtained by previous statistical inquiries, which appeared to establish the following conclusions:

1. That the disease is communicated by Texas cattle, or those from Florida or other parts of the Gulf coast.
2. That the disease itself is unknown in Texas.
3. That the cattle communicating it are not only apparently healthy, but generally improving in condition.
4. That while local herds receiving the infection nearly all die, they never communicate the disease to others.
5. That either a considerable increase in elevation, or a distance of two or three degrees of latitude from the starting point, is necessary to develop the virus into activity and virulency; and a further progress of two degrees of latitude or a few weeks in time is sufficient to eliminate the poison from the system.
6. That Texas cattle removed to other miasmatic sections, as the Mississippi bottoms, up to the thirty-sixth parallel, communicate no infection to local herds.
7. Medication has thus far been of little avail.

The conclusion was thence derived that the disease could not generally spread and involve the cattle of the country; that New York stock would not take the infection from sick western cattle, though they might from steers recently from Texas, or from cattle cars infected by such animals, and that the danger might be averted by the arrest of the Texas cattle movement during the summer months, or by separating them in the transit from the native cattle, and thoroughly disinfecting the boats and cars in which they are borne; but that the safer plan would be to carry them to eastern markets only in winter, when the virus is inert, or after a winter's grazing in safe seclusion on the borders.

STATISTICAL INVESTIGATION OF 1868.

In the autumn of 1868 a circular was sent to all portions of the country in which the Texas cattle disease had ever appeared, in which the Commissioner of Agriculture intimated his purpose to give the subject "official attention until its character is definitely known, and the traffic in southwestern cattle so regulated by law as to give safety to our farmers, and furnish an outlet to the surplus stock of Texas, and cheap store cattle to the feeders of Illinois and Missouri." The following questions were asked:

1. In what town or locality did this disease first appear in your county?
2. At what date was the first arrival this season of southwestern cattle?
3. By what route, and from what section did they come?
4. What numbers of such cattle have been received in your county during the present season?
5. What was their condition on arrival? How many were diseased? How many subsequently sickened? If death occurred, at what interval after sickening; and were the symptoms the same as those of native stock dying from the so-called "Texas fever?"

6. How many days elapsed from their introduction to the breaking out of the disease among the native stock?

7. What number of natives died, and in what proportion to the whole number attacked?

8. Has the disease been communicated, except to animals that have fed upon pastures or in lots soiled by the excrements of the southern cattle?

9. Has a case occurred of the infection by one native animal of another?

Responses were prompt and general, of a tenor similar to those of former years, but indicating a wider diffusion and greater losses than ever before. A synopsis of this material will convey its essential features, and avoid something of its reiteration. The States suffering most severely were Illinois, Indiana, Missouri, Kansas, Arkansas, and Kentucky. Those in which the disease was communicated by droves coming in on foot will be first considered.

Arkansas.—In accordance with information previously received from this State, the returns showed that certain locations were liable to the introduction of this disease, while others, generally near the Mississippi or the Arkansas River, were wont to receive Texas droves with impunity. Mr. Tennison, of Arkadelphia, Clark County, stated that he had been pasturing droves of cattle for two previous years, and as long as they were kept separate from his native stock, no outbreak occurred; but in 1868 he penned two droves with his own herd and lost six out of eighteen, and at the date of writing feared he should lose them all. The symptoms were "depression of the eyes, falling of the ears, discharge from nostrils, hair dry and rough, body swollen, no disposition to eat or drink, bloody discharges mixed with water; death occurred in from two to three days."

About three thousand cattle from Western Texas passed through Drew County, all in good condition, though not fat, and no disease resulted. Drew is in the southeastern portion of Arkansas, in a latitude and location in which no infection would be expected.

In Crawford County neither the "Spanish fever" nor any disease resembling it has ever occurred. A very large cattle trade has been going on between the citizens of Crawford and those of Texas, for years before and since the war. Van Buren (the principal town) is immediately on the north bank of the Arkansas River, and is the main crossing on the route from Northern and Eastern Texas, droves of Texan cattle numbering from one hundred to one thousand head crossing at Van Buren Ferry almost every month for years past. Herds of long-horned Texan cattle are continually pastured in the county, mixing and intermixing with the native stock, so that fully one-half of the stock owned there are Texan cattle.

In Washington County the first cases occurred in the vicinity of Cincinnati. Cattle coming through the Indian country, Choctaw, Creek, and Cherokee Nations, and entering the State a few miles above Cincinnati, began to arrive about the 10th of April; two or three thousand passed through in 1868, and about half that number remained in the county, all in healthy, thriving condition. The disease broke out about three months after their introduction, in the latter part of July, and destroyed about four per cent. of the native cattle, four-fifths of the whole number attacked.

Kansas.—Since the legislative prohibition of the passage of Texas cattle through the State at any point east of the hundredth degree of west longitude, except on the Union Pacific railroad, the cattle of the State have been generally exempt from the disease.

The returns from Osage County state that no Texas cattle were allowed an entrance, and hence there was no disease; but that in 1866, native cattle sickened in about a week after the introduction of a drove from Texas, and fifty died.

About two thousand head of cattle from the Cherokee country passed through Morris County without communicating the disease.

The fever prevailed in the northern part of Bourbon County, and destroyed six hundred head of the native stock, ninety per cent. of the whole number attacked. About five hundred head of the Texan cattle have entered the county after the 1st of June, coming via Fort Smith and Baxter Springs. They were in good condition and apparently healthy. The disease broke out in from four to ten days after their introduction.

Ten steers arrived in Troy, Doniphan County, July 15, all apparently healthy. In about five weeks after their introduction twelve head died, and several more were sick at the date of the return. None recovered. In former years (before the prohibitory law) the native stock suffered severely from Texas fever. The opinion obtains here that the disease is communicated by the feet,* for if Texan and native cattle are kept in adjoining pastures, merely separated by a fence, the native stock remain healthy, but if they pass over the track of the Texan cattle, they are almost sure to become diseased.

Our correspondent in Butler reports that probably one hundred thousand passed through that county in 1868, and at least ten thousand remained to winter. They were generally healthy, and in fair condition; probably one per cent. lame, with matter oozing out at the top of the hoof, but without any symptoms of Texan fever. He assumes that the time from their introduction to the outbreak among the native cattle varies according to the temperature—in hot weather from nine to ten days only may elapse before the development of the disease, but as the cold season approaches, much longer time is required. In colder weather a larger proportion of the native stock attacked, recover. No case occurred except among cattle exposed to the Texan herds. Texan cattle, after passing two winters in Kansas, take the fever as readily as the native stock on being exposed to animals recently from Texas.

In Greenwood County large numbers of cattle died with splenic fever, in September, 1865. Our correspondent lost fifty-two per cent. of his cattle on the home range, through which lay the highway traveled by Texas cattle, while three other herds, four or five miles away, were perfectly healthy. The experience of his neighbors was of the same character; and the watering and camping places of the droves were everywhere marked by carcasses of domestic cattle. The period of incubation was ten to twenty days.

The loss from "Spanish fever" in Dickinson County was over $6,000 in 1868.

Ten head of oxen died in Republic County in the fall of 1867, after feeding on the track of Texan herds. In Butler and Wyandotte several fatal cases were reported.

Missouri.—The losses from this disease in Southwestern Missouri for several years prior to the war, and from 1865 to 1868, when legal restrictions on summer driving were quite generally enforced, have been extremely burdensome. Vernon County appears to have suffered more than other counties. The losses there in 1858 are estimated at $200,000. The arrival of Texas cattle has uniformly been the prelude to prevalent disease and heavy

* The facts are correct, but the deduction may be faulty; a better conclusion would be that the virus comes from the excrement.

loss. A full report of the symptoms and ravages of this disease was made by Dr. Albert Badger, of Vernon, from which the following extracts are taken :

"This disease was first recognized as having been propagated by cattle driven from Texas twelve or thirteen years ago; it having been in the county some two seasons previous to its having been traced to the Texas cattle.

"From the first breaking out of this fever it was found to be confined to the large roads or highways running through the county from south to north, and, finally, was centered on the Texas cattle, I believe, in the year 1853, by its being confined to one highway through the county over which these cattle passed that year. On this road the disease was quite fatal, killing about fifty per cent. of all the cattle on the road, and persons living near the water-courses over which the road crossed lost as high as ninety per cent. Captain Freeman Barrows and Peter Colley, the one living at the ford of the Osage River, the other near by, lost ninety per cent.; one of them owning about one hundred head, while the other had considerably above that number. Mr. Collins, living at the ford of Clear Creek, south of the above, lost an equal proportion. The disease being in no other part of the county that year satisfied the people, on this road at least, that they had found the true origin, as it had been among the cattle in the county for two summers past. In a season or two after almost every settler of the county was convinced that the Texas cattle in some way communicated this fever to our stock, although a few persons, living secluded from the great highways, were unbelievers, and still remain so. In fact, the way this disease is propagated, the obscurity surrounding it, together with the different opinions of persons familiar with it, give them, at least, a reasonable excuse for doubting the prevailing belief. Two things are agreed to by all: the symptoms of the fever and its fatality, the latter being much greater in a warm dry summer than in a cold wet one; the disease always ceasing when the frosts have killed the vegetation.

"The first symptom of the fever, discoverable several days before any appearance of sickness, is a dry cough, noticeable by careful observers. In a few days after this the nose becomes dry and the ears slightly drooping, and more flies will collect than on healthy cattle. At this stage the breath will be found to have lost its sweetness and assumed the sickening feverish smell generally, if not always, found in the Texas cattle, which I can best describe by comparing it to the smell of our slaughter-houses, or constantly crowded stock-yards in cities. From this condition in one or two days the fever gains its highest stage, and is found to have disseminated itself over the whole body, the heat being very great; the arteries of the neck are seen to beat in short, heavy throbs; the ears becoming very much lopped; the hinder parts reel in walking, the animal getting up or lying down with difficulty; the breath and exhalations are very disagreeable; the end of the tail usually hollow for two or three inches; the pith in the horn has commenced to decay, if not already decayed; the animal refusing to notice the herd, remaining stupid, if not disturbed, neither seeking food nor water. Some, in this stage, will pass water mixed with blood, and dung naturally, others will pass water of a natural color and not dung at all, or but very little, and that in a dryish lump. In another type of the disease, which will occur perhaps in every eighth or tenth case, after being taken the same way, and having the same symptoms as those described, even to the hollow horns and tail, the animal does not get weak, sluggish, or stupid, but is always to be found on its feet, in a watchful attitude, with head turning to any noise, which, if close by, it rushes toward, even through fences or against trees, the eyes being of a green cast, very glaring and wild; those of the first type have a dead, sleepy, and glazed appearance. Both these classes die, as I have described them, without any change, except that the hair deadens before death and has the appearance of that on a dry hide.

"The drove mentioned as having passed through the county in 1853, was owned by Mr. Richard Burris, of Spring River. They were driven from Texas the fall previous and wintered about fifty miles south of here, near Sarcoxie. In the early part of June Mr. Burris came into this county with his cattle, apparently healthy, in good order, and no lame ones in the drove, numbering about four hundred and fifty head. He made a slow passage through the county, grazing on the best grasses near the road unmolested, as no one knew at this time that this species of cattle communicated a disease to ours. Early in July the fever broke out on the road traveled by this drove, lasting until the frost put a stop to it, with the fatality previously mentioned. As the disease this year was in no other locality except where these cattle were driven and grazed, the citizens, after carefully tracing their route through the county, in all its windings, came to the conclusion, for the first time, that this fever was engendered from the Texas cattle. This was fully verified in the next year; and up to the outbreak of the war hundreds of cases occurred to prove that they were not mistaken. No Texas cattle, until this year, (1866,) except two yoke of oxen worked here in the fall of 1865 by Mrs. Box, have passed into or through this county since 1860; neither has there been a case of Spanish fever during this period, or any other fatality among our cattle. Mrs. Box's oxen, so far as could be seen, were healthy, and not lame. The neighbors whose cattle came in contact with these oxen were Mrs. Smalley, Mr. Cothran, and Mr. Packard, all having the Spanish fever among their stock, and losing some notwithstanding the lateness of the season. About three thousand head of Texas cattle passed through this county in the month of June, in 1866, and a portion of them reached six or eight miles into Bates, the adjoining county, before being turned back by citizens of that county. They returned on the same road previously traveled, making no delay in their passage either way more than was necessary. The disease did not break out for some six weeks after the passage of the droves—many more recovering than usual, and about forty per cent. dying—extending into Bates County to the point where they were turned back. It proved more fatal on the crossings of water-courses, killing about seventy per cent. In 1858 my stock were exposed to this fever by coming in contact with a drove of Texas cattle. The fever was very bad among them, one or two dying every day through the month of August; they were in daily contact with Mr. Millender's stock, who kept a herder, not suffering them to reach the ground that had been used by the Texas droves, yet he had not a single case of fever. When spoken to about keeping my stock from coming in contact with his, he told me there was no danger of our own cattle diseasing one another. I have since watched many such exposures, and in no case has the fever been propagated. The farmers have each an opinion as to how the disease was propagated to their cattle, some thinking it is through the lame ones, a few of which will be found in almost every drove coming from Texas. Their feet become worn out and sore from long travel, matter forms between the hoofs and is left on the ground and in the water through which they pass, and, it is contended, this inoculates our cattle by being taken in the stomach or otherwise. Others think it is done by the excrements left by those that are lame or diseased, while some think it is through the slobber or froth which is left on the grass. On one thing they agree, that the fever is communicated in some way, raging until the cold weather puts a stop to it, no remedy appearing to have any effect. From the few cases mentioned, which are selected from many of like nature, I have been led to believe, first; that the disease is conveyed to our cattle by those from Texas; second, that the feeding of a large herd one winter in this climate does not prevent the spread of the infection from them the next season; third, that Texas cattle, in apparent good health, give disease to ours; fourth, that the disease is not contagious from our own cattle to each other; fifth, that killing frost will stop the disease; sixth, that no remedy has been found to cure this fever.

"By a very close observation of this disease among my own and neighbors' stock for the last thirteen years, I have generally found, on opening those that had died, but very little blood, and the following results: In those that passed water mixed with blood the kidneys and surrounding parts were entirely decayed, the other parts of the body sound; those that did not dung at all, or but little, with manifolds perfectly dry and partly decayed, while the large stomach would be more or less mortified, other parts healthy; those that appeared to dung and pass water naturally, with a liver more or less decayed, the gall always swelled to its greatest tension; other parts healthy; those that were on their feet in a watchful attitude, the brain was found more or less decayed. This leads me to believe the disease is in the blood, which finally becomes congestive, destroying the parts in a few hours after it becomes seated, and no doubt in many cases could be cured if we knew exactly where it had located itself, blood-letting not being sufficient of itself to check the inflammation. The hollow horn and tail no doubt is caused by the fever destroying the blood in the extremities before it does in the vessels, which it does, in a great measure, before death. The present law is very defective. First, it only precludes the sick ones from passing through the county, and few men under oath can say that because a steer has an unhealthy smell he is sick; second, in order to separate the lame or sick ones, if any, the drovers, under the present law, are required to impound them in order that the selection may be made, &c. But it is little use to select the sick ones when there is equal danger from those that are apparently well."

Mr. Nathan Bray, of Mount Vernon, Lawrence County, Mo., attested to the infection of whole districts in Southern Missouri from 1853 to 1868, except during the period of the exclusion of southern cattle by the late war. He states that immediately after possession of Forts Smith and Gibson had been regained, the traffic was renewed, and the farmers along the military road in Kansas suffered losses of cattle. Away from the route traveled by Texas cattle no such losses occurred. Soon these cattle were distributed through the interior, and, as a result, heavy losses of horned stock were sustained. Mr. B. declares untrue the statement that the Texas cattle do not themselves have the disease, and states that he has seen many sicken and die with it.

Mr. William Montgomery, of Stockton, Missouri, a dealer in cattle, stated that from 1861 to 1865 there were no Texas cattle, and not a single case of splenic fever, in Southwest Missouri.

Mr. Huron Burt, of Calloway County, Missouri, referred to a lot of oxen driven through that county early in the spring of 1865, and states that wherever they grazed a virus was left which infected cattle feeding on the same ground, and that it retained its power to infect until the rains of September came. Nine-tenths of those affected died. Several gentleman are named, each of whom lost his entire herd.

The loss in Newton is estimated at three hundred; in McDonald five per cent. of all native cattle; in St. Louis one thousand four hundred milch cows and two hundred and fifty to three hundred heifers and steers; in Henry two hundred to three hundred; in Montgomery forty-five, and but three recovered; in Mississippi forty; in Dade twenty-five per cent. of the stock; and small losses occurred in Benton, Bates, Butler, Cedar, Clark, and Polk.

Kentucky.—Occasional outbreaks of splenic fever have occurred in Kentucky, originating in conjunction with the importation of southern cattle, since the first introduction of such stock. In Anderson County, in 1868, the disease first appeared on Salt River. A drove of southwestern cattle arrived on the 15th of May. They were shipped at Bayou Sara, Louisiana, and brought up the river to Louisville; ninety-six head were received into the county during the season, all in fair condition and apparently healthy, and but one sickened subsequently, about the 1st of October, which recovered, after displaying the same symptoms as the native stock, viz: "loss of appetite, droopiness, stiffening of the joints, contraction of the muscles, and foaming at the mouth, shrinking away of the flesh, and when first observed they are generally traveling around in a circle until they get down; most of them showing symptoms attendant upon lock-jaw." About twenty native cattle died, and but one or two affected with the disease have recovered, most of them dying within twenty-four hours of the first observable symptoms. One farmer claims to have cured a cow by administering a pint of whisky as a dose. The disease broke out five months after the introduction of the foreign cattle, and was only communicated to animals fed in pastures which had been occupied by southern herds, and no case has occurred of the infection of one native by another.

In Jefferson County the disease appeared in and around Portland. Cattle coming by steamer from New Orleans and by the Mobile & Ohio Railroad began to arrive during the winter months, but no disease broke out till the June arrivals. About 6,000 head were received into the country during the season of 1868, all apparently healthy, and some in such good condition as to be immediately forwarded to the New York market, others being sent to pasture. About fifty or sixty native cows died at Portland, (a part of the city of Louisville, and one of the principal landing and crossing places for Texan stock on the Ohio River.) No deaths occurred beyond this range, and no secondary infection was communicated.

No disease has occurred in Franklin County since 1866. The Texan cattle, coming by the turnpike from Louisville, passed through the county in June or July, 1866; they were very thin in flesh and sore in the feet, but otherwise appeared healthy. None of them remained to be fed or grazed in the county. About one week elapsed from their introduction to the outbreak of the disease among the native stock, of which about twenty head died, being all that were attacked. The disease was communicated to animals passing over the same road as the Texans, but no case occurred of infection of one native animal by another.

Texas fever prevailed in Henry County in 1859, since which time no Texas drove has traversed it except one in the winter of 1866, which communicated no disease.

Infection was brought to Carroll County by fifteen head of Texan cattle coming up the Mississippi and Ohio Rivers from Louisiana, which the citizens were unwilling to receive until assured that they had been out of Texas a full year. They did not understand that they might as safely have come from Texas as from Louisiana. The outbreak occurred seventy to seventy-five days from their arrival among cattle pastured with them, of which ten died and three recovered.

Illinois.—The disease first made its appearance at Cairo, about the 10th of June, 1868, among the cows of the town, causing much fatality and pecuniary loss; but it did not extend through the county, from the simple fact that the migrating cattle were not distributed through the country, but were sent northward by rail.

The heaviest losses occurred in Champaign County, where fifteen to eighteen thousand head were reshipped or distributed from Tolono, the junction of the Illinois Central and Toledo and Wabash Railroads. The number lost in this county has been estimated at five thousand, worth $150,000 at a low valuation. Our correspondent reported as follows: "Spanish fever has prevailed in this county, commencing on the 27th day of July, 1868, and cattle have continued to die of the same disease up to January 1, 1869. In this township the loss is ninety per cent.; entire county seventy-five per cent. It is a blood disease; the blood under a powerful glass proves this. It has been argued, and tried to be proven, that it is a disease not easily taken. I have now in my possession a large amount of evidence from good men, showing it to be a disease very easily given. A number of cases can be given where the only exposure was by driving a short distance over the road where Texas cattle had passed, from tame pasture to barn lots, the natives being kept up all the time only when in transit from lots to pasture. Blood examined in the earliest stages of the disease shows a diseased condition of the same. As the disease progresses from day to day the blood, examined by a good glass, shows the gradual destruction of vitality, and at dissolution is a mass of putridity."

In the southern part of Cook County the disease, communicated by contact with cattle shipped to Chicago, prevailed for a short period; in Ford County the loss was estimated at five hundred head; in Grundy one hundred died in a single town; in Douglas there were forty fatal cases; in Clinton nineteen; in Du Page one man lost eighteen head; fatal cases were also reported from St. Clair, Pulaski, Effingham, Pope, Massac, Macon, and Iroquois.

Indiana.—A drove of one hundred animals coming from Texas, by water *via* New Orleans, was landed at Evansville, and after a stay of six hours taken by rail into the interior. They appeared to be in good condition; none died on the way, and very few after reaching their destination; but the symptoms of those that sickened were the same, a day or two before death, as those of the native stock attacked. Nearly a month elapsed from the passage of the Texas drove to the outbreak among the native stock, of which fifty died, only one case (and that of doubtful convalescence) is known to have recovered.

In July, 1868, sixty Texas cattle were pastured on the farm of S. A. Fletcher, jr.; near Indianapolis, Indiana. His domestic cattle were separated by a fence from the Texas stock, and watered at a stream flowing through their pasture. A neighbor had thirty cows in a pasture also adjoining the long horns, but the infected water did not pass through it. In ten days two of Mr. Fletcher's cattle died, and five others gave evidence of the disease, to which all but one succumbed, in periods ranging from twenty-four to forty-eight hours from the outward manifestation of the disease. None of the other herd were attacked, though the cows were only separated by a fence from the Texas cattle.

A drove of Texan cattle from New Orleans to New Albany by steamer, crossed White River at Wood's Ferry, five of which died near that point. A Mr. Cobb subsequently lost eight milch cows that pastured along the road they traveled. A Texas steer of another lot sickened and died, the symptoms being profuse bloody discharges from the bowels, ears drooping, and a generally dull, stupid appearance. From two thousand to two thousand five hundred Texas cattle were received by steamer from the mouth of the Red River. They were apparently healthy on their arrival, though in poor condition; some died on the way up. Few of the Texan cattle died at New Albany. About three weeks elapsed from the introduction of the Texan cattle to the outbreak of the disease among the native stock, of which seventy-four died out of eighty-one attacked. The disease was only communicated to animals fed on the pastures occupied by the Texan cattle; in pastures adjoining the cattle remained healthy; and no positive case has been reported of the infection of one native animal by another.

About three hundred were received in Washington County, coming up the Ohio in boats to Louisville and New Albany. Some came in March, others as late as June. No disease was communicated to natives. About four hundred cattle were received in Bartholomew County, coming by boat up the Mississippi and Ohio Rivers to New Albany, thence overland, beginning to arrive in May. There was no infection of native stock.

In Warren County about four thousand head of Texan cattle were received in or driven through the county, coming either by the railroad or driven from Cairo, Illinois. After being landed from the steamer, some were poor, others in good condition. Some were taken off the cars dead, but this was supposed to be owing to bad treatment. The Texan cattle commenced to arrive about the 1st of June, and the fever appeared about the 25th of July. About one thousand five hundred of the native stock died, being about nine-tenths of the whole number attacked.*

---

* James Park, of Williamsport, Warren County, Indiana, gives the following particulars, in a letter to Gov. Baker, of one of the principal of the infected herds sent east:

"On the 27th day of April, 1868, a herd of nine hundred and thirty head of Texas cattle was purchased in Colorado County, Texas. They were driven to the mouth of the Red River, a distance of about six hundred miles, reaching that point May 31, 1868. They were at once shipped from that point on steamboats, and arrived at Cairo, Illinois, June 4, 1868. From thence they were shipped on the Illinois Central Railroad, and reached Tolono, Illinois, June 7, 1868. From this point they were driven into Warren County, Indiana, a distance of about sixty miles. They came into the western boundary of Warren County on the 12th of June, 1868. There was a loss of forty-four head, only eight hundred and eighty-six of the nine hundred and thirty head reaching Warren County. These cattle were from four to six years old, all apparently in good condition, nothing indicating any disease whatever. There were ticks on very many of them.

"This herd of Texan cattle on the 12th day of June, 1868, passed over a certain piece of prairie pasture on the western boundary of this county, (Warren.) On the 19th day of June a lot of native cattle, numbering ninety-five head, weighing over one thousand three hundred pounds each, was permitted to graze upon the same pasture, and continued to feed upon the same until the 4th of August. One of the herd was noticed to be sick on the 28th of July, and, up to the 4th of August, eleven were sick and three had died. On the 4th of August eighty-four of this lot of ninety-five were driven to the West Lebanon station of the Toledo and Wabash Railroad, and shipped for the New York market. There were eleven head of another lot that had not been on this pasture, or in any way exposed to the Texas cattle shipped with the eighty-four. None of the eleven head were taken sick on the road to New York, but the sickness was confined to the eighty-four head exposed to the Texas cattle, at least herded upon pasture passed over by the Texas cattle.

"On the night of the 12th of June, 1868, this lot of Texan cattle herded on another piece of prairie where a lot of one hundred head of native cattle were feeding. On the morning of the 13th of June the Texan cattle were driven to the north of the county. Fifty-five of the one hundred head of the native cattle were three years old, the rest were one and two—all in good growing condition.

"On the night of the 12th of June, 1868, there were twenty-six head of native fat cattle in an adjoining inclosure to the ground occupied by the Texan cattle. About four weeks after the 12th of June, these twenty-six fat cattle broke out of their inclosure and grazed upon the prairie where the Texan cattle had been on the night of June 12. On the 29th of July, one of the twenty-six was discovered to be sick, and died on the night of July 31 On the 1st day of August, two of the one hundred head died, and some twenty-five more were sick. From that time up to the present, the entire herd have been taken sick, eighty-eight head out of the one hundred have died; twenty-two out of the twenty-six have also died; total, one hundred and ten out of one huudred and twenty-six. The remaining sixteen head have all been sick, and are now very poor and stupid, but have the appearance of getting well.

"As a fact, wherever native cattle have passed over ground where this Texan herd have been, the native cattle have sickened and died. It is also a fact that other Texan cattle have been brought into this county, have been herded with native cattle two months, and, as yet, no disease has made its appearance."

The first arrival of southern cattle in Jasper County was between the 25th of May and the 1st of June, and six thousand eight hundred were received during the season, coming from the Red River country up the Mississippi *via* Cairo, Illinois. About forty-two days elapsed from their introduction to the outbreak among the native stock, of which four hundred died, or ninety-nine per cent. of the whole number attacked. The disease was only communicated to animals fed on pastures soiled by the excrements of the southern cattle, and no case occurred of the infection of one native animal by another. In one instance, in June, a small drove of Texan cattle was driven across the grazing ground of a native herd; the drovers pushed them across as fast as practicable, not allowing them to stop. In six weeks the native cattle in that range were taken sick, and several died. About six hundred head of cattle, which had wintered in the Louisiana marshes, passed through Jasper County about the 25th of May. They were very thin, and about thirty died on the road. The disease broke out among the native cattle in from seven to eight weeks, and fifty head died, being nine-tenths of the whole number attacked.

About eight hundred head of Texan and Cherokee cattle were herded in the adjoining county, and four hundred natives died from coming in contact with them or their trail, and the citizens of Jasper County would not permit them to enter that county unless the owners deposited money to make all damages good. The loss was heaviest among the milch cows.

On the 20th of July a lot of four hundred Texan cattle were purchased in Chicago, and driven through Lake County, stopping over night in the prairie west of town, all in apparently good health. All the native cattle which fed upon or ran over that prairie were attacked in about twenty-eight days, and sixty died; only four or five recovering. No other southern cattle passed through the county, and no other outbreak occurred.

In Marion County about one hundred died of splenic fever; and some losses occurred in Hendricks, Lawrence, Newton, and White. Our correspondent in Benton reports the loss of four hundred to six hundred head, and makes a statement which conflicts with the uniform testimony from other sections, and which therefore should be taken with allowance for a possible misapprehension of the facts, so far as it favors the idea that the infection can be carried by the wind. It is as follows: "In a neighboring county a herd of Texas cattle were driven about eight miles along a road, and, the wind being from the south, cattle along on the north side of the road took the disease, without either being driven along the road traveled by the Texas cattle, or drinking water that had been exposed in any manner. These facts induce the belief that the disease was communicated by the wind." Joseph Poole, of Attica, Indiana, reports the case of a cow which took the disease in fifty-one days after Texas cattle had passed by the inclosure, which was separated from them by a board fence. Another cow in the same inclosure was not infected. It is not impossible that contact was effected through openings in the fence; otherwise infection must have been carried in the air, as the animal was at no time outside of the inclosure. He gives another instance, occurring five miles from the depot, forty-seven days after exposure to Texas cattle passing along the road, a fence separating the native cow from the traveling herd.

Ohio.—Thousands of Texas cattle have been carried through this State in the cars, usually after pasturage in States further west for a sufficient time to eliminate the infectious matter from the system, and almost invariably without reshipment. Hence the disease is little known in this State.

Several infected cows were brought from one of the western counties to Columbiana, where they all died, but did not communicate the disease to others. A few cases appeared in Hamilton County; ten or twelve deaths occurred in Greene, from exposure to passing Texan stock; and in Wyandot a loss of six occurred in two car-loads brought from Chicago.

New York.—This State received many Texas cattle, some of which were in condition to communicate disease, yet such were the precautions taken by the State commissioners, Messrs. M. R. Patrick, Lewis F. Alden, and J. Stanton Gould, and the metropolitan board of health, that outbreaks occurred at only few points. Quarantines were established at Buffalo, Erie, and Jameston, and a rigid inspection of all animals coming into the State by rail was vigorously enforced.

A lot of eighteen Illinois cattle was brought to Sing Sing, July 30, six of which died in a few days, and others, believed to be diseased, were slaughtered and disposed of.

A lot of sixty-five western cattle, driven from West Albany, August 9, lost one at Copake, Columbia County, August 17, and four at Millerton, Dutchess County, between August 14 and 19.

At Campville, on the Erie road, the disease appeared August 9, and eighteen or twenty head of western cattle, taken from the cars on the previous day, died within a few hours.

A lot of eighty-three head was shipped, August 3, from Arrow Rock, Saline County, Missouri, and at St. Louis two cattle were added to the herd, which arrived at Bull's Head, New York, August 19. On the 22d, the two from St. Louis were taken sick and subsequently killed, revealing strong indications of the disease. It does not appear that any of the eighty-three were infected.

One of a lot of nineteen head of Illinois cattle was killed at Bull's Head, September 19, and found to be diseased. The others were quarantined, but none were diseased.

September 12, twelve cattle died at Pier 12, East River, on the steamer Fah Kee, and subsequently five more; the remaining twenty-three survived the quarantine. The *post mortem* appearances were unmistakably those of the Texan cattle disease.

During September, isolated cases occurred which proved to be identical in character with those already mentioned.

Travel-worn Texas cattle were quarantined and subsequently discharged. When killed for beef, the spleens were generally larger and darker than those of northern cattle, and old cicatrices of the abomasum appeared, and signs of erosions and congestions.

In October, "a number of sudden deaths" occurred at Hamptonburgh, in Orange County, attributed to the Texas cattle disease, assumed to have been taken from other native cattle brought from Painesville and other points in Ohio. Dr. Morris, Mr. Gould, and Dr. Montfort, made *post mortem* examinations of two heifers, and Dr. M. afterward examined a cow; and these gentlemen entertained no doubt that this was the Texas disease. The commissioners report the fact as follows: August 25, forty-four cows and heifers, purchased at different places in Ohio, arrived at Hamptonburg, and one died a few hours after arrival. Four days after, two of the cows were turned into the dairy pasture of John Moul, where they remained till September 1, and, on the 8th, one of them died, the other on the 10th. On the 12th, thirteen days after exposure, one of the cows in the pasture of Mr. Moul was taken sick, and died on the 13th. On the 14th, a second cow was attacked, and died on the following day. A third cow sickened on the 18th, and died the same day. No examinations were made. The two cows of the original herd were buried in a pasture in which were two pairs of oxen and two heifers. In about two weeks one of the oxen became sick, but recovered; another ox was found dead in the pasture, and subsequently both of the heifers. A *post mortem* examination revealed large livers and spleens, and engorged and softened kidneys. These symptoms suggest splenic fever; but is it positively ascertained that one of the cows placed in Mr. Moul's pasture was not a Texan? The forty-four cows of the two car-loads have been traced to different points: seventeen to Hambden, Lake County, Ohio, eleven to Huntington, Lorain County, nine to Clarksfield, two to Wakeman, three to Plymouth, and one of the two others came from Kentucky. It is but just to say that Dr. K. V. K. Montfort, who reports the case, thinks, from conversations with dealers who saw the cattle, that there were no Texans among them. Yet no positive evidence to that effect has been presented; and a shadow of doubt must continue to rest upon the case, while it is undeniable that thousands upon thousands of exposures of cattle to sick natives have been attended with perfect immunity from disease in many latitudes and through many years.

New Jersey.—A large number of Texas and Indiana cattle were brought into the cattle-yards and abattoirs of Hudson County in August, sick with Spanish fever. The State agricultural society forbade any more being brought into the State; and those sick were quarantined, and, after a thorough examination, were put into rendering vats, and the yards and pens disinfected with carbolic acid. No disease appeared afterward. Three inspectors were appointed by the State Society, who quarantined all the suspected cattle on arrival.

August 9, one hundred and forty-one of Mr. Alexander's cattle, sent from Homer, Illinois, on the last day of July, were sacrificed at the rendering tanks to avoid all risk of public injury by the sale of the flesh. *Post mortem* examinations proved the existence of the disease in many of them.

An arrival of about seventy infected cattle, a portion of the Campville lot, at the Bergen yards, Hudson City, was reported to Governor Ward on the 10th of August, and on the following day the sanitary commissioner, Dr. Stephen Smith, found fifteen animals in a dying condition. These animals were a part of the lot of eighty-four which were shipped, August 4, reported in the letter of James Park, (quoted in a note on page 192,) from West Lebanon Station, Indiana, and were a part of the drove of nine hundred and thirty starting, April 27, from Colorado County, Texas, and driven six hundred miles to the mouth of Red River, reaching that point May 31, for shipment up the Mississippi by steamboat.

Pennsylvania.—A lot of western cattle were driven through Westmoreland County, stopping over night on a farm three miles south of Greensburg. Some eight or ten head took sick during the night and were left with the farmer to be killed. The symptoms were said to be those of splenic fever.

Georgia.—A disease supposed to be the splenic fever prevailed in several counties; among them are named Chattooga, Hall, and Pulaski.

RECENT INFORMATION.

The passage of laws to prevent the summer driving of southern cattle, and their strict enforcement, have limited the losses from this disease in a marked degree. A few cases have been reported in 1870. One in Chester County, Pennsylvania, furnishes another illustration of the invariable and peculiar features of this disease. In 1869 a lot of cattle from North Carolina stopped at Avondale; soon after they had left, other cattle turned into the meadow they had occupied became sick. Some twenty were attacked and about three-fourths of them died. No other cattle were turned into the same inclosure and the disease did not spread further. Many believed the ticks, which infected the North Carolina cattle, and were communicated to the natives attacked, caused the disease. There is no evidence that these parasites have anything to do with its diffusion or virulence.

Our correspondent in St. Louis County, Missouri, says: "We had no Spanish fever last year, Texas cattle being effectually kept out by the provisions of our law during the season they would be likely to spread contagion." In Benton County, "there has been no loss by Spanish fever. The vigilance of the people and stringent legal enactments have prevented the introduction or the transit of Texas cattle through this county." "Owing to the stringent laws of this State, but one small drove of cattle direct from Texas succeeded in entering or passing through this county (Vernon) last summer. This drove passed hastily along the east border of this county a short distance, through a district sparsely settled and containing but a few cows, oxen, &c., for home use. The Spanish fever broke out about six weeks after their passage, and continued until after two or three white frosts in October, when it ceased to spread, and those with fever at the time mostly recovered. About forty-four per cent. of the cattle which grazed on the grounds this drove passed over had the fever, two-thirds of which died, the remainder slowly recovering. No other drove is reported as having entered the county till after frost had killed the vegetation. Many thousand then passed through without a known case of fever." A report from Bates says: "There has been no Spanish fever. The inhabitants of the county are organized and will not allow cattle to be driven through, although the laws of the State allow them to come in from December to April. I have known of two herds being driven over in the winter, one in 1867, the other in 1869, and in both instances many of the native cattle which came in contact with them died of the disease a short time after grass became of full bite." This instance appears to invalidate the certainty of exemption from infection received through stock introduced from the South in winter.

Last summer tens of thousands of Texas cattle were driven into the southwestern part of Butler County, Kansas. There were but few domestic cattle in that locality, but they all died. Several herds of Texas cattle, brought direct, during the past winter, from Texas and the Indian Territory, have been pastured and fed in Jefferson, Kansas, among some of which were occasional losses, but none could be clearly charged to Spanish fever. Our correspondent says: "I have wintered (1869) a herd in my pastures in which, afterward, my Durham cattle fed, and no harm has been witnessed." In Franklin, Kansas, the splenic fever appeared about the 1st of September. About one hundred head of native cattle died, mostly cows. The infection was taken from a drove of Texas cattle passing through the county. It is reported from Shawnee, in the same State, that the disease has not prevailed since the shipment exclusively of Texas cattle by rail from

Abilene. The law preventing the herding of Texas cattle in summer has been generally enforced, so that few points have been infected.

A few cases are reported in Washington County, Nebraska.

The Missouri law has been well enforced; but a few droves went through Greene and Cedar, communicating the disease, which resulted fatally.

There has been some splenic fever in St. Francis, Arkansas, caused by permitting native stock to be penned in lots used by Texas cattle passing through the county; loss very light.

A lot of Texas cattle brought into Washington County, Virginia, communicated disease to the native stock, resulting in one hundred and fifty deaths. The disease is now fatal in Salem, Fauquier County, Virginia, and sixty-seven deaths have been reported of cattle owned by nineteen farmers and villagers; the loss amounting to $3,000. It is traced in every case to contact with Texan cattle. The people of the village express a determination not to allow another carload to disembark there.

LAWS RELATIVE TO DISEASES OF FARM ANIMALS.

In closing this partial history of the Texas cattle disease in the United States, a brief digest of the laws relating to it may be appropriate. Several of the States have enactments bearing upon all contagious and infectious diseases, without a distinct specification of any one; and others have laws relating mainly to pleuro-pneumonia, while including other diseases. Greater uniformity in their legal requirements and restrictions is desirable. This digest is condensed from a more extended statement in the Report of the Department of Agriculture for 1869. Either the general Government should enact a law providing for the suppression of contagious diseases of farm stock and for the regulation of the transportation and movement of farm animals, or the State governments should be induced to act simultaneously and harmoniously on the subject. Pleuro-pneumonia has a dangerous footing among the cattle of the Middle States, and is spreading south, and is liable to scatter contagion among western herds from which come the principal meat supplies of eastern cities. It is far more to be dreaded than the splenic fever communicated by Texas cattle, as that infection does not pass in continuous progression through one sick animal after another. Yet there will be no safety for northern cattle coming in contact with those from the southern coasts during the summer months; and effective prohibition of the movement of such cattle from May to November should be secured by efficient legislation. There are other infectious or contagious maladies of other kinds of farm stock over which legislative control should be obtained by a general enactment.

There are seven different laws on this subject now temporarily in force in England, and it is there proposed to consolidate and perpetuate them, with suitable amendments The dreaded rinderpest, the ravages of which increased with accelerating ratio until the passage of the law requiring and compensating the destruction of infected cattle, was very rapidly subdued by compulsory and summary destruction of infected and exposed animals.

In the sea-board States the laws relating to contagious diseases were generally framed with reference to pleuro-pneumonia, but in many of them the provisions are sufficiently general to embrace all communicable diseases.

A board of commissioners has authority, in Massachusetts, to control the introduction of diseased cattle and take measures to prevent the spread of disease within the State;

and the orders of this board supersede those of selectmen of towns and mayors and aldermen of cities. The law provides that cattle diseased or suspected of disease can neither be removed to another State, nor killed, except by permission. Owners of animals killed on account of disease are indemnified. Town authorities may brand infected animals, and for selling animals so branded a fine of $500 may be imposed, or imprisonment for one year.

The law of Rhode Island punishes the offence of bringing diseased cattle into the State with a fine of $100 to $500.

Township committees in New Jersey, upon notice of a cattle disease supposed to be contagious, are required to cause the separation of animals presenting symptoms of such disease, five hundred feet from any highway or the premises of neighbors. Penalties are inflicted for storing the hide or any other part of a diseased animal, and for permitting the admixture of convalescent with healthy animals without permission of the committee. These committees are empowered to prohibit the passage of cattle through their townships, and their authority is enforced by a fine of $100 for each animal driven in disregard of the prohibition. The State agricultural society is also authorized to take active measures for preventing the introduction of disease.

A fine of $500, or imprisonment not exceeding six months, are penalties in Pennsylvania for selling infected animals; and cattle and sheep are prohibited from running at large in sections where contagious diseases prevail.

Only healthy animals are allowed to be driven through the States of Virginia and North Carolina. In Virginia, when diseased cattle are found at large, or driven in violation of law, a justice may require the owners to impound them, and upon failure thus to restrain them, the animals are killed by order of the justice and buried at the depth of four feet.

The owner of "distempered" cattle in Kentucky is liable to a fine of ten dollars each for such animals driven or permitted to run at large through the State; and a penalty of five dollars each punishes a neglect of burial of cattle dying of disease.

Laws bearing more directly upon the Texas cattle disease are in operation in some of the States west of the Mississippi.

In Missouri the county court of each county may appoint three competent and discreet persons to act as a board for the inspection of cattle supposed to be infected with the Texas cattle disease. This board is empowered to stop any drove, and to order the removal of the suspected cattle from the county, and by the same route of entry if practicable. Owners complying with such order are not further liable; in case of refusal or neglect to comply, the president of the board may direct the sheriff to drive the cattle out by the route upon which they came, or to kill them if the slaughter shall be deemed necessary to prevent the spread of the disease. The owners are liable for all costs of examination, removal, or killing. The act to prevent the introduction of diseased cattle into the State provides that no Texas, Mexican, or Indian cattle shall be driven or otherwise conveyed into any county in the State between the 1st day of March and the 1st day of December in each year, but this does not apply to any cattle which have been kept the entire previous winter in the State. Cattle may be carried through the State by railroad or steamboat, provided they are not unloaded, but the railroad company or owners of the steamboat are responsible for all damages which may result from the Texas fever, should the same occur along the line of transportation; and the existence of such disease along the route shall be *prima facie* evidence that the disease has been communicated by such transportation. For every head of cattle brought into the State contrary to law a fine of twenty dollars may be recovered, or the party may be imprisoned in the county jail not less than three nor more than twelve months, or may be subjected to both fine and imprisonment. It is lawful for any three or more householders to stop any cattle which they may have good reason to believe are passing through any county in violation of the act.

Illinois has a law prohibiting the introduction of Texas or Cherokee cattle into the State between the 1st day of October and the 1st day of March under penalty of a fine of not less than $500 nor exceeding $2,000. These fines shall be paid into the county treasury for the purpose of distribution *pro rata* among persons who have suffered losses by the introduction of such cattle. Persons and corporations are made liable to injured parties for losses. It is made the duty of any circuit or county judge, or justice of the peace, upon oath of any householder setting forth that Texas or Cherokee cattle are spreading disease among the native cattle, to forthwith issue a warrant to any sheriff or constable of the county, commanding him to arrest and impound such cattle and keep them by themselves until the 1st day of October following. "Texas and Cherokee cattle" are defined to mean a class or kind of cattle without reference to the place from which they may have come.

A law of Iowa, approved April 8, 1868, forbids the introduction or possession of Texas, Cherokee, or Indian cattle, but permits their transportation through the State by railroads, and the driving of such cattle when wintered north of the southern boundary of the State of Missouri or of Kansas. The penalties for a violation of this law are a fine not exceeding $1,000, imprisonment not exceeding six months, and payment of all damages accruing.

A special enactment of Kansas forbids the driving of cattle from Texas or the Indian Territory between the 1st day of March and the 1st day of December in every year, except in the remote and sparsely settled territory of the plains, and then not within five miles of any highway, or within that distance of any "ranche" except by consent of its proprietor. The penalties for its violation are, for first offence, a fine of $100 to $1,000 and imprisonment from thirty days to six months; for subsequent offences the penalties are double.

The general convention held in Illinois, in which most of the States were ably represented, considered carefully the subject of restrictive legislation and adopted the following resolutions:

"Whereas a malignant disease among cattle, known as Texas fever, has been widely disseminated by the transit of southwestern cattle through the Western and Northwestern States during the warm season of the year, occasioning great loss to our farmers and possibly endangering the health of our citizens: Therefore,

"*Resolved*, That this convention earnestly recommend the enactment, by those States, of stringent laws to prevent the transit through their limits of Texas or Cherokee cattle from the 1st day of March to the 1st day of November, inclusive.

"*Resolved*, That the interests of the community require the enactment of laws making any person responsible for all damages that may result from the diffusion of any disease from animals in his ownership or possession."

CONVENTION OF CATTLE COMMISSIONERS.

Accepting the invitation of Governor Oglesby, of Illinois, the cattle commissioners of the several States met in convention at Springfield, December 1, 1868. There were present, representatives from Illinois, Indiana, Maryland, Massachusetts, Michigan, Missouri, New York, Ohio, Rhode Island, and Wisconsin.

Various views were presented, and many facts elicited, of a character similar to those recorded in these pages; it was made perfectly conclusive that the infection came from Texas cattle, and that restrictive legislation was necessary, and rigid inspection of suspected cattle, with provisions for greater care in transportation.

The convention recommended the enactment of stringent laws to prevent the transit of Texas or Cherokee cattle through their respective States between the first of March and the first of November, and to make the owner responsible for damages caused by the introduction of such cattle.

It recommended the appointment of State boards of commissioners who should have power to appoint assistants, when needed, to take measures to prevent the spread of diseases of domestic animals, to give public notice of the outbreak of any dangerous disease, establish regulations for the transit of cattle, place diseased animals in quarantine, and cause them to be killed if neccessary to the public protection. It proposed the empowering of commissioners to inspect all cattle brought into the State, to exclude any animal deemed capable of diffusing dangerous diseases, and to stop cattle trains in which no opportunity had been afforded during the preceding twenty-four hours for food and water; and recommended penalties for resisting or interfering with such officers in the discharge of their duties, and for the bribery of officers charged with the execution of the law.

RECAPITULATION.

In conclusion, the following peculiarities of this singular disease are presented by a systematic sifting of the mass of testimony brought out during the respective investigations so briefly chronicled in the foregoing pages:

1. The disease is communicated by southern cattle.

2. The cattle communicating the infection, though showing signs of splenic enlargement or evidence of once-existing disease, when slaughtered, are apparently well and actually increasing in weight and vigor.*

3. Infection is not usually communicated in winter, and fields may be safely depastured in spring which have been occupied in winter by southern cattle. In a single case reported an apparent exception is presented.

4. Animals receiving the infection from southern cattle do not communicate it to other natives. This exemption is a rule so undeviating that probably not one farmer in one hundred, whose stock has suffered by this disease, would fear a dollar's loss by communication of their uninfected with sick animals. The authenticated exception is

* While southern cattle possess the germ of virulent disease, it is rarely, if ever, developed in themselves, at least with the same manifestations and intensity. As prisoners, coming from unventilated jails, have communicated typhus to judge and jury, without active manifestations of similar disease in themselves, so Texas cattle, coming from miasmatic pasturage, infect cattle of other climates, and cause a disease, unknown in degree, (or perhaps in kind) among the stock in which the infection originates.

the case, recorded on page 194, at Hamptonburg, New York, and in that no positive proof is given that the animal communicating the infection was not a Texan.*

5. Southern cattle removed to localities characterized by the same climatic conditions (as from one portion of the Gulf coast to another, or upon the same parallel of latitude,) do not communicate disease to local stock.

6. The virus appears to be eliminated from the system after a stay of a few weeks or months in a northern climate, so that no infection is communicated to the cattle with which they come in contact.

7. A preponderance of testimony tends to establish the theory that the infection is conveyed through the voided excrements. It does not appear that the disease has ever been communicated "except to animals that have fed upon pastures or in lots soiled by the excrements of the southern cattle."

8. The period of incubation is not of uniform length. From causes which may be left for medical investigation to determine, the potency of the virus is variable. Sometimes a week intervenes between the exposure and the attack; frequently a period of ten days or two weeks elapses; sometimes two, three, or six weeks intervene; and in one case in Washington county, Arkansas, the time of incubation was three months. In portions of Arkansas, in which the climatic conditions are similar to those of the region from which the migrating cattle come, no infection occurs; and in proportion as a section assimilates in climate to such region, it is reasonable to suppose the liability to the disease is lessened, and, probably, the period of its incubation extended.

9. The disease runs a brief course of a few days, generally but three or four, often but one or two, and proves fatal in nine cases of every ten.

10. Liability to infection is so imminent that few exposed animals escape. When circumstances favor the greatest virulence of the disease, whole herds have often been destroyed, and the cattle of entire districts nearly all swept away, while beyond the line of exposure, distinctly marked as the boundary of a sweeping conflagration or resistless tornado, not a herd nor an animal has been touched.

11. Medication has been of little service, though the testimony gives color to the probability that a slightly reduced mortality might be secured by skillful medical treatment and feeding with soft mashes.

12. The losses from this disease for a few years prior to the war, and for years since its close, cannot be accurately stated, but undoubtedly amounts to several millions of dollars. The greatest fatality has been in Missouri and Kansas. In 1858 the loss in Vernon County, Missouri, was $200,000. Losses were widely distributed and severe throughout southern Kansas and southwest Missouri in 1866 and 1867; in 1868 they were less in these States, as the result of general enforcement of restrictive laws, but were heavy and alarming in eastern Illinois and western Indiana, when the prairie pastures

* Joseph Poole, a commissioner representing Indiana at the Illinois convention in 1868, said, on this point: "My own experience, and all the authentic information I have been able to obtain, goes to show and prove most conclusively that in the most aggravated cases of the disease among native cattle, and where they are dying by scores, and other native cattle are in a field or inclosure at a proper distance from any point that may have been infected by Texas cattle, you may drive native cattle, sick with this disease, into the field with the native cattle in good health, and not one of the healthy cattle will ever be infected or sick with the disease." Such were the facts elicited and generally admitted by all at the convention, after the most strict inquiry and quite a spirited discussion upon the subject. The New York commissioners, in an official report dated September 5, 1868, (before the outbreak at Hamptonburg,) said: "We have not heard of a single case of the disease having been taken by any animal that has not been in contact with Texas cattle or with their excretions. We have had authentic evidence that Texas cattle that have passed over a road, dropping the excrement thereon, have communicated the disease to native cattle that passed over the same road forty-eight hours afterward."

of those States were for the first time occupied by cattle direct from Texas. The deaths numbered about 5,000 in Champaign County, Illinois; 1,500 in Warren, 600 in Benton, and 400 in Jasper, in Indiana; and many counties in these and other States were involved to a less extent. The mortality of 1868, reported by our returns, amounts to at least 15,000 cattle, involving a loss of not less than $500,000.

13. While meat of diseased animals can never be deemed wholesome food, the milk and flesh of cattle affected with this disease do not generally cause immediate sickness.*

From these characteristics of this climatic disease it is clear that it can never involve in general destruction the cattle of the country by successive "generations" of the virus, as in the case of the European rinderpest, and that its ravages may be easily confined to circumscribed limits, if not prevented altogether, by judicious legislation which shall not interfere seriously with the freedom or the profits of the cattle trade.

J. R. DODGE.

Hon. HORACE CAPRON, *Commissioner*.

* Of the testimony bearing upon this point, that of Mr. Eaton, in charge of the Broadland farms of Mr. Alexander, in Champaign county, Illinois, is very strong. He states that 140 head of native cattle died there in 1868 from Texas fever, and among them nearly all the cows on the place, whose milk was used with apparent impunity until they ceased to give milk; the calves sucked as long as their mothers could stand, and in one instance a calf sucked three cows alternately until each died; and in some cases the hogs consumed the carcasses of dead cattle. Not a single case of disease or injury resulted from the use of meat or milk.

INDEX.

K.

L.

M.

N.

O.

P.

R.

www.ingramcontent.com/pod-product-compliance
Lightning Source LLC
LaVergne TN
LVHW050531100826
845148LV00002B/524